Paul Baker
and the Integration of Abilities

Paul Baker
and the Integration of Abilities

Robert Flynn and Eugene McKinney ▪ editors

TCU Press ▪
Fort Worth, Texas

Library of Congress Cataloging-in-Publication Data

Paul Baker and the integration of abilities / Robert Flynn and
Eugene McKinney, editors.
              p. cm.
Includes bibliographical references and index.
    ISBN 0-87565-271-9 (cloth : alk.paper)
   1.   Baker, Paul, 1911– 2. Dramatists, American—20th
century—Biography.   3.   Theatrical producers and
directors—United States—Biography.   I. Flynn, Robert, 1932–
II. McKinney, Eugene, 1922–

    PS3552.A4335 Z84 2003
    812'.54—d c21

*The editors are indebted to all the photographers whose work appears
in the book, especially Linda Blase, Andy Hanson, Windy Drum,
and Mary Ann Colias.*

Jacket & Book Design/Margie Adkins Graphic Design

Table of Contents

BALCONY

BALCONY

Ruth Taylor Theater,
Trinity University,
San Antonio, Texas

Opposite page: Model of the
Baylor Theater,
Baylor University,
Waco, Texas

Theater Dedication

Read at the opening of the Baylor Theater, 1941; read at the opening of the Ruth Taylor Theater, 1966

This theater is dedicated to the young at heart, to the dreamer, to the imaginative creator of beauty for others. This theater exists to challenge the best in its devotees—the living, the inspired part of each of their lives. It aims to reach out to the roots of our soil and our people . . . to interpret, to portray what is truth—to select what is good, what gives joy, what is real.

This theater starts with the needs of a people and reaches out through the child, the student, the man—touching each with its varied endeavor, showing each the nobility of man: his weakness, his greatness.

This theater attempts to be new in its concept, to offer only the best to its advocates. May it stand firm—sure of its footing—resolved to hold fast, through the treacherous times, for its friends and neighbors, to our basic dreams and realities.

The doors are open; bring in your thoughts, bring in your rarest desire, bring in your best. Here you may find expression and growth; here you may find a gateway to service; here you may find real understanding.

To those who want to keep alive the dream and help to weave a finer dream for the future, we dedicate this theater. Enter—it is yours.

Paul Baker

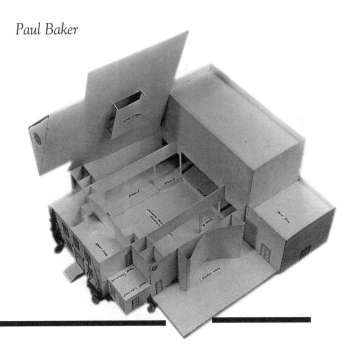

Introduction: A Tale of Five Cities

Eugene McKinney

I have a long-standing relationship with Paul Baker and his wife, Kitty. Supposedly, that resulted in an intimate knowledge and understanding of them. I do possess that knowledge about them, and I think I understand Kitty. But I don't understand Paul Baker. Never have, never will.

Kitty Baker is a brilliant mathematician, teacher, artist, and children's theater pioneer. And somehow, she found the time to be the mother of their three individualistic offspring. Paul Baker is an impractical visionary, driven more by inspired intuition than by earthbound logic.

Early in his teaching career, Baker originated a course with the strange title of "The Integration of Abilities." It had very little to do with drama. It had everything to do with your realizing your own potential as a creative person. Crazy! But it changed the lives of thousands of students and is still being taught across the country by advocates of Baker's approach to creativity. Design and build a theater at Baylor University with stage space surrounding the audience seated in swivel chairs? Insane! But it worked, and influenced theater design from that point on. Tear up copies of Thomas Wolfe's eight-hundred-page novel, *Of Time and the River*, hand out segments to small groups of students and say, "put this on stage?" Mad! But it worked, and the production drew national acclaim.

These are only a few examples of the unorthodox, imaginative, and "impractical" approaches that Baker used in bringing vitality and creativity to theater throughout his long career as a director and educator.

The story of that career can be summed up under the title: "The Tale of Five Cities."

Waco. Baylor University. In the early years Baker taught and directed plays in a classroom on the third floor of Old Main. There was no drama department and few courses, but he built a department, a curriculum centered on the integration of abilities, and a new theater with those revolving chairs.

Paris. In the early fifties, Baker took a group of Baylor drama students abroad on a summer work-and-study program, presenting a play, *Green Grow The Lilacs*, in Paris and exploring that city's contemporary art museums. The impact of the summer's study was strong, and when the group returned to Baylor Baker set out to translate modern art techniques into drama. The resulting stagings of both Shakespearean plays and original scripts were startling, and the influence of that

1

summer's study had a lasting effect on Baker's career.

Dallas. After twenty-four years at Baylor, Baker was asked to be the founding director of the Dallas Theater Center. He agreed on the condition that he would continue his work at Baylor and that Baylor's graduate program would be an integral part of the Dallas Theater Center. Another irrational idea. But it worked. Baker commuted to Dallas while teaching and directing in Waco and built a flourishing theater program with a large permanent resident company and a large focus on new play stagings. He also became the founding director of the Dallas Independent School District's new Arts Magnet High School, one of the first such schools in the nation.

San Antonio. Later, he moved the Waco drama program, along with the Theater Center's graduate work, to Trinity University. And he did for Trinity what he had done at Baylor. Again, he started from scratch, codesigning an innovative theater building and placing in it an exciting large-scale curriculum and production schedule.

Waelder. The fifth city is actually a small town named Waelder. The Bakers retired to their small ranch between Waelder and Gonzales but not from life or creativity. Among their many projects, some still ongoing, they designed a revolutionary curriculum based on exercises from the integration of abilities class. Called "Sensory Learning," it used the arts as a vital part of the classes in the Waelder Elementary School. Baker wrote and his wife edited a book, *Making Sense with Five Senses*, for use in the curriculum.

Baker demanded more of actors, designers, directors, writers, students, and teachers than they wanted to give, but he gave more

I am a West Texan. That means I come from sun-conquered and wind-conquered country. As a child I was overwhelmed by the tremendous sky and great flat land—the tremendous space. This class in creative work began, its formulation began, out of the experiences in space, rhythm and time, sound and silence, direction, line, movement silhouette which I had as a child.

Paul Baker
Integration of Abilities

than he demanded. He gave them his respect; he gave them public credit for aiding him in making his classroom as innovative and exciting as his remarkable productions. Baker encouraged his students, even non-drama majors, to participate in creating scenes in his productions. In staging *Of Time and the River*, the students developed most of the scenes. Baker and his students and associates were a team. He gave them the freedom to dream lunatic dreams and to fail to achieve them. He gave them the freedom to grow, and he expected them to grow strong.

The road wasn't always smooth, but Baker fought for whatever cause he felt was worthy. Early in his career, the fight was over departmental money matters. Baylor believed in charity but not at home.

After World War II and after I joined the faculty, Baker stopped me in the theater lobby. I noticed that his neck was bowed, his head was jutting forward, and his chin was out. I recognized immediately that this was his "going into battle" mode, as though he was about to use his head as a battering ram. Possibly on me. He stared at me and asked curtly: "Do you think I look poor and need money?"

Of Time and the River, Baylor Theater

I had never viewed Baker as a natty dresser, but on this day he looked dreadful. Ancient sports coat and tie, baggy pants too short, exposing the GI olive-drab socks from his army days. But it was his shirt that distressed me. Frayed collar, faded color, but even worse, one cuff was held together by a large paperclip.

I decided evasion was the better part of valor. Timidly I responded to his question with a Socratic answer: "Why do you ask?"

He said: "I'm on my way to the administration to battle them about next year's budget. The drama department needs a lot more money. I thought I might help our cause if I went over looking as poor as our department is. I'm trying for the sympathy vote."

"Well," I said, "you certainly look like you need a lot of help." He smiled grimly. I wished him luck but deep down I knew that under most circumstances battering rams don't get the sympathy vote. He launched himself through the front door, his head jutting forward.

When he returned from the meeting, his head had returned to its normal position and he looked tired—but semi-triumphant. I asked him how he did.

"Not great. But better than last year," he said. "I think it's because this year I added the GI socks and the paperclip. I think they're starting to get suspicious."

Or, I thought, they're starting to worry about his sanity.

In the early sixties, Robert Flynn, of the Baylor drama department decided to direct *The Skin of Our Teeth* during the summer term. There were not enough students to fill all the roles. The drama department had a children's theater begun by Kitty Baker, so he used two of their mature students. They were both African Americans. Baylor children's theater was integrated. Baylor University was not.

One day, during a break, the students went next door to the Baylor Drug Store for coffee. Baylor Drug was owned by a Baylor trustee. One of the students returned and said he thought Baker and Baylor Theater were in trouble. The owner/trustee refused the students service because they sat with blacks, and the trustee believed it was a Baker/drama-inspired sit-in. The trustee talked to President Abner McCall. Flynn assumed his career at Baylor was over. McCall called Baker who was in New York. Baker called the instructor, asked what had happened, and said, "I'll take care of it." And he did.

Baker believed that it was the job of an administrator to make it possible for his staff to do their work free of unnecessary interference. Of all his crazy ideas, this may have been the most insane.

Only a year later a major crisis in Baker's career occurred. President McCall abruptly closed Baker's production of Eugene O'Neill's *Long Day's Journey into Night* because of profanity in the play. He had notified Baker by phone (Baker was at the Dallas Theater Center) to cut the play's profanity. Baker refused. The contract, okayed by McCall, did not permit the play to be cut.

4

McCall shut down the play in the middle of its run.

The closing of the play made national news. My mother called me from her home in Nashville. My brother, who was overseas, sent me a wire. The local paper gave the story a big spread on the front page. And certainly it was the hot topic on campus. The student newspaper criticized the action. The student council passed a resolution protesting the closing, as did the Baylor Chamber of Commerce.

When Baker returned from his usual stint at the Theater Center, he was greeted by a group of students sitting on the front steps of his house, waiting for him. None were drama majors, but he recognized several students who had taken his integration of abilities class, and he knew they were considered to be campus leaders.

They were angry over what had happened. They were willing to lead a boycott of classes, picket the administration, or organize protest rallies. "How can we help?" they wanted to know.

Baker told them he appreciated their support. But they could help best by not doing anything. He said he was hopeful that the furor would die down, that he and the department wanted a peaceful outcome. Student demonstrations would hurt the chances of the department's getting back on course. The students left quietly. There were no riots. We were relieved, because we hoped that we could survive the crisis. And we tried.

We believed we could reach an accommodation with President McCall. Paul Baker and Baylor Theater had a national reputation. Baker's integration of abilities class was a favorite with students, and Baker and McCall were longtime friends. However, soon McCall made additional demands restricting the selection of plays that we could produce and limiting the subject matter of plays written in our playwriting classes.

Baker received a program from a church worship service. It appeared to be a form letter that McCall had sent to all who supported his position. The letter said, "I have been somewhat saddened to discover that there are so many people today who confuse academic freedom with the license to stand on a stage and shout vulgar and profane words to the public, including children. . . ."

Baker asked for a meeting with McCall and invited me and another faculty member, Robert Flynn, to accompany him. We asked McCall about the form letter. He said he stood by that letter and that it represented his sentiments—that in presenting the play we were doing nothing but standing onstage shouting obscenities.

We asked if he could have also included in the letter a statement of his confidence in the Christian character and the work of our faculty. He said, "Yeah, I could have. But I didn't." We asked, "Will you make such a statement?" "No," McCall said. "I won't."

In a letter to a friend, McCall would confess that Baptists were suspicious of him because he was not a preacher and that he saw this as an opportunity to gain their support by creating a common enemy, and he took that opportunity. Baker, Flynn, and I walked back across the campus in silence. As we neared the theater, Baker said, "It's all over, isn't it?" He had built a drama program of national significance. He had designed a theater space that had drawn students, critics, architects, and theater artists from around the world. It was gone in a moment.

We had lost our long investment in Baylor. Our past had been rich. Our future looked empty. Each member of Baker's staff would have to find a new position. In my sixteen years of teaching, I had never filled out a job application form. Baker tried to reassure us that somehow we would stay together. All twelve of us.

When the play was closed, causing all the media attention, Baker started to get inquiries from a number of institutions and theaters asking him if perchance he was in the market for a new position. For his faculty, however, the number of job offers was, to overstate it, rather underwhelming.

Baker responded to each of these opportunities by saying that if he accepted an offer, that institution would also have to take his faculty. Another crazy idea! What university would hire an instant department, fully staffed and with a large curriculum?

Trinity University would. And did, thanks to another visionary, President James Laurie. In addition to accepting Baker and his faculty, Trinity also wanted our graduate program at the Theater Center. In the past, Baker had pulled off some minor miracles. This was a whopper.

After we resigned and just before finishing our last semester at Baylor, Baker and I went to San Antonio for our first formal meeting with Dr. Laurie and several of his staff. We arrived at the administration building a few minutes early and paused on the steps to compose ourselves.

I looked over at Baker and suddenly flashed back to that earlier year, another time, when in the Baylor Theater lobby he showed me to what extremes he would go to fight for what he wanted. But on this day he did not look like a homeless man. He looked neat, if not natty. One thing was not different, however. He was in his "going into battle" mode—neck bowed, head jutting forward. In his hand he had a folder containing his demands, subtly listed under the heading: "Suggestions." He was ready to fight. He squared his shoulders and launched himself through the doors. I followed.

Several hours later, we came out of those doors shell-shocked. Totally exhausted. Baker's head was still in battering-ram position, but he looked like he was about to fall on his face, having missed the target. There had been no battle. Laurie had enthusiastically given us everything we had asked for and even volunteered a number of items not on Baker's "suggestion" list.

I felt ecstatic, relieved, jubilant, incredulous, and thankful that we had a new academic home. Baker felt the same, but I sensed while we were walking toward our car that he also felt somewhat deflated, perhaps even a little disappointed. Baker has always loved a good fight. But he had met the enemy, and they turned out to be already on our side.

Our department left Baylor and moved to Trinity, lock, stock, and curriculum. We had everything but a theater. To Baker, it must have been déjà vu—a theater constructed in a classroom space on a building's third floor! To see a play, the audience had to walk up six flights of an outside staircase. An actor could enter or exit the stage only from stage left. An actor exiting stage right would experience defenestration.

But we had freedom to dream again, freedom to imagine. And the excitement was back. The last three or four months at Baylor had been a nightmare of accusations, rumors, slander, anonymous phone calls, and less oblique forms of harassment. Baker not only launched into a new season of plays and a new curriculum, he also began planning the Ruth Taylor Theater.

In three years we had a great new home—classroom space, offices, workshop—and three theaters. The biggest space was Theater One—a remarkable theater based on the flexibility of Baylor Theater but greatly improved by the years of experience gained from working in it and in the Dallas Theater Center. It was the architectural realization of all of Baker's dreams.

Trinity planned a huge event to celebrate the opening of its new theater. The day before its dedication, students were hanging long banners from the building roof. Baker and I went up to check on how the students were doing. Of course, while the building was being constructed, Baker had prowled every inch of its interior. But this was his first visit to the roof. He immediately spied a sizable flat space. He said, "Gee, what a great space to do a play!" Baker was standing on top of a building that housed his realized dream. And he wanted to do a play on its roof! But then he always believed that any empty space is a stage.

With our new facility, our program expanded, our staff was enlarged, we had an ever-increasing number of majors, and we presented a hyperactive season of productions. Eventually, each semester we had eight sections of the integration of abilities class and with more than 140 students enrolled. For years, the Ruth Taylor Theater was a truly remarkable place, with its students, both majors and nonmajors, learning a creative approach to the arts and to their lives, and staging productions that enriched the campus and the community. And Trinity gained national recognition.

Baker's energy, drive, and creative thinking had always earned for him strong friends and strong enemies. After he retired to Waelder, the enemies laid siege to his ideas. In Dallas, new management took over direction of the Theater Center. No one who had worked with Baker remained.

In San Antonio, Trinity had a new administration that viewed the arts as an extracurricular activity. Within a few short years, all those who taught the integration of abilities classes

Playwright Paddy Chayefsky, director Burgess Meredith and Dallas Theater Center managing director Paul Baker prior to the world premier of *The Latent Heterosexual* starring Zero Mostel.

8

were no longer in the department or no longer at Trinity. The course itself was canceled. The celebrated Theater One was remodeled into a permanent orthodox proscenium theater, beginning the twenty-first century with a retreat into the nineteenth. But the concept of that once-flexible space survives.

Proving that you cannot kill a brilliant idea, the once-unique Baylor Theater concept has been replicated in theaters nationally—four of them in Texas—and internationally. The integration of abilities concept is taught in such countries as Korea, India, Guam, and New Zealand, and in many colleges and public schools in the United States by those who have read Baker's books and by those students we may have forgotten. They have not forgotten the lessons they learned.

And, by the way, Baker's directorial genius is still active. Recently, at a large party at his ranch, some of us were on the porch talking while watching his herd of cattle grazing in the distance. Baker got out of his chair, cupped his hands around his mouth, and bellowed: "All right, you cows, slowly move to stage right!"

Right on cue, the cows, as a group, started moving stage right until they disappeared from view. Now, several of Baker's neighbors there on the porch were astonished. But we who have known the man for a long time just nodded our heads and said to ourselves, "Yep, he's still got it."■

Trojan Women, Trinity University

9

Creative workshop at Trinity's Children's Theater

10

The Integration of Abilities:
Exercises for Creative Growth

William M. Doll

The integration of abilities (IA) philosophy and methodology developed by Paul Baker serves as both a course of study and a creative process. First taught at Baylor University in the 1930s, it is the basis for all creative work by Baker, his students, and the professionals who worked under his supervision. Baker has recorded the philosophy in his books, *Integration of Abilities: Exercises for Creative Growth* and *Making Sense with Five Senses*.

The core of both of Baker's books and of his thinking/creative process is the exploration of the elements of form, which he outlines as: space, movement, line, color, sound/silence, rhythm, silhouette, shape, and texture. These elements serve as a connecting force for all learning and creative activities and are referred to and used as a "common language."[1]

Integration has been taught to elementary school students and teachers, to children in children's theater programs, to teens in teen theater programs, to undergraduate and graduate students at Baylor University in Waco and Trinity University in San Antonio, and to graduate students at the Dallas Theater Center.

Baker has shared his methods and philosophies with hundreds of practitioners. Their extension of his work in their methods and philosophies of art, arts education, and personal development reveal the depth of his influence. Theoretical and historical examination of successful methodologies has long been a part of education and the arts. Throughout history there have been innovators and creative figures whose ideas remain "alive" through the reexamination and continued use of their work by scholars, educators, and artists who establish new perspectives on such work. So it is with Baker: a variety of applications continue to be found for his approach to creative development.[2]

The primary goal of the Baker method is to open doors to the student's creative self and therefore enhance individual creativity through self-discovery. Students keep journals of their life experiences to understand how they think and express themselves most effectively. The journal is also used to record students' impressions of the work generated by the exercises practiced in IA. This self-examination is intended to help students remain open and receptive to all their creative ideas.

In his dissertation, "A History of the Development and Growth of the Dallas Theater Center," John Marder III refers to the IA class not as a course in the study of drama but a caldron

11

of ideas, experiments, and discoveries. "The purpose of the course was to acquaint students with their own minds, stimulate the emotions to a response, force the body to act as an instrument to carry out the commands imposed on it by the mind and emotions, and ultimately, to show how these three forces can be integrated through discovery of the individual's creative ability to enable him to find his direction in relation to space and time. Once this integration was accomplished, great works could result" (Marder, 1972, 49–50).

The process increases students' awareness of the ability to create and an understanding of the different ways individuals best learn and create. Baker has pointed out that because our society is structured and focused on the ability to learn via text, it stifles the creativity and self-respect of those who learn and express themselves most effectively through other senses and other ways of processing information. Persons who are not primarily word-oriented have difficulty in the academic world where their individual learning strengths are ignored.[3]

Baker worked to liberate those who learned and expressed themselves most effectively though visual, aural, kinesthetic, and tactile means. Students begin by discovering their own "original" self. Without understanding of self, originality and creativity are not possible. Baker discusses his own humble childhood in West Texas in the preface to his book, *The Integration of Abilities*:

I'm a West Texan. That means I come from sun-conquered and wind-conquered country. It is a cruel country, and the faces of the old men who have lived there all their lives show the sand, wind, heat, and dryness of it all. West Texas is a great space. As a child I was overwhelmed by the tremendous sky and great flat land—the tremendous space. That space, bounded by very distant horizons where flat earth met the sky, seemed to me an infinity of distances. That was the first great space I knew.

I remember the dramatic silhouette of the windmill; the windmill at a distance; the windmill, which brought water to our house, as it sat in the backyard impressed against the sky. On moonlit nights or in dust storms, barely visible, or on beautiful spring days when the weather changed from warm sunshine to a blizzard in only a few minutes, there was that windmill. Every kind of weather and wind and cloud silhouetted that windmill—lonesome, stark, friendly, grotesque. So, we had space. We had that space cut with a windmill—a gigantic character etched against the sky, drawn there. (vii)

Acknowledgment and examination of the world in which one grew up is rudimentary to discovery of the original creative self. Certainly anyone who devoted time to his past experience would have a clearer understanding of his or her own behavior than would a person who ignored the past.

Space concept as exploited in the Baylor production of A *Different Drummer*.

"This course in the integration of abilities starts at that point when we were very young, before we had words to put the feelings together, or words to destroy the feeling. It starts at where we were when we were very alone and very private people" (*Integration of Abilities*, viii).

Much of Baker's philosophy and methods are based on relearning childhood freedoms and unlearning the barriers, fears, and inhibitions to creative expression. What we know often inhibits our creativity and stifles the imagination, and we must relearn how we became the individuals we are, discover what Baker calls our personal "landscape." Thus, journaling is expected of all students.

Each student begins by writing his or her life story to the present and recording reactions to the class in a notebook. That story should include the student's background, significant moments or events, and a study of the attitudes, values, and philosophies of the family, hometown, and schools attended.[4]

Baker asks students to discover what kind of persons they are or want to be and challenges them to consider four growth levels to discover which are most appreciated and what limits them from attaining the highest level. He explains:

1. To some, growth is almost all memory and recollection. Names, faces, events; the latest slang, movies, athletic and social activities; what to wear, to eat, to buy; the continuous enumeration of places, times, occurrences—these are the preoccupations at this level.

2. To some, growth lies in learning how gadgets work—how to put motors together, how to attach pipes, mix formulas, solve problems. The purpose is never to develop a new method but to become extremely adept at the old one. Redoing, becoming faster than someone else, competing by telling others how to improve in their performance are ends in themselves.

3. To some, growth is the extension of ready-made faith. It sets the follower apart and makes him superior to the common herd. He applies well-worn formulas, recollects, memorizes, improves standards and talents, develops cults. He projects systems whereby he can estimate how far below his own standards other people have fallen. He joins, dictates, slaps backs, smokes cigars in back rooms. He belongs to important committees; becomes a pseudo artist, musician, actor, prophet, preacher, politician, drops names and surrounds himself with position.

4. To some few, growth is the discovery of a dynamic

As for the Baker philosophy, world-renowned avant-garde artist and playwright, Robert Wilson says he took from the Baylor Children's Theater the Baker dictum that "we each have a landscape, a vision which is individually ours."

14

power of the mind. There is a long period of intense study, criticism, and self-examination. Directions are not easily found; words do not come easily; the growth process is of little immediate interest to anyone else. The stimuli to growth come from within the person. They are fed by ideas and sensations from nature, books, works of faith, bodily movement. The growth is precious and very private. It cannot be put on display or put to immediate use. It does not deal in mass or grow in a gang. It has no formula. It has faith, love, steel guts, impatience with mediocrity. It demands utmost extension of the body it inhabits. It works and slaves; engulfs whole ideas; absorbs; performs surgical operations on pat formulas; laughs heartily at mediocrity and opens new worlds of insight. This mind is at home in any period, in any place where genius has produced lasting works (*Integration of Abilities*, 13–17).

Three Zeros and One One, Baylor Theater

Baker insists that theater training, for example, does not make a person creative but that students must discover their own creative imagination and creative drives that can be expressed through their art or discipline. He criticizes teachers' attempts to mold students into images of themselves. Instead he contends that the goal of IA is helping students escape traditional molds.[5] He cautions teachers of IA not to teach but rather to let the course be the students' course, to allow freedom of expression, to give each student the luxury of failing and making mistakes and looking foolish. A teacher who knows what he wants from a student and forces that on him has failed the student. The teacher's job is to help the student determine in which of the elements he is strongest and to give him the confidence to express that strength.[6]

The first exercise that Baker uses establishes that the class is not a theater course but one about the discovery of creative ability and the way each student works best. The student moves across the stage twice, expressing tragedy one time and comedy the next. There is no time limit, no words or storytelling, no copying, no result orientation. In preparing the exercise, students are to write all of their ideas and to watch the process by which they prepare.[7]

Baker believes that when a student is confronted with a

Charles Laughton "discovered" the Baylor Theater on one of his national reading tours, was stunned by its revolutionary design, and became a fervent supporter of Baker's productions. He returned to Waco often, and was instrumental in Burgess Meredith's decision to appear in a one-month run in the Baylor Theater's initial production of *Hamlet*.

16

problem, the mind will consciously and subconsciously work on the problem. The student will become aware of mental activity, and learning the patterns in which his or her mind works is the integration of abilities. Baker's definition of "mind" is borrowed from Frank Lloyd Wright. "But the Mind should be not only a matter of the head (the intellect) but an affair of the heart and of the imagination and of the hand (or what we call technique). But I believe that until those three (intellect, heart, and hand) become one, become operative by inspiration, going to work all together, you do not have a true work of the Mind" (*The Works of the Mind*, 50). Imagination, emotion, and the craft of the hand are as important as the head.

Others have used similar approaches. Ramon Delgado echoes Wright's definition in *Acting with Both Sides of Your Brain*. "You will note that the left-brain functions are verbal and logical; the right-brain functions are nonverbal, kinesthetic, spatial, and interpretive. In the creative processes of acting, creative and interpretive right-brain specialties combine with the logical, recognition abilities of the left brain to collate their abilities into an integrated performance that is both emotionally sensitive and intelligently controlled."[8] Delgado analyzes the issue in a more scientific manner than does Baker; yet Delgado's process is quite similar to Baker's, using journaling and the elements in his training of actors.

Baker warns students that the comic and tragic walks will seem absurd but that growth will come if they record their resistance by writing their inner dialogue (*Integration of Abilities*, 24–25). He reminds students that in every activity we have space, direction, or movement, time or rhythm, silhouette, and sound. Space, as the core of creativity, is a universal principle.

This is made clear by Karl Jaspers' definition of space and time in *General Psychopathology*. "Space and Time are always present in sensory processes. . . . They are not primary objects themselves but they invest all objectivity. Kant calls them 'forms of intuition.' They are universal. Everything we experience comes to us in space and time and we experience it only in these terms. . . . Space and Time are real for us only through their content" (Jaspers, 79).

All creativity begins with an empty space. To construct a building, you first clear a space. To create a painting, you begin with a clean canvas. Space and time are shaped by related elements. Space is shaped by line, shape, texture, direction, movement, color, silhouette, rhythm, light, and shadow. Time is shaped by tempo, rhythm, duration, sound, and silence.

After addressing space, Baker asks the student to look for comic rhythm and tragic rhythm. Not all comic rhythm is fast, and not all tragic rhythm is slow. The student is going to cut that space with his or her silhouette. The student must decide at what point to enter the stage space and what direction movement will take. And for how long? There are thousands of different points that may be used to enter the space, thousands of directions available in that space, dozens of silhouettes that may be used to cut the space, and hundreds of rhythms, all of which can be used in various combinations. He or she doesn't have to use a direction, shape, or rhythm that anyone else has used. The possibilities are staggering to the student, but from those choices can evolve a fresh discovery, a unique, new idea. That is what the class is about, the student becoming an original.

Some students perform the exercise without giving much thought to it. In much schoolwork, students who get the answer quickly get the best grades, but those who distill the material and relate to it with mind and imagination will develop a method of meeting problems, an understanding of what it is they do well and in which areas they are weak. They must keep their notebooks by their sides as they work, jotting down the way their minds respond to the problems.

Thus they examine not only the possibilities of the elements that shape space and time but also of how they themselves think. Creative products result only from work, and without taking the small steps at the beginning, no work of value will ever result.

The second exercise uses automatic writing. The student is given a word and writes whatever comes to mind, any associations. When first enthusiasm wears off, the student is encouraged to take the word and begin again. The goal of automatic writing is to see what happens.

Free drawing follows the writing exercise. The student is shown a line drawing and begins drawing in response. It is a challenge to some students to express themselves freely, to respond to a word or a line without fear of failure. Students are required to keep all of their writing and drawing in notebooks, to date each entry, and to study the work to recognize old patterns, words, or shapes and to see new patterns emerge.

The third exercise studies visual and auditory rhythm. We all receive rhythmic stimuli and respond to them muscularly, either tensing or relaxing to the rhythms we experience. These can be specific or they can be a part of a broader context.

Cities, countries, regions, ages, and people have unique rhythms. Our individual rhythm is a composite of heredity and experiences. Baker suggests that rhythmically we might often be confused by our frantic lives; therefore, finding our basic rhythm is important to self-awareness. In the rhythm exercise, study of another person's rhythm is central.

Students select two people that they know well in different circumstances and environments, someone eighteen or older so the personality has begun to form. They observe and record as much about these two people as possible: postures (slumped or erect), tensions (tight or relaxed), strengths (developed or undeveloped, where?), tempos (fast or slow), etc., and what kinds of events might change them. Then they look at the person's philosophy or basic attitudes toward life.

The students reduce that information on each subject to a rhythm and clap out that rhythm with their hands. The teachers of the class, which for this exercise is broken down into small groups, respond to a student's clapping of the individual by relating what those rhythms tell about the character. This is the exercise most difficult to visualize because of its high degree of abstraction. It is also the exercise that is most convincing to students when Baker or one of the instructors correctly describes the subject.[9]

In the fourth exercise, creative self-discovery becomes clearer through the exploration of all the senses using a common focus: an inanimate object out of nature. The student writes down what he sees, not what he thinks he ought to see, not some moral lesson or universal precept. The student describes the color, texture, line, mass, and rhythm of the object, describing it from many angles, at various times of day, and when the student is in different moods, looking for the elements from as many perspectives as possible. Patience is important, and Baker cautions students to fight resistance and not to fear or block their ideas and responses.

The student then creates a character from the written description and the rhythm of the inanimate object and puts that person in a real setting with dialogue. The assignment demands honesty, time to distill the work, revisions, patience, and self-discovery. The goal is "discovery action" and not "result action," even though the scene is intended to be shared with the class. Discovering how creative work is performed on a personal level and what is involved in experiencing creative work are the goals of the exercise.[10]

The fourth exercise is a prelude to a more intense yet similar process in the fifth exercise. Reducing the fear of trying is a benefit of the previous exercises. In addition, the students are by then more accustomed to allowing themselves to think in their own ways. This is new to many who have been taught that free expression is not necessarily acceptable.

The fifth exercise, which extends through most of the semester, begins like the fourth exercise with an object of nature, one that has at least three kinds of lines in it. The student also needs large sheets of drawing paper, notebooks, and drawing tools such as pens, pencils, paints, and crayons. Being comfortable in dress and in the workspace is vital throughout the exercise, because this exercise is based on motor responses, not intellectual ones.[11]

As children, we seem to be most creative when we are moving, and it is fun. Our muscles have not received the training and conditioning that our intellect has; therefore, a muscular or kinetic reaction is more honest, more distinctively individual, than an intellectual reaction. Students are asked to listen to the way their bodies tells them what feels right or good and what doesn't feel good or is unpleasant as they try to recapture the childhood joy of movement.

The first step is to draw the object on a page and bring it to class. The next step is to walk out the lines of the drawing, transferring the shape into movement through space. As the student walks the pattern repeatedly, he or she experiences the object's rhythm. The student is to perform the movement until it is comfortable and then to eliminate the part of the movement that is not kinetically pleasing and enlarge the part that is. Repeating and trying new and different approaches to discover what works

Baylor Children's Theater,

well is a key to the activities in the exercises. With each alteration, the student notes why it has been altered and records the internal dialogue between body and mind. Then a new drawing is made, enlarging again what is liked and eliminating what is disliked. In this way, the students let their muscles tell them what is right.

From the movement and drawing come rhythm, sound, and color. The student records the process, describing feelings, choices, and observations, and making drawing after drawing. Some students spend additional time experimenting with and developing different media. Teachers encourage this as long as all sensory experiences are worked and are allowed to have influence on the others. Some students develop complex sound compositions from movement or color studies, and others find that sound influences movement studies.[12]

The last step of the exercise is built on five activities. The student transfers the motor experience into a three-dimensional sculpture,[13] into literary form such as poetry, drama, or short story, into a dance or stage movement, into music or sound composition,[14] and a two-dimensional art work such as a painting or watercolor. The concluding activity is a three- or four-minute staged scene; as in exercise four, the student is to develop a character from the elemental qualities that have been discovered, creating and placing a real character into a real situation with real dialogue.

Each new work should begin with a return to the source—the walking of the design, a recording of whatever thoughts or feelings come, a review of previous activities to see how they have grown, and further development of ideas that have emerged. Baker encourages students to visualize themselves performing the activities. Visualization and freedom are vital, providing the independence to work and not be afraid of the activities or the discoveries.

Everyone is gifted differently. Some express themselves more creatively in words, others in sound, movement, or color. Results are not important. Results can take on such import that they become a distraction, inhibiting the creative process. The process of discovery is the primary objective.[15]

The five exercises may appear simple, and they are, as activities. The self-study combined with the activities and the perspective brought by the course creates complexity. Perhaps its simplicity accounts for its broad implementation and continuing impact. All disciplines have their rudimentary exercises, and these are repeated at every practice or study session from the beginning level to the professional level.

Sometimes we allow some of our abilities to atrophy, to become weak and dull. This weakness in one or more areas may inhibit the creative process. According to Baker's philosophy, it takes all of our abilities, working in unison, for our creative selves to function most effectively, and his goal is to see these abilities strong and integrated.[16]

The Baker philosophy has been used across the discipline barriers in the arts: visual arts, music, dance, creative writing, and architecture. It is not an end-all to art or to education but rather seeks to find new rewards in all areas of creative development.[17] Baker says it clearly:

> I have learned to never underestimate the potential of anybody and to not be a judge or a critic, but to share an experience of discovering with all those whom I meet. From my students I have learned that there is genius in all of us and that that genius must be discovered and exercised and given a chance to express itself (*Integration of Abilities*, ix).

To discover and love the creative impulse in oneself and to find a way of communicating that impulse is what all art hopes to accomplish; what Paul Baker has provided is an approach to aid in the achievement of this goal. ■

End Notes

[1] IA provided me with a language . . . understandable to those on the outside. I work for Walt Disney World Entertainment. Artists from varied disciplines, meeting together to create a product, struggle to communicate ideas and concepts. This language meets this need. *Steven Peterson*

I've used the elements in approaching characters (good technique to have for cold readings and soap work), analyzing scripts, designing, and communicating to others. *Jessamy Tomlinson*

I provide state of the art equipment for international concerts. It's an exciting business filled with creative people. I've been working with Mark Fisher, a British architect acknowledged to be the world's foremost concert stage designer. When I communicate with Mark on big projects, I use line, rhythm, texture, shape, etc., and he immediately understands what I'm saying. My job as production manager (coordinating between design and production, and between Japan and England or the U.S. or Germany or wherever) has been made much easier by my command of these concepts. *Yoichi Aoki*

The "elements" have stayed with me for all these years. . . . It is one of my main tools in my arsenal of director's tricks. *David Cotton*

[2] It may appear to be a fairly broad leap from drama major to insurance executive, but what I learned in IA has served me well. *Mike Bathke*

My first job out of college was as a window trimmer for a large department store chain in Washington, D.C. My display windows earned me a window display manager position at the age of twenty-two. *Donna Sullivan Everage*

I have used what I learned from Prof directing plays, motion pictures, television, slide/tapes, and multi-image productions, stage directing operas, designing and building sets for stage productions, pageants, motion pictures. Because of the people we met through Prof—Charles Laughton, Burgess Meredith, Bob Hope, Brooks Atkinson, etc.—when I had the good fortune to direct Jimmy Stewart in a motion picture, I was able to do my job professionally with no fear of the man. *Jerry Ratliff*

I am a musician-record producer and contributed original music to *Paris, Texas, The Border, Streets of Fire, Long Riders,* and *Alamo Bay,* among other Hollywood films. I have produced or recorded with musical artists from Arlo Guthrie and the Rolling Stones to Aretha Franklin and Carmen McRae. I have passed on what I learned from Prof to two generations of artists. *Jim Dickinson*

Paul Baker caused me to do more thinking about life and important issues than anyone else. I got my master's degree in social work from Columbia University and it all fit together. *Carol Smilley*

Corner stage of the Baylor production of *Othello*

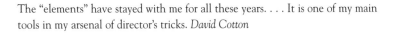

23

When I couldn't find a play to direct for my church, I knew I could write one, and I did. I've since written and published several plays. *Barbara Terrill Rowland*

Upon recent publication of one of my plays, Prof said, "That just goes to show you, something good happens if you live long enough." I remember the joy of risk. *Sally Netzel*

I travel, capturing events with photographs and words, detailing in mathematical precision costs and repairs. I have been able to integrate my fascination with machinery, catastrophe, and human nature with an ability to see and capture a form, retell a tale, and translate this into a practical product, enabling me to have a good life. *David S. Holder*

I have taught school, developed a chain of sporting good stores (Academy) with my former husband, directed television commercials, and worked in film. I have used integration of abilities in everything that I have done. . . . I once worked for Francis Ford Coppola in the film *Cotton Club*. I remember thinking how he could have benefited from IA. *Sara Hess Roney*

[I] express gratitude . . . for his creativity and how he used it to teach and instill in so many of us who have studied with him and known him the kind of values and life skills that actually have changed our lives and given them direction. *Robert Johnson, president, The Johnson Group (creative media producers)*

[3] My family tended to be methodical, systematic, efficient, goal oriented. Feeling free to express myself in unconventional ways makes me a better parent and a better therapist and teacher. IA taught me the value of seeing in myself and in others a limitless potential for tapping into new and exciting areas of growth. *Mary Ann Brawner Barnett*

Prof did not try to force us into some mold; he helped us escape. I escaped. *Ladelle Dennis Bisel*

Prof taught me that every child comes to class with gifts. If you do not accept them, they stop bringing them. *Joe Kagle*

[4] I remember sitting in Brackenridge Park, with my portable typewriter perched on the tailgate of the station wagon, typing (it seemed like) hundreds of pages of autobiography. *Rachel Anderson Tayar*

I dug through the trunk of college stuff and buried down deep—the daily journals and writings I had kept during my integration of abilities years. I could not believe the raw emotion and fears and joys that I expressed in those journals and how I poured my soul into those writings. I learned how to channel my creativity, not only with drama and art but in life itself. *Donna Sullivan Everage*

Prof trained us to set the highest possible standards —not his, but our own— and to risk them in a principled and disciplined manner. I remember him saying so often, "The one thing in life you must not do is nothing."

Robert Johnson
president
The Johnson Group

24

5 For fifty years Prof taught each of us our uniqueness, to trust our own vision, to find our own way; to confront and face down mediocrity in ourselves; that if we can imagine something, we can achieve it; if we can dream it, we can become it. *An address delivered by Orlin Corey at the annual Distinguished Alumni Awards Dinner, Baylor University, February 18, 1983*

6 I found . . . that what I thought of as my 'gift' was only one among many and maybe not even my best one. I found I had an artist's eye and a gift for three-dimensional media, despite the fact that I never could draw or paint or do any of the things I thought of as artistic. *Rachel Anderson Tayar*

7 The task seemed simple and clear enough, but my attempts to plan a response released a cloud of resistance. I finally walked that stage and learned how challenging it was to stand before others and give some expression. Scores of students like me came into that space for all kinds of reasons and emerged having learned something powerful and profound about themselves and their relationship with others, about their place in the world and about what it means to occupy something as open as an empty space. *Jim Laurie*

I love starting to rehearse a show and walking into an empty theater because the elements will all come together to create a new work. When I teach a class I use the exercise of walking across the space using the feeling of comedy and tragedy. It is where I discovered myself as an artist and individual. *Ron Pirette*

8 One of my favorite assignments was the resistance-to-work paper. I wrote about the things that kept me from sitting down and writing the paper. I think of it often when I find myself procrastinating. *Jocelyn Crews*

9 I was confused and skeptical. Here was a way of working that was designed to bypass my linear and logical editor that public schools had forged so well. I began to believe again in intuition, metaphor, and magic as I 'clapped' the rhythm of my father, then listened as Baker described his impression of this clapped character as if he'd known my father a lifetime. *Rachel Anderson Tayar*

10 I remember a short scene that grew out of my inanimate object character. That may have been the only time I was ever able to leave my fear and inhibitions in the wings long enough to give a credible acting performance on stage. Possibly because the character was at once a totally fictional creation and at the same time a deeply personal and unrecognized piece of myself. *Rachel Anderson Tayar*

11 It was where I became aware of the importance of movement. I didn't continue as a dancer but I am a fight director. I've performed and staged fights from sword duels and battles to fights with umbrellas and purses. I conduct workshops in stage combat. *Ron Pirette*

12 I loved the freeing experience of exploring an idea or feeling through sound, movement, and the elements of form rather than simply through words. I have used these techniques in several of my productions over the years, notably on shows that require actors to find an intuitive wellspring of emotion outside the boundaries of what can be neatly explained verbally. I take them through the process of creating a physically-based metaphor for a feeling or force and then drawing the metaphor, moving what they drew, drawing what they moved, and so on through the process, until they're left with something very personal, vivid, and fully explored. *Tom Rowan*

13 I studied a rock I picked up on a Hill Country outing. I studied it morning, noon, and night, when I felt good, when I felt bad. I recreated it in a clay sculpture. While we lived in Terlingua, outside of Big Bend National Park where Trent taught in a one-room schoolhouse for five years, I had a full-fledged ceramic pottery business going. *Olga Jones*

14 I remember the panic when we were told to prepare a three-minute 'sound and movement exercise.' What was that? Where was the script? I'd never been required to create something so abstract and so wholly my own. It doesn't matter that I don't remember what I did. It matters that I did it. *Josie Whitley*

15 We made music, wrote, created characters from twigs. I started sculpting in stone and metal. When I went to The Goodman School of Drama for my MFA, I always went into the art studio to create a metal sculpture of the characters I played. *Ron Pirette*

I created three hundred drawings, a sculpture, a poem, a short story, and a character. The volume of work I created in a six-week period amazed me. But that amazement was nothing compared to the awe and internal stirring when I saw the combined work of all of my classmates at the end of the exercise. I've never been the same. That class vivified for me the limitlessness of human imagination when it's combined with persistent effort and freedom from criticism. I believe in people's ability to find solutions to any problem. *Josie Whitley*

16 I serve as professor of electronic media & film at Eastern Washington University. In addition to my career as a teacher, I have produced, written and directed over five hundred television programs, authored a textbook, created a radio station, continued an active career as a painter, and am completing negotiations for the sale of my first feature screenplay and a commercial cable television series. I use the exercises and discipline I learned in IA as the beginning point for every script, every character, every interview, every program, every sketch for every painting. It is the organizing principle for my life. IA allowed me to nurture my most precious commodity—my inner voice. I have merely done what Baker asked me to do, searched for the truth in myself and reported it to the world. *Marvin Smith*

26

[17] . . . most things in the classroom in college are like you go in, the bell sounds, the professor starts talking, you take notes wildly, the bell sounds, and you're out again. And this (IA) was something that there were just no limits and it kept challenging you to think further and think about things you'd never thought about before and do things you'd never done before. It was just a wonderful experience. I'm sure the things I learned in there are just integrated as they told us to do . . . integrated into your potential. It was so great. I wish I'd kept a diary of it. I was always so grateful to Trinity for it. And again, it was one of those visionary things that Dr. Laurie did. *Joe Armstrong*

Works Cited

Baker, Kitty, and Jearnine Wagner. *A Place for Ideas—Our Theater*. Foreword by Paul Baker. San Antonio: Principia Press of Trinity University, 1965.

Baker, Paul. *Integration of Abilities: Exercises for Creative Growth*. San Antonio: Trinity University Press, 1972.

———— *Making Sense with Five Senses*. Waelder, TX: Paul Baker Enterprises, 1993.

Durham, Willard Higley, and John W. Dodds, eds. *British and American Plays 1830–1945*. New York: Oxford University Press, 1947.

Jaspers, Karl. *General Psychopathology*. Translated by J. Hoenig and Marian W. Hamilton. Chicago: University of Chicago Press, 1968.

Heywood, Robert B., ed. *The Works of the Mind*. Chicago: University of Chicago Press, 1947.

Marder, Carl John III. "A History of the Development and Growth of the Dallas Theater Center."   Ph.D. diss. University of Kansas, 1972.

The Dallas Theater Center's Minority Theater (later called The Janus Players). Pictured is Reginald Montgomery

27

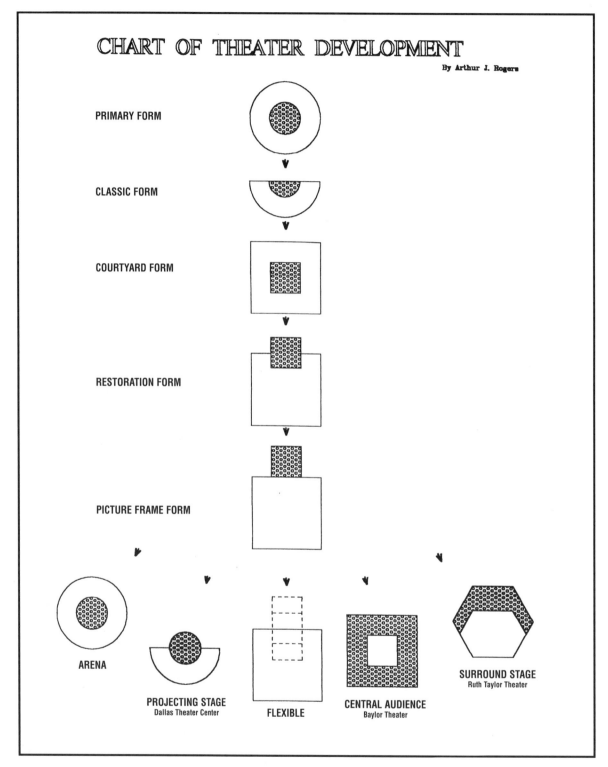

CHART OF THEATER DEVELOPMENT

By Arthur J. Rogers

PRIMARY FORM

CLASSIC FORM

COURTYARD FORM

RESTORATION FORM

PICTURE FRAME FORM

ARENA

PROJECTING STAGE
Dallas Theater Center

FLEXIBLE

CENTRAL AUDIENCE
Baylor Theater

SURROUND STAGE
Ruth Taylor Theater

28

Paul Baker and Theater Architecture

Arthur J. Rogers

In the long history of theater architecture, from its primitive beginnings to the incredible proliferation of entertainment facilities built in the post-World War II era, no single person has contributed more to its development than Paul Baker. Early in his career he constructed a new theater form of historical significance and went on to bring invaluable insights to enrich both drama and architecture, as they come together in theater architecture.

Architecture for the theater has its fundamental essence in the place where the union between architecture and theater occurs. More than a stage from which to perform and seats from which to watch, more than a physical place, that essence is the spatial relationship between the audience and the actors. It is a complex quality that is, at the same time, metaphysical and prosaic, abstract and concrete. Understanding this relationship requires a grasp of the concept of space and time as indivisible, as space/time, and a dedicated realization that the relation of the actors and the audience is, above all, a space/time relationship.

The arts of theater and architecture develop in much the same way in that they move from the abstract to the concrete, from ideas to plays and buildings, from the poetic to the prosaic and, if successful, to an eventual end as a poetic, abstract reality. Paul Baker's contribution to art is that he brought all of this together in a way that had not been done before and invented a language for the arts that made possible dialogue between artists rather than only dialectic discourse. It is a language that, should we care to use it, enables us to construct buildings that are not only workplaces for creating significant theater but have the potential for great architectural design. Baker, always the teacher,

A theater should be a space awating the wildest flights of imagination.
Paul Baker

29

has illuminated the obvious with a way of thinking that encourages an ongoing, ever-evolving creation of new theater and new architectures for it.

From its beginnings in early Greek culture, architecture for the theater evolved progressively for more than two thousand years, reaching a plateau in the early part of the seventeenth century with the establishment of the proscenium theater form. This form, in which the audience in one room views the actors in another room through an opening (proscenium), remained in use for the next three centuries and was presumed to be the end point in the development of the genre. Architectural technology, spurred by the Industrial Revolution, the development of steel and ensuing engineering advances, as well as inventions like the electric light and air-conditioning, brought many innovations to the proscenium form, improving and perfecting it. However, the form itself, the relation between the actor and the audience, did not change or improve. The world was not to see a change in that regard until the late 1930s, when Paul Baker built a new form of theater at Baylor University in Waco, Texas. With this form, one in which the actor-audience relationship became a unified space, Baker earned a place in the history of world theater as the creator of the first new form of theater architecture in three hundred years.[1]

Paul Baker had studied under George Pierce Baker at Yale and was heavily influenced by the writings of Adolphe Appia and Gordon Craig. Appia was a theater theorist and visionary who wrote about the art of the theater in the 1920s and '30s. Craig, son of famed actress Ellen Terry, was an early-twentieth-century playwright and director who wrote *On the Art of the Theater* and *Toward a New Theater*.

Craig and Appia emphasized and clarified metaphysical concepts of space and time in their ideas about the theater. They introduced the idea of artistic space and time as a unity, or space/time. It was an idea not commonly held or understood. Baker embraced their thinking and followed with a language for using this abstract approach that enabled artists to utilize this concept in making their art in the theater, and, potentially, elsewhere. This language identified components of space/time such as light and dark, sound and silence, shadow, texture, color, and proportion. Baker showed how these elements could be manipulated with movement and rhythm.

With these basic elements, an entire world of creative possibility opened up. It was a new way of looking at things. When Baker had an opportunity to build a place for performing his ideas, he adapted a structure at Baylor University to that purpose, and in a very un-architectural way, created a new form. He did this by constructing a U-shaped stage with the audience in the middle. The three stages created in this manner surrounded the audience with the action, making them all part of the same space. To facilitate this, Baker placed the audience in swivel chairs, so the spectators could turn as the stage action went back and forth, making the audience itself another actor. The genius in this theater form was the way it took abstract, metaphysical thoughts and made them into a concrete reality that could be used to manipulate ideas into creative, artistic performances. The Baylor theater of 1939 demonstrated the creation and use of space/time. Baker had begun to make a vocabulary for architects as well as dramatists.[2]

Modern architecture had its genesis in the the Industrial Revolution and the subsequent development of steel in the late nineteenth century. Louis Sullivan and his erstwhile protégé, Frank Lloyd Wright, were major figures in the new architecture made possible by those developments, and their designs marked the first departure from formalism as well as the design formulas of the Beaux Arts era.

The Beaux Arts was a formal system of teaching the arts originating in France in the late nineteenth century and lasting until the 1930s. It eventually became so rigid and dogmatic that many artists reacted against it. In the case of architecture, the pedagogy centered on neo-classical revival, ignoring modern needs and ideas about architecture. It was used in many American architectural schools until just before World War II, when it fell into disfavor. The return of servicemen from the war and their demand for wide-based and practical architectural training brought an end to the Beaux Arts era.

The design advances of Sullivan, Wright, and others were interrupted by the 1893 Columbian Exposition in Chicago, an eclectic collection of World's Fair buildings done in the European neoclassical style. Sullivan claimed that it would set architecture back fifty years, and his prediction proved eerily accurate. For Sullivan, one of America's preeminent architects at the time, the exposition marked the beginning of his professional and personal decline, and he died in poverty about ten years later.

Frank Lloyd Wright, however, continued to design contemporary buildings, albeit in his own esoteric way, for sixty more years. During most of that time, the influence of the Columbian

Exposition dominated American architecture, and the Beaux Art method was the mainstay of American architectural education. It was not until the 1940s, with the influx of the Bauhaus architects fleeing Nazi rule and their subsequent influence on the postwar building boom in America, that the Beaux Arts was abandoned and contemporary architecture took hold, fifty years after Sullivan's prediction.

The Bauhaus, an art and architecture school in Germany, was founded in 1919 by architect Walter Gropius and others. Gropius emigrated to the United States after Hitler came to power and established the foundation of contemporary architectural education at Harvard. Mies van der Rohe replaced Gropius at the Bauhaus and eventually left Germany after Hitler started World War II to go to Chicago, where he practiced architecture and influenced American architecture until his death in 1969. The Bauhaus movement died out in 1939, but it had influenced architectural and industrial design worldwide, the result being what the general public commonly knows as "modern" design. This new "contemporary" style of architecture, while demanding a high level of professional artistic skill combined with equally strict engineering competence, created a fertile field for creative design in architecture, and the period from the end of World War II until the mid-1960s brought forth some of America's greatest architecture. It was a time of individual architects,—Wright, Stone, Yamasaki, the Sararinens, Harrison and Abramovitz, Mies van der Rohe, and, at the end, Louis Kahn,— each noted for his own creative way, a pantheon of architectural gods. It was the time of the Lever Building, the TWA Terminal, the Guggenhiem, the Museum of Modern Art, Illinois Institute of Technology, and the St. Louis Arch, all of them creative landmarks and none of them of a certain style or similar to each other. It was a time of creative individual accomplishment. This was true not only of architects, but generally for all American artists. Certainly it was true of Baker.

As the history of architecture tends to be additive and linear in that its artifacts remain in place over time, the history of the theater is collective and impermanent. While theater continually evaporates, it is constantly renewed as its body of work expands. The only tangible historical residue of theater art is the architecture in which it is performed. This residue is the evidence of the origin of the meeting of these two arts.

It is commonly held that the first places for theater in the Western world were the alonia, or circular stone threshing floors, found in the grain fields of ancient Greece. The essence of this first form was an audience surrounding performers. There is no question that the actors and the audience shared the same space or space/time. This actor/audience relationship can be analogized as a fried egg with the actors being the yolk and the audience the surrounding egg white. One can trace the evolution of theater form from that point forward by extending the analogy.

The next evolution of the stage occurred when the Greeks replaced the alonia with a round stone floor next to a hill, increasing audience capacity and improving acoustics. The actor/audience space was altered in that the egg white now surrounded only part of the yolk, like the letter C. The Romans took this a step farther and cut the fried egg precisely in half, turning the actor/audience relationship into a more frontal presentation and away from a relationship of inclusion. Collateral with this development in Greco-Roman culture was the advent and growth of theater in the Near East, in Asia, and later in England. Early Japanese theater, the No drama, was acted in the same fried egg form as the alonia, with the audience around the actors. This form was a natural way for performing and viewing and can be seen in the dance-based drama of the preindustrialized cultures of Africa and pre-Columbian America.

As the Dark Ages overtook western civilization, the structured drama of Greece and Rome was lost. In Iran and England, and probably in many other cultures, theater consisted of traveling storytellers and loosely knit groups performing in town centers from carts or wagons. The players stopped in an open area and performed for an ad hoc audience that gathered around them and their vehicle stage. This became known as the courtyard form. It is not hard to visualize the next step, which was to push the cart next to a building, with much the same effect on the actor/audience relationship as the Roman theaters. The half-fried-egg form returned.

To this point in history, theater was performed outdoors. While the essence of the place for theater, the actor/audience space relationship, was inherent in the architecture that was built for the theater, the structures involved were shapes built on the ground without roofs or walls. Technology eventually progressed so that it was possible to cover performing spaces, and housed drama came into being. It was a small step from a wagon stage placed next to a building to a permanent stage built into the side of a building and eventually to a building that housed both the stage and the audience.

At this juncture a critical change took place in the actor/audience relationship. The proscenium arch was born. The proscenium arch changed the relationship radically. The fried egg, cut in half in courtyard theater, lost its circular characteristic and became rectangular. While the arch had been employed in the classical architecture of Rome and later in medieval churches, pedestrian architecture in the fifteenth century relied almost entirely on post-and-lintel engineering. Post-and-lintel construction was rectangular and limited by the size of trees and the relationship between the height of a tree and its diameter. Simply stated, the taller the tree, the bigger around it has to be to keep it from bending when laid horizontal.

Thus, when stages went indoors, there was, for the first time, a wall separating the actors and their audience. The audience was forced to view the actors through an opening in the wall. The limitations of post-and-beam construction dictated that this opening be relatively small, with the result that the proscenium arch (a misnomer, as it was not an arch) became a standard feature as theaters moved entirely indoors and evolved into a distinct building type. The forestage, or thrust stage as it later became known, was a step in this development and had parallel developments with the Kabuki theater that emerged in Japan. The integrated surrounding space of fried-egg form in early theaters had become two rigid squares separated by a wall with a hole in it, and the actor/audience space relationship was strained and restricted.

From the time the development of enclosed theater matured in the mid-1600s until mid-twentieth century, not much changed in terms of theater form. The proscenium stage persisted, and although manipulated and altered (as in thrust stages, horseshoe seating, movable seating etc.), the form of theaters remained essentially the same, with the actor/audience relationship diluted to the point of separation. There were other types of theater spaces built in that three-hundred-year period, but those forms, such as arena theater and thrust stages, were forms resurrected from an earlier time. While architecture and engineering made great advances in the early part of the twentieth century, there was no growth in theater development itself for nearly three centuries. Theaters got bigger, were lighted and heated and cooled, acquired movable scenery and sophisticated acoustics, but the actor/audience space relationship remained stagnant.

Paul Baker's theater in Waco was an innovation, and by the mid-1950s Baker and his drama program at Baylor University had gained national attention and recognition in American theater.

34

Baker started a professional acting company and by 1959 had developed another new theater for that company with the construction of the Dallas Theater Center.

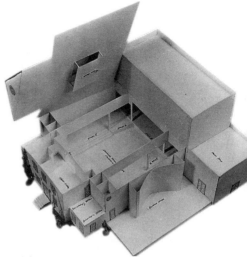
Model of the Baylor Theater

In that era of creative individualism, Frank Lloyd Wright, the prototype for architects, was selected to work with Baker in creating the building. The Theater Center, while not a new theater form as the Baylor Theater had been, benefited from the advances made at Baylor and the growth of Baker's own theatrical thinking.

Baker's intrinsic understanding of architecture and space had evolved into a way of working with architectural elements. He used architecture for his own theatrical purposes and understood it that way. That his understanding was metaphysical rather than philosophical must have been a large factor in his relation with Wright during the course of the design and construction of the Dallas theater. Wright, with his immense ego, had little time or interest

THE NEW THEATER
DALLAS THEATER CENTER
FRANK LLOYD WRIGHT ARCHITECT

Frank Lloyd Wright

in Baker's architectural insight, and most probably never differentiated between the dramatic gesture and the art of the theater. Wright's philosophy, although interesting and useful to Baker in directing the Dallas Theater Center in the years that followed, was to a great extent written after the theater was designed and was more of a result of the architecture than a basis for it.

Each man's thinking had little effect on the other as far as the building was concerned, and the compromises that Baker forced out of Wright were more for technical theater reasons than for aesthetic ones. Ironically, the theater had a superb actor/audience relationship. That this was true is less a happy accident than the result of one man making a fine instrument and another being able to compose music with it, without each discussing their endeavor with the other. As can be seen in the chart of theater development, the form of the Dallas Theater Center was an improved version of foregoing thrust stages that broadened the field of theater architecture, even if it did not extend it. In that elusive but essential element of the actor/audience space relationship, it achieved an artistic success that is hard to match.

In the early 1960s, Baker moved from Baylor University to Trinity University in San Antonio. There, working with architect Arthur Rogers, Baker built the Ruth Taylor Theater, the third and last theater he was to develop.[3] Rogers was an associate in the architectural office of O'Neil Ford and Associates. O'Neil Ford, in association with Bartlett Cox, was the architect of all the buildings at Trinity University at the time.

This theater, a hexagon with three surrounding stages, was a powerful space that placed the audience in the middle of the action, in a way similar to that of the earlier Baylor Theater. With this unified actor/audience space as its central theme and in combination with an extended and uniquely equipped central stage, the Ruth Taylor Theater could accommodate any form of theater, including proscenium and arena. It encouraged both experimental and traditional staging, resulting in the creation of new plays and new drama forms as well as bringing fresh clarity to classical plays and traditional styles.[4] The Ruth Taylor Theater incorporated features from both the Baylor Theater and the Dallas Theater Center, the most important of which was the sanctity of the actor/audience relationship.[5] While apparently of vastly divergent architectural styles, these three theaters have one thing in common: the spatial quality of that relationship. The Ruth Taylor Theater was completed in 1966, providing Baker with an adjunct facility to the Dallas Theater Center.

Ruth Taylor Theater, Trinity University

It is troublesome that the theater world at the end of the twentieth century did not recognize the significance of Paul Baker's work in theater architecture and that it subsequently has gone largely unnoticed.[6] The same could be said at the beginning of the twentieth century of Adolphe Appia and, to a certain extent, Gordon Craig, names known to few in contemporary theater. Baker is in good company with these two great masters of the theater, however, with the significance of his thinking. In concrete terms, he probably surpasses them, having actually built three theaters that embrace and promote his insight into art in general and the art of theater architecture in particular.[7] However, in light of the theaters that have been built all over the world since 1966—and there have been an incredible number—his impact has hardly been felt.

The theater at Baylor in 1940, the Dallas theater in 1959, and the Ruth Taylor in 1966, all were hallmarks of their time and all were heralded as breakthroughs in theater design. Sadly, through ignorance in the theater community and unfortunate crosscurrents in the architectural world, these buildings have been destroyed or eroded by remodeling to a point where their significance is hardly visible. The Baylor Theater is gone entirely, the Kalita Humphrey Theater (the name that appears on the Dallas Theater Center Building) is denigrated as a technical monster, and the Ruth Taylor Theater has been emasculated through massive remodeling of its interior.

Hopefully, a time will come when Baker and his work will be discovered again and his thinking put to creative use. Nonetheless, he has earned a place in history as one of theater architecture's foremost innovators and pioneers. ∎

End Notes

[1] The multistaged design of Baylor Theater's Studio One was the result of academic need. Paul was determined to offer to the Baylor drama students a course of study as strong and comprehensive as the courses offered in the other outstanding academic departments of science, math, English, and music. A one-proscenium stage did not bring enough flexibility into the teaching of the many historical forms the theater architecture had encompassed. Therefore, he designed a large flexible space having within its structure the possibility of presenting all the major theater forms as well as facilitating the study of historical production: Greek, Roman, medieval, Elizabethan, Restoration, theater-in-the-round, and contemporary theater forms. *Kitty Baker*

[2] A climate of inquiry and discovery permeated the theater at Baylor. Encouragement was given to explore and compare, to understand and apply.
There was discussion of the why and how in the design of Studio One where the audience sat in swivel chairs in the middle while the stage encircled the viewers. Then came the purchase of the little Mexican restaurant around the corner that was long and narrow but just right for a small, shallow stage whose vertical space was visually sectioned by horizontal and vertical pipes, (a Mondrian-type stage) where a play was directed in a single plane vertically rather than in depth. Character relationships were defined in the height and size of the spaces as focus was made on a hand or foot or face in contrast to the full figure. Baker's idea (with Virgil Beavers) of housing a large space that could be constantly redefined in shape and size for both audience and performer became the Weston Studio with final designs by Bill Tamminga. *Ruth Byers*

[3] The space was gorgeous—large, expansive, polished, extending into and around the audience so that the action took place among us and not only before us. It was as large as the generosity of Vernon and Ruth Taylor. It was as radical and challenging as the vision of Paul Baker. *Jim Laurie*

[4] The Ruth Taylor Theater was a radical wide horizon with the intimacy of a womb or a tomb or an ancient Greek theater. The opening performance of *A Different Drummer* showcased the experimentation from the Baylor days and demonstrated the potential of the new space. Thornton Wilder's *The Skin of Our Teeth* chilled audiences with its end-of-the-world flood scene and the passing of the hours on the back wall. In *Journey to Jefferson* the movement of the Bundren family wagon across the stage was like an etching in the great open space of West Texas. *Sallie Baker Laurie*

Theater One was open-ended and vast and awesome—an architectural maze to be explored and celebrated—a playground for creativity. One had to take its stage, use its space, fracture its boundaries. To harness its potential required courage, energy, and wit. It brooked no timidity, had contempt for small efforts, punished banality. It demanded before it gave. *Mary McCullough*

39

This marvelous tool, the Ruth Taylor Theater, meant that creativity and ingenuity were directed at something other than reinventing the wheel. *Charles Beachley*

The Skin of Our Teeth utilized the main stage, the two side stages, the stage steps, and part of the floor. *The Seagull* was performed on the floor in the midst of the audience. There were seats on the stages. *A Comedy of Errors* used the whole theater including dummies falling from the catwalks and a chase scene up and down the riser steps. The first happening, in 1968, employed every space in the theater—a vaudeville show in the Cafe Theater, repertory class scenes in Theater One, featured scenes developed in repertory class, improvisational theater in the Attic. What an incredible thing that was. *Mike Bathke*

The wonderfully whimsical set for Peter Lynch's production of *The Journey Of The Fifth Horse* filled the whole Theater One stage and also involved screens with slide projections. Peter experimented with every creative thought that entered his brain during rehearsals, and I learned much about the value of giving one's imagination unfettered reign. *Mary Ann Barnett*

I saw the versatility of Theater One contained, twisted, and utilized in ways that only that space would allow: the tower from the light booth to the floor and the many runways of Indians, the in-the-round production of Seagulls, Will Brann's assassination bullet moving over the swivel seat audience, the Camelot arches complete with medieval banners overhead. It was the creative spirit and energies of the artists involved and the knowledge and experiences we gained that made Theater One the special and unique space we remember. *Stephen Treichler*

In Mary Ann Colias's show *The Women*, the set contained five large department-store display windows. Even though the action shifted from 'window' to 'window' there were always women standing as living models in the inactive windows. This created strong images of the false, superficial world of the characters. As the action shifted the audience made real use of their swivel chairs! *David Cotton*

[5] Theater One commanded the use of extraordinary amounts of energy to fill and effectively use the space. This had an impact on all of the participants: from actors it demanded more of the voice and body than tends to ever be required in any other setting. Designers and directors had to come up with newer, more creative ways to communicate ideas and literally fill the visual and auditory space. Even the audience was required to change their concepts of what a theatrical experience would be. *Charles Rucker*

I remember spending hours at a time in that great huge space that was Theater One—feeling it, listening to it and becoming comfortable enough to fill that space with a character and with my voice. *Pam Gorham Iorio*

"The stage design enabled the audience to be one with the production, with no fourth wall to separate the audience and actors. It had flexibility and elements of surprise that make going to the theater a communal occasion." *Tom Adams*

[6] When I was a senior at Trinity, I was showing two well-known French directors the campus. When I opened the door to Theater One both men gasped, "My God! But this is *not* a theater for amateurs." *Sallie Baker Laurie*

[7] I was weaned on *Ruthie's Magic Barn*. We were 'Baker Babies' which gave us a cloak of invincibility on campus. We were students with a mission and a purpose. *Blair Tarley*

Theater One was a fantastic place in which to create. As students we were given the tools to go about our work, and we could learn as much as we wanted because such a big and expansive space welcomed large ideas and thoughts for all areas of the theater. *Jessamy Tomlinson*

The first production I saw at Trinity was The *Fantasticks*, staged between the downstairs seating and the upper-level seating. I remember the magic, and I knew I had made the right decision to come to San Antonio, Texas, from Stratford, Connecticut. The next performance I recall was *Hamlet ESP* The uniqueness and imagination were awe-inspiring, and I was excited to know that Paul Baker, the man who created this incredible work, would be my teacher. I remember the fun and excitement of being on that incredible stage. It was freeing creatively and at the same time a spiritual experience. I knew I was performing on one of the most innovative stages of the time. *Ron Pirette*

Othello, Baylor Theater

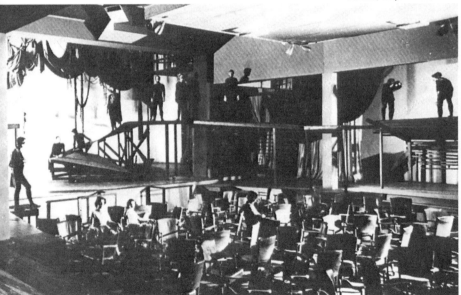

41

I could not escape the parallel between what Baker taught about the creative process and what occurred in the original Creation described in Genesis and echoed in Chapter One of St. John's Gospel.

Harry Thompson

Three Zeros and One One, Baylor Theater

Baylor Theater: The Phoenix Rises

Baylor Theater was razed. The Ruth Taylor Theater has been renovated beyond recognition. However, the dream that was Baylor Theater lives on in other places, some unlikely, such as Seoul[1] and Manila.[2] Cecile Guidote, a former Baylor student, founded PETA (Philippine Educational Theater Association) in 1967. PETA staged English translations of Philippine plays and adaptations, translations, and new plays in Filipino in an open-air multistage theater in the Fort Santiago ruins.

Because the open-air theater could be used only at night and in the dry season, PETA is building a new theater center that will "enable it to pursue its vision of a Philippine Theater that is truly integrated and vital to the development of people and society." The Theater Center will feature a resource center, two training centers, and a four-hundred-seat "black-box" theater that permits multiple stage and audience configurations.

The Drama Center in Seoul is an older theater being remodeled to expand "the possibilities of performance while preserving the influence of the traditional Korean performing arts." Other theaters, similar to Baylor Theater, exist not far from Waco in Sherman, Abilene, and San Angelo.

The Editors

A Stage Is an Empty Space

Harry Thompson

The concept of a theater with stages surrounding an audience in swivel chairs was first brought to my attention in 1950 in a class on play production taught by Orlin Corey at Georgetown College. Paul Baker, who designed this revolutionary arrangement, said that his concept of a theater was an empty space artistically defined by four walls but plastic enough to be modeled to the needs of the creative artist.[3]

Both Orlin Corey, director of theater, and Irene Corey, head of the art department at Georgetown, had completed graduate study with Baker. Their high regard for Baker, his faculty, the drama curriculum and details about theater productions at Baylor intrigued me. In 1954, I decided to study with Baker and satisfy my curiosity about the imaginative use of theater space embodied in Studio One.

In addition to the curriculum at Baylor Theater, I discovered the magic and wonder of productions in Studio One and in the newly added Weston Studio. I audited the integration of abilities class three times. The career-shaping and life-influencing principles espoused by Baker in IA account for most of my success as a university professor, theater director and designer, motion picture and television producer and director, and as a consultant and designer of several theaters and performing arts centers. In the course, watching Baker's directing, I came to understand the correlation and significance of such terms as space, sound, light, color, rhythm, texture, line, and angle and the way Baker's extensions of space were implemented in Studio One and later in the Weston Studio.

Each studio encouraged interaction with the witnessing and participating audience. Performance spaces and seating spaces were interchangeable according to the requirements of the script. My goal in designing theater spaces and directing within them became to enjoy and validate for myself and audiences the ingenious insights that I had experienced under Baker. Baker's extensions of theater space and his approach to the creative process were manifested in every production I directed and the theaters I was privileged to design.

I could not escape the parallel between what Baker taught about the creative process and what occurred in the original Creation described in Genesis and echoed in Chapter One of St. John's Gospel. In every process of creation, the same elements are present that existed in the original Creation. "In the beginning God created the heaven and the earth, and the earth was without form." Before form there must be a space for it to occupy. Form presupposes space.

"And darkness was upon the face of the deep." Darkness is one of the primary elements present in the creative process. "And God said . . ." Until God spoke, there was silence. Space, silence, and darkness exist before creation begins. God moved upon the face of the deep. "And he said, Let there be light." The light opens the darkness and reveals whatever movement there is in space—showing whatever form has been created.

However flawed it might seem, I concluded that there is a "creative ratio" in these elements. Movement is to space what sound is to silence and what light is to darkness. They correlate. What occurs with one element affects the other two, and relationships among them must be respected.

In 1956 I had an opportunity to confirm and exhibit what I learned at Baylor Theater. I was invited to join the faculty of Hardin-Simmons University in Abilene as director of the university theater. For productions I had the use of the chapel/auditorium and a double classroom that had been modified for a limited arena staging capability, principally for use as a chapel. The theater was a small platform behind a proscenium arch.

The day before Thanksgiving of my second year, students hurried from the chapel to holiday time with their families. Within minutes, the chapel and its stage were in flames, and the building was reduced to rubble.

Dr. Evan Allard Reiff, university president, engaged an architect to begin designs for a "chapel/auditorium." Because theater was involved, I was asked my reactions to the initial designs. The drawings submitted reflected a typical eighteenth- or nineteenth-century design of a box for the audience who watched and listened to speakers or performers in another box behind a proscenium arch. My opinion was candid.

The president said that unless I had something better to propose, they would move forward with the submitted drawings in order to have convocation space available. I replied that I did have something better to offer and asked for fifteen minutes to retrieve materials from my office files and to explain my alternative to the drawings we had reviewed.

I had begun work on the alternative theater drawings, variations of the Baker concept, as a result of my experience at Studio One and had continued to work on them after I took my position in Abilene. The president was interested in the rationale for the drawings and my explanation of their advantages. Convinced of the validity of these substitute designs, the president called the architect and told him that he was to incorporate the new design concepts that I would explain to him. In less than a month, the new design was approved by the administration and the board of trustees, and fund-raising and construction began for a chapel/auditorium.

The chapel/auditorium filled two basic functions: assembly space for convocations and a theater performance space with the associated support spaces.

The main stage, situated between the theater and the chapel, was open on both the theater and chapel side allowing an unobstructed view from either house to the other. The dimensions of the openings to the stage from each house were the same—forty feet wide and twenty feet high. The space offstage on each side was twenty feet by forty feet. The fly loft above the stage allowed repositioning of the head blocks for battens supporting lights and curtains. Because there was no hard cyclorama wall, a cyclorama curtain could be lowered to serve the needs of either house.

The theater incorporated side stages approximately forty-five feet long, fifteen feet high and fifteen feet deep on each side of the audience; these were at a ninety-degree angle to the main stage. An actor could move from one side stage to the other or to the main stage area by means of a forestage approximately four feet wide. Additionally, each side stage had an arch leading to the main stage. These arches could remain open or be closed as needed by means of an overhead door. Because the space for seating and staging was flexible, a stage could be positioned at the rear of the audience area, between the two side stages.

The audience seating area was approximately thirty-six inches below stage level. Swivel chairs had three-hundred-and-sixty-degree rotation so that the audience could follow the action from one stage to another in a sequential pattern, across the audience from one side stage to another, or from the main stage to the rear stage. Stage and seating were interchangeable, and all or part of the side stages could be used for additional seating.

The chapel/auditorium provided comfortable seating for convocations of the student body, commencement ceremonies, guest artists, concert series, and use for theater productions as well. Those seated in the thousand-seat house faced a proscenium stage opening forty feet wide and twenty feet high.

To capitalize on the dramatic impact of *Lamp at Midnight*, both the theater and the chapel/auditorium were used. In the play by Barrie Stavis, Galileo is forced by the Catholic Church to recant his scientifically based findings that the sun is the center

We must break out of the concept of the theater being two boxes pushed up against each other —one box for the audience and another box for the actors.

Paul Baker

46

of the universe. The vast space provided by the theater and auditorium amplified the power of the Church against an individual. As the scene closed prior to the recantation scene, the stage lights went down and a bell tolled. The scene that followed was barely pulled out of the darkness into light, and the enormity of the dark empty space made the silence overwhelming. To underscore the interplay of sound and silence, speakers for the bell were mounted against the underside of the main stage between the theater and the auditorium. The vibrating sound was felt as well as heard in the two houses.

The audience seated in the theater looked through the two arches of the main stage into the cavern of darkness in the auditorium. A solemn procession came through the remote central doors and advanced through the darkness. Monks preceded the cardinals and the pope himself, carrying candles on staffs as they moved toward the main stage along a narrow strip of light. They mounted steps and moved across center stage toward the audience in the theater. Dividing into two columns they moved around the dais in the center of the main stage where the pope took his position, flanked by candle-bearing monks.

The chief inquisitor was at the pope's right. The cardinals and remainder of the monks continued their procession to positions on the side stages and on the stage in the rear of the theater. Galileo was led to an interrogation box on a dais in the center of the audience, standing alone while the cardinals and the pope took their seats. The audience in swivel chairs surrounded Galileo, isolating him from those who persecuted him, leaving him in the laps of the audience. The use of space created a physical and visual metaphor of sympathy for his circumstances.

On cue from the chief inquisitor, a document stating his refutation was thrust into Galileo's hand. Forced to read it aloud, lighted by a single flickering candle held by a monk, Galileo's weak and aged voice was almost lost in the immense space and silence that surrounded him. When he was required to sign his denunciation, the scraping of the wet quill on the parchment of the document scarred the silence. The candle flame wavered with uncertainty as the monk carried the document to the chief inquisitor. He passed it to the pope, who scrutinized Galileo's signature.

Again, the tolling bell was simultaneously felt and heard, cueing the pope and his somber entourage to retrace their earlier path through the darkness out of which they came, crossing the side stages, the main stage, and through the auditorium. Their shuffling feet and the tolling bell reverberated in the dark and hollow space while they moved up the aisle and out of sight into the dark and empty space of the lobby.

Galileo, left alone in the embrace of the audience, knelt in the restricted space of the interrogation box. A lone monk in black helped Galileo to his feet and escorted the aged and near-blind scientist through the audience and across the side stage. Together they moved out of sight as the stage lights dimmed to darkness.

Women and Oxen, the first play of a trilogy by Ramsey Yelvington, begins with a group of settlers brought to Texas by Stephen F. Austin and ends with the men of the group joining those who eventually perish in the Alamo. This production utilized the entire theater space, including the side stages and the auditorium. The opening scene re-created the wilderness into which the settlers moved. In the vague dimness as the house lights went down and the sun began to rise, the sounds of alligators, animals, hawks, and other birds came from the various stages and the auditorium, their calls answered and echoed throughout the two houses. Silhouettes of Native Americans crouched and stalked across the sides stages toward the main stage and into the darkness of the auditorium. In the top center of the auditorium balcony, 280 feet from the theater audience, a shaman chanted his greeting to the sun. As he completed his hymn, the stage lights rose on the main stage, revealing a rustic wagon coming to rest and the settlers dismounting to stretch.

After Hardin-Simmons, I worked on the design for a performing arts center that included space for theater, art, and music at Eastern Kentucky University in Richmond, Kentucky. In 1969 I was invited to join the faculty of Austin College in Sherman, Texas. My experience in theater design appealed to the college because a member of their board of trustees, Cecil Green, assured them of a gift to build a communication arts center that would include theater and television facilities.

When completed, the physical facilities for the communication arts center at Austin College included classrooms, offices, a large conference room, art gallery, box office, coat check room, and refreshment center in the lobby area. Closed-circuit television facilities linked it with five other colleges and universities, capitalizing on curriculum and faculty among the separate institutions. There was a television studio, television control room, and a proscenium theater, with a thrust stage, on the ground floor that seated nearly one thousand.

A second theater on the lowest level of the four-level structure provided a highly flexible space for staging and seating. This theater was a large, open, carpeted area, two stories tall, approximately eighty feet square. A complex overhead tracking system permitted different sets of curtains and a sky cyclorama to be used in various configurations, making it possible to reshape or subdivide the room.

In Baker's concept for theater design, work presented for viewing moved around the audience. An audience member might be on the front row for one scene, the back row for another, or at one side or the other. One's point of view changed. As a motion picture camera might provide different perspectives, similar opportunities prevailed for the audience in a spatially free theater.

Conventional proscenium theaters depicted various locations for action by revealing one scene after another when the curtain dropped and time was taken for scene changes. Some attempts were made at simultaneous sets by subdividing the picture within the frame of the proscenium. Sometimes one or more cubicles or mini-sets were stacked atop another or placed side by side with the cubicles revealed in sequence as actors shuttled back and forth from one mini-set to another. Regardless, the view was still limited to facing the picture in the opposite space.

If a stage is an empty space, as Baker said, then viewing the action of the play could be much like viewing sculpture. Action could penetrate and move within an audience that would be free to experience the play from many sides. The open space of the flexible theater at Austin College prompted such a use of simultaneous staging for Hellman's *The Little Foxes*. Swivel seating was arranged around the various rooms required for the play's action, providing an X-shaped hallway connecting the separate areas. As the action in one area concluded, the light dimmed and rose in the area into which the characters moved. This disparate arrangement of the rooms reflected the separation in the lives of those who lived there.

Horace struggled within arms' reach of members of the audience, attempting to retrieve his medication from upstairs. Responding to Regina's cry for help, Cal rushed from the upper left corner of the dining room through the center of the audience to the landing in the down-right corner of the set. The servants raced through the audience from the up-left dining room quadrant toward the down-right quadrant. The visible and vocal alarm and agitation gave way to a deliberate calm and silence as Regina descended the stairs with the telltale hissing of her rustling taffeta dress. The scene exploited the effectiveness of simultaneous staging made possible by the theater design.

A *Cloud of Witnesses*, by Ramsey Yelvington, includes a reenactment of the battle of the Alamo. The characters explore introspectively the significance of what they did during the siege and fall of the Alamo and the extent to which their efforts gave freedom a forward thrust.

The audience came into the theater and sat in swivel chairs inside the walls of a skeletal Alamo. The set was characterized by simplification and stylization rather than realistic imitation. As the house lights dimmed and darkness engulfed the audience, the men who died at the Alamo took their places within the walls of the set, like saints in the niches of a cathedral. They moved into position with the sound of rushing wind and the whir of wings made by doves settling on a plaza.

The lights came up cool and low, presenting the characters in silhouette as they questioned each other across the audience. Warm lights illuminated the features of the characters as the soldiers anxiously discussed the tenuous situation. With rifles at the ready, sentries walked their watch on the lower and upper level around the walls of the skeletal outline of the enclosure.

The Mexicans attacked with suddenness and fury, appearing in the space between the bones of the set and the theater walls. Makeshift ladders were thrown up as they attempted to scale the walls. Volleys of rifle and pistol fire passed across the audience as the battle increased. Through the open work of the sets the hand-to-hand combat was clear around the perimeter of the audience.

The audience was caught in the battle that raged around them, at one moment on the front row, then at the side, and soon

> The play should surround the spectators so they are actually involved in the play and are not just onlookers.
> *Paul Baker*

50

on the back row distant from combat. Following the reenactment, there was a reprise of the introspection that occurred at the opening of the drama. The characters returned to their niches in the walls of the Alamo and again assessed the merits of what they had done to advance the cause of freedom. An echoing of the opening sounds of wind and whirring wings was heard as the audience witnessed the heroic characters in silhouette. Movement ceased. Darkness swallowed light. Silence replaced sound.

Paul Baker instilled the truth that we are alive as long as we are open to growth and change and that theater space also must either grow and change or die. We who are privileged to have a voice in the designing and shaping of theaters and others who write for it, act in it, and create the sets, costumes, and lighting for the productions must work to protect and advance the extensions of that free space. ■

The Modular Theater at Angelo State University

Raymond E. Carver

Paul Baker's Baylor Theater in Waco was the inspiration for the design and construction of the Modular Theater at Angelo State University in San Angelo, Texas.

As a student with a minor in drama at Baylor from 1951 until 1955, I worked as an actor and occasional technician in Baylor Theater. The first time I saw Studio One, I thought, "Of course! This is how all theaters should be conceived for maximum flexibility."

The Baylor Theater was not appreciated universally for its greatest value—the flexibility of the building. It is a simple, stunning realization of sophisticated concepts, yet it has been over-looked by theater historians in published records of innovative theater designs. My teacher at the Yale Drama School, John Gassner, author of *The Theater in Our Times*, concentrated on European innovations and failed to acknowledge Baker or his theater; his colleague, George Izenour, an engineer and author of *Theater Design*, also snubbed Baker and others by excluding the work of all contemporary theater architects who did not have hard-earned design and engineering credentials.

At Angelo State University I worked in a black-box theater where I designed in-the-round shows with platforms for audience seating surrounding the performance area. I located settings in corners or sides of the room, moving the platforms to new positions. I put the audience in the center, stages on four sides, served pizza, and called it supper theater.

In 1970, President Lloyd Vincent, a tough-minded but discerning administrator, recognized initiative and willingness to experiment and urged me to start planning a new theater for ASU. Within months, with help of all faculty members involved, we had drawn up plans. Vincent agreed that a theater on the order of Baker's might serve as an ideal teaching facility as well as a creative stimulus for writers and directors. Vincent also saw the Baker theater concept as a public relations enterprise, a "jewel box for showcasing ASU talent." He sought private funding and made it possible for the ASU theater to be a state-of-the-art facility. Without Vincent's commitment to excellence, the theater could not—and would not—have been built.

I requested the services of a theater consultant, Jules Fisher, Inc., to ensure that design and engineering components would be certifiably correct. Izenour's concerns were not lost on me, and Fisher's credentials as consultant for the California Institute of the Arts were perfect for our purposes. We had a most amicable relationship: administration, architect, consultant, faculty, and I, working without conflict on ideal theater plans with enough money to do it right, ignoring recommendations of the architects that the building would cost a million dollars less if certain concepts were abandoned.

The construction took a little over a year. One night, when Baker was visiting, I brought him to the unfinished theater and showed him around, describing it as a dream theater based on his dreams. He was very complimentary and, I think, delighted to see that his concepts were the basis for the design. He was also pleased with the technological add-ons: a modular floor and wall system, designer swivel chairs, a winch system for raising and lowering scenery by remote control, an electronic dimming system and patch panel with more than a hundred outlets located on steel catwalks in the ceiling, a quadraphonic sound system, ample storage space with lifts for raising heavy set pieces, and I beams that made it possible to avoid building a permanent proscenium frame.

ASU had a three-hundred-plus seat proscenium auditorium, so the new facility was called the Modular Theater—a term denoting units and systems flexibility—to distinguish it from the fixed-seating auditorium. The performing area could be located virtually anywhere, and audience seating could be stepped to view the stage accordingly. The modular theater was a forty-by-forty-foot pit, three feet deep filled to floor level with forty-two-inch-by-forty-two-inch-by-twenty-six-inch modules that could be stacked like building blocks to provide stepped rows for seating. The wall around the pit was constructed of three-foot six-inch modules stacked on end (allowing for stanchions between each stack), and wherever an opening was needed, the wall modules could be removed to storage. For some shows, all four walls were removed to enlarge the theater. The floor surrounding the pit, ten feet wide on each side, allowed the theater to be expanded to sixty-by-sixty feet overall for large shows or contracted to the pit dimensions for shows that were not expected to attract large audiences. In effect, the Modular Theater's design achieved Baker's objectives and added a rear wall as large and flexible as any sidewall.

If there is a negative aspect to a highly flexible theater, it is an impulse to change arrangements arbitrarily. Moving modules from one location to another or to storage is labor intensive, and damage to the modules is inevitable and costly. Even with a full season of plays, admission income and student fees do not offset expenses. The theater could not have been maintained without administrative financial support.

During the seventeen years I worked in that theater, staging an average of four shows a year, I never doubted that a flexible theater was infinitely superior to a fixed-purpose facility, except for cost of operation and labor. We might have entertained larger crowds, but we could never have given our students a more exciting playground for learning what matters most when producing shows. ■

End Notes

[1] During my last hiatus in Japan, I went to Seoul, Korea, on business and ran into Duk Hyung Yoo. He took over his father's theater in Seoul and decided to renovate the old theater making it much more exciting—similar to the Ruth Taylor Theater and Baylor Theater. I went to see the space and found it to be one of the most exciting theater spaces I've ever seen. *Yoichi Aoki* (Letter to Paul Baker)

² It may be of interest that the architectural space that at first made Baylor Theater and later the Ruth Taylor Theater unique was incorporated in the design of another theater, with which I was associated in Manila in the Philippines. Imelda Marcos and Cecile Guidote were the driving forces behind the construction of this theater (I also participated). The Royal Fort Santiago Theater is situated in a national shrine, a three-hundred-year-old fort. . . . The open-air theater, which more than once was a fortress prison, consists of a thrust stage and side stages that surround the audience on three sides. Like at the Baylor Theater and the Ruth Taylor Theater, the audience at the Royal Fort Santiago Theater sits in swivel chairs. *Randy Ford* (Letter to Paul Baker)

³ It was my first class on my first day in college. Paul Baker took the stage and asked, 'What is a stage?' He asked repeatedly, moving from answer to answer, pushing us to think. Finally he said, 'a stage is an empty space.' At that moment my entire worldview shifted. I thought, "At last, a teacher who makes sense." *Sherry Kafka Wagner*

Othello, Baylor Theater

Paris and Beyond

Paul Baker

Living theater demands experimentation and point of view. . . . When (it) becomes pompous, self-satisfied, a follower of dead rules; when theater forgets its soil, its people, its heritage, its religion; when it goes academic, losing its driving vitality, its honest two-fisted search for understanding, it becomes a cheap streetwalker and dies. (From Paul Baker's commencement address, Trinity University, June 2, 1958)

The summer of 1952 was a turning point for the Baylor Theater. That summer, with the cooperation of Baylor University and Reynold Arnould, outstanding young artist of Paris, and his wife Marthe, longtime student and art historian of the Louvre, we established Baylor University's first art school in Paris, France. My wife, Kitty, and I took our three daughters, my mother-in-law, and twenty-five drama students to Paris. Our purpose was to study the ideas of the French modernist painters. Two months later, we returned home with enough ideas to spark a small revolution in theater.

During the first two weeks in Paris we performed *Green Grow the Lilacs* by Lynn Riggs at Theatre Babylone, a small avant-garde theater in Paris. (The musical *Oklahoma* was derived from *Green Grow the Lilacs*.) Our art school schedule began with morning painting and drawing classes taught by Reynold Arnould in his studio; in the afternoon Marthe Arnould taught art history classes in the Louvre. I used the afternoon sessions to visit the art museums, focusing on the canvases of the modern artists whose works were on display there: Pablo Picasso, Henri Matisse, Georges Rouault, Fernand Leger, Marcell Duchamp, George Braque, Raoul Dufy, Piet Mondrian, and others. Beth Wear, a playwright and graduate student of the Baylor drama department, accompanied me. She took copious notes of my reactions and later published a master's thesis documenting the evolution of our production of *Othello*.

I had little idea that the analysis I had made of each artist's canvas would change my theatrical philosophy and practices or that my reaction to the work of these artists would revolutionize our artistic philosophy at Baylor. It would govern our relationship to the space of the stage, our relationship to the actor, the relationship of the actor and audience, and the entire theater practice. From the Paris canvases I had studied, I was empowered to view directing plays in an entirely different manner.

I had developed the basic theatrical philosophy that a stage was an empty space surrounded by four walls. Lying dormant in that empty space for the use of the theater artist were the following elements: rhythm, movement, color, texture, line, planes, sound, silence, light, and dark. I began to see that the artist's canvas was similar to the empty space of a stage. The artist, by using his own interpretation of the elements of form, was able to communicate a fresh and unique view of reality.

Thus began the thrilling adventure of transforming creative ideas from the canvases of those painters to theater productions. It is clear from Ms. Wear's notes that the analysis of the works of Picasso, Rouault, Braque, and others changed our whole concept of the importance of the ground or floor in theater space. "Picasso, use of heavy raked or ramped tabletops," I said to Ms. Wear.

Mandolin and Guitar, Braque, heavily raked or ramped tabletop for still life. *Music Sheet*, Rouault, figures seem to be part of the background. The painter accomplished merging background by the breakup of color and line in actor's background. He shows only a few characteristics of each face that stand out. Remainder of face and figure part of the background. How to make the head of a character fill the whole stage as Rouault does with *The Old King?*

Repeatedly Ms. Wear recorded that the artist saw the object "against or in relation to ground or floor." The artists seemed to find new angles, new viewpoints. Often they seemed to see objects from many directions at once, as in Picasso's canvases. These artists had broken away from the tradition of painting as though seeing an upright on a horizontal plane and seeing it at eye level. Yet, in the theater, the actor was always seen as a vertical figure against a flat horizontal plane. The actor was almost never seen in relation to the floor, except by the audience in the balcony.

In Picasso's *Portrait of Femme* the woman's neck was made into a cube and then outlined in blue and black. Picasso built planes at one side of the face. Roger Risset's *Figure de Femme* was a study of the breakup of planes in the face through strong color. Blanchard built up faces of actors and in some way built up the background with splashes of color. Braque's *Le Duo* made atmosphere with location more important than the characters. He set characters by outlining the characters' silhouettes.

I noted simplicity in my study of the artists:

Pablo Picasso, *L'Portrait of Femme*, plain background. Stark simplicity of background important. Blanchard, how to get still-life quality and simplicity into a stage picture? Need much more color in floor ground cloth and sharp contrast in the background. Against these, keep simple form. Leger's *Woman with a Book*, do more to elongate faces and simplify face planes for style. Dufy, important thing is strong color in the ground cloth with rhythm of all lines very important. Rouault, *The Wounded Clown*, all forms are simplified. Interesting to do a play in simple planes. Break up of body into simple geometric shapes. Edward Pignon, try simplification of stage design and stage shape. Merrand, simplicity of forms and close grouping of body surrounded by wide expanse of sky and sea in his picture *Le Pocha Moracuteuse*.

The ground shifted under our old theatrical images. With challenging new concepts coursing through our heads, the faculty and students returned to Baylor to develop a fresh and dramatic approach for our fall production of *Othello* and other scheduled shows.

The Baylor drama faculty—Virgil Beavers, design; Gene McKinney, playwriting; Mary Sue Jones, assistant director and acting; Beth Wear, assistant—played an integral role as we developed our understanding of the play. All scenes were listed and located as to time and place. Then each of the staff studied each scene for its form. Was it an angular scene? Did the shape seem to be softer, curved, or round? Was it short or long? What was the tension level of the scene? The general theme of the scene? The conflict? In what direction did the scene seem to move? Often the ideas thrown into this discussion seemed to have no connection with the problem being discussed, but ideas grew out of ideas from other discussions.

The students shared in the direction of the production to a great extent. They blocked many scenes themselves as they worked in rehearsals; the director needed to change only a few movements or placements.

In her thesis, Wear described how the chorus worked:

The students worked for hours without a specific result or outline. They worked in groups of three or four and in groups of twenty or thirty. Sometimes they worked alone trying out some idea they had. Sometimes one of the chorus members gathered three or four others together before a scheduled rehearsal and worked out an idea, presented it to the group for approval, suggestions, and sometimes use.

They took words—maliciousness, hatred, jealousy—and tried to express that word in movement, both realistic and abstract. They worked to control body movements and to learn what impression they gave with a specific movement. They discussed together and with the staff and director their ideas of the meanings of scenes of the play, of moods and impressions they wanted to create. No idea was dismissed without consideration, and usually trial.

The group decided maliciousness indicated its center to be at a low body level; from this they tried out movements in crouching positions, in bent-over positions, in low, stooping positions, to discover how they could best express maliciousness. In rehearsals the director would say, "We want to get the feeling of deserted streets late at night, and the feeling of evilness and ugliness about the streets. Wilson, you and Jones and Betty cross from up close to the cyc (cyclorama) and work down to the circular platform, and give us that feeling. And the students would do it.

As the analysis and discussion of *Othello* continued, it became clear that the principal character of Iago had several distinct psychological facets to his personality. There was the side Iago showed to Othello, the evil cunning side he kept hidden from the Moor, and the hail-fellow army officer. Why couldn't two or three actors working as a single unit be used to do on the stage what Picasso had done? That way we could show the varied

Othello

sides of the character.

Three sides of Iago emerged—the ancient, the sadist, the puppeteer—with three actors simultaneously playing the same role. Othello was portrayed as the barbarian, the soldier-lover, the jealous husband. The three facets of love, obedience, and strength were presented in Desdemona.

Just as space had been treated as an unimaginative restricted and tragically ignored stepchild, so had light been little used. Another characteristic of the *Othello* production was the treatment of light and darkness as a living element. How could light and darkness as living elements be used almost as another actor to heighten and clarify the meaning of the play as well as to give the desired visual effect?[1]

Sound in the theater usually is conceived of as series of single elements. One speaks, another answers. We wanted to use sound the way we tried to use perspective, from many different angles. Several points of view and meaning could be embellished and enlarged by adding texture in sound, by having several different pitches that made up a recognizable tone. The theater had lost much of the excitement of sound, and we tried to rediscover that excitement. We wanted to fill the silence with as many layers of sound as the meaning of the play required, using rhythm, texture, attack, pitch, and tone. We tried to find the sounds, the level, the tensions, the rhythms, the timbre, the qualities suited to and growing out of each production or play that we produced. This was particularly true of *Othello* where we tried to use sound as a complement to the spoken word and not merely as an effect.

There were long hours of work experimenting with the voice in sound and the body in movement. Three actors working

as a unit would portray the character as: the thinker—who gave most of the lines related to planning and inner thoughts of the character and most of whose action centered around the neck and head. Outward appearances—making contact with other characters and centering this action in the chest and arms. The physical section centered his movements on the hips and legs.

After the play was cast, the actors worked together outside of regular rehearsals studying and discussing the lines of their character until they believed they had it divided correctly into three parts. They worked to move as one body and one mind. They developed rhythmic tension of their character and worked together with such constancy during the production period they moved as one person even when they were offstage, as if spiritually joined by an unseen link.

The early planning for the presentation of *Othello* revolved around two ideas: first, the play should surround the spectators so that the audience would be actively involved in the problem of the play; second, the play must be of vital interest to an audience more informed about atomic bombs and supersonic airplanes than crossbows and slave-propelled galleys.

Studying the Paris notes, we worked to change the actor's relationship to the stage space. No longer was he viewed only as a vertical actor on a horizontal plane, but he was seen from other angles and perspectives. This required changing the actor's relationship to the audience. We had been thinking of him in only one restricted relationship.

Henry Hewes, revered drama critic for the *Saturday Review of Literature* wrote of the production of *Othello*:

> The triad system of breaking up the characters into three parts is most effective when all three aspects are in conjunction and directly reinforce each other, or when they are in valid opposition and battling intramurally. Another benefit of the system is that it often results in the repetitions of a particular line. This is excellent in Shakespeare where strong images often become obscured in the rigid rhythmical flow of poetry. In general there are many advantages of doing *Othello* in this manner, in the manner the Baylor group has attempted. It relieves the actors from having to do too much acting. Therefore, they can concentrate on sound and movement. For the spectator it provides varied patterns of action which have the same compulsive fascination that is found in music. This is true when the

import and the emotion of the action are slight. It is apt to please even those that are not familiar with *Othello*. It has accomplished what Orson Welles in motion picture tried and failed to do: applied the visual arts to a great play without allowing them to be inundated (February 13, 1954, 27-28).

Othello, Baylor Theater

John Rosenfield, critic for the *Dallas Morning News*, headlined his review of *Othello*: "Baylor Forces under Paul Baker Offer Daring *Othello* Synthesis." The following are excerpts from his March 30, 1953, review:

Our reportorial vocabulary stops with the description that this *Othello* is the goldan-gedest thing you ever saw. Otherwise, the creative processes of Texas Dramaturgy never took a higher, more uncharted flight. Yet it was eccentricity in handsprings. The Baker project seems to find something new and valid in the living theater the likes of which are not in the annals. Nobody who sees this *Othello* is wearied. To the contrary, he is stimulated much as an 1860 music lover was after his first pilgrimage to Bayreuth. With personalities split almost like the atom, lines of speech are tossed from one Othello to another, among the Iagos, Desdemonas, and the rest. It is a Shakespeare not in histrionic bravura but in psychological essences. But it is Shakespeare nevertheless in rhetorical witchery and dramatic impact (Part I, p. 10).

Gynter Quill, amusement editor of the *Waco News Tribune*, wrote,

When developing a fresh interpretation for Shakespeare's *Othello* the Baylor Theater Staff and Director deliberately set out to break all the rules and to find new ways to use them. The finished production of *Othello* was hailed for its daring and doubly hailed by the audience and critics for its effectiveness. . . . Shakespeare's characters were already split personalities. Baker and his staff divided them among several actors which gave each (self) a voice and individuality. The parts sometimes speaking alone, at times speaking in unison, at other times in tandem to emphasize a line. United against others but at times at war among themselves. . . . Diagonal flooring, an adaptation of Rouault, put the action on a different plane, almost as though seen from above. Movement up and down the ramp on the stage. Scaffolding on another stage and a circular platform in the center stage gave the actor new dimension and new relationship to the audience and to each other. The unity of costumes and facial makeup—gobs of black paint—emphasized characters' traits. Sinuous hanging of cloth, paper, and shaped metal moving as wisps of smoke and clouds in casting eerie shadows. Sound effects from the wings—simulations of trumpets, the raucous sound of pounding on an open piano strings, speaking a whispering chorus—all created great excitement, much of it drummed up throughout the land by the excitement and prestigious convert Charles Laughton.

Charles Laughton saw two performances of the play, and summed up his feelings in the following way: "It is one of the finest performances of Shakespeare I have ever seen." He said the activities of the Baylor Theater, under the direction of Paul Baker, offer the American Theater a needed breath of fresh air. "I think that Paul Baker is one of the most important minds in the world theater today. He seems to have invented new ways of doing things, and I think something big will come out of it" (Second Edition of *Othello* at Baylor Strange, Effective," December 5, 1953, 11).

Three Othellos, Baylor Theater

In the summer of 1953, following the spring production of *Othello*, the theater group began experimenting with movement, color, and human sound, working from the ideas generated in Paris and by the *Othello* production. A core student and faculty group worked together for six to eight hours a day over an entire summer, experimenting with selections from the Old Testament and poetry. Color, movement, sound, and rhythm became key components of the explorations. For instance, rhythm was given a primary role in the study of selections from poetry and the Bible. Charles Laughton had suggested the importance of a steady underlying beat throughout a piece of poetry. Against that base rhythm, the readers could overlay a myriad of counter rhythms, syncopations, repetitions, etc., while still maintaining a unity and forward action. The summer company was divided into small groups, with each group assigned a number of selections that they explored through rhythm and sound. The resulting production, entitled *New Dimensions in Sound and Form*, consisted of a series of experimental presentations, including staged choral readings and a short comedic piece written by resident playwright Eugene McKinney. [2]

The title of McKinney's play, *Three Zeros and One One*, was a response to Edward R. Murrow's question following Hiroshima. Did the atomic bomb mean twenty-four hundred, midnight, or zero, zero, zero, one, the beginning of a new day? In the play, a series of flats of differing sizes and colors were carried across the stage in a variety of planes, utilizing a range of rhythms. Flats exploded out of other flats. Some flats deserted other flats. Conflicts arose and were resolved. A baby flat was born. Sometimes flats were lifted slightly to reveal rows of feet. "Words" were reduced to a wild variety of sounds, and the actors' bodies was extended through two-dimensional shapes in vivid colors and textures, organized through a rhythmic pulse throughout. An actor came out from the flats and spent a long time pulling a knotted rope down from the catwalk. The rhythm of those knots and his reaction to them left the audience in gales of laughter.

Choral speaking techniques developed during the summer's experimentation became integral to the theater's work, as did the use of planes, level, sound, and rhythm. Ideas generated by this concentrated study were to influence all the playwriting, theatrical design, acting, and directing collaborations for major theater productions to follow at the Baylor Theater. [3]

As the second production of *Othello* was in progress in Studio One, a new studio was being built. Weston Studio, a large square empty room (sixty-four by sixty-four feet and twenty feet high), was designed by Virgil Beavers and me working with the architect, Bill Tamminga. This theater gave directors and designers freedom to choose the position and shape of the spaces encountered by the actors and the audience. The stage was not defined, the entire space being stage, but chairs on movable platforms were provided so that the stage could be placed anywhere in the room. This new space would allow the artistic team to continue explorations and experimentations with acting planes, shapes, and patterns in space.

To open Weston Studio, the theater staff chose Ramsey Yelvington's *The Long Gallery*. The set—a small-town street and a particular house with several galleries—was built along the entire length of one wall (sixty-four feet). In this play, the direct plane between the actor and the audience was examined. In rehearsal, the director strung lengths of yarn in straight lines between each actor and a particular point in the audience, dramatizing the angle of contact, connecting the eye of the actor with the eye of the audience. The actors contacted each other directly through the audience, playing full front with great simplicity and strength. This resulted in an acting style of classical simplicity such as one might see in a painting by Grant Wood or Amedeo Modigliani. A three-person chorus backed each of the two leading characters, repeating and emphasizing key lines and speaking the characters' inner memories and thoughts directly to the audience.

The Long Gallery, Baylor Theater

65

A new play, *A Cloud of Witnesses*, by Ramsey Yelvington was produced in Studio One in the spring of 1954. This play, examining time at the events of the Alamo and the women of Gonzales who prayed for their men, provided a natural vehicle for spatial exploration. The starting point for the play was the image of witnesses. A number of general ideas quickly led designer Virgil Beavers to create a skeletal structure that was a replica of the front of the Alamo. When actors took their places within the structure, the characters were immortalized as heroes before a word was spoken.[4]

The heroes of the Alamo were seated on one side of the structure, and the sixteen women of Gonzales were seated on the other. Each actor's space was outlined by a structural design so that every character established a clear image in space. When the lights came up on the play, the shapes and silhouettes of the set with the actors inside created an immediate impact upon the audience. The actors standing or sitting in their respective niches spoke their lines directly to the audience, sometimes singly, sometimes in chorus. Their speeches, always delivered directly to the audience, established the rhythm of the heartbeat; the rhythms of fear, courage, and tragedy vibrated throughout the production.

While the women of Gonzales mostly maintained their positions in the structure of the Alamo set, the Alamo battle scenes erupted from the structure, covering all three stages of Studio One, even spilling over to the back balcony above the audience in the rear of the theater. The audience was ultimately surrounded by the action of the siege of the Alamo, much the same as the heroes of the Alamo themselves. Throughout the production, the skeletal design loomed as a subliminal message of a critical moment in time and its impact on the future of the state of Texas.

Eugene McKinney's *A Different Drummer* was produced in the spring of 1955 in Studio One, using all the stages and highly simplified and abstracted scenery. Royal Barnhill, the central character, cannot follow in his father's footsteps but marches to a different drummer. The play called for a four-member chorus to comment on the action, a chorus of three actors to represent Royal Barnhill's imagination, and an ensemble to play the multiple roles of townspeople, scenery, dancers, and other characters.

The artistic team quickly saw the relationship between McKinney's writing in *A Different Drummer* and the earlier explorations in *Three Zeros and One One*. The latter play used sounds rather than words, and the actors were mostly stage flats of various sizes and colors. The artistic team wanted to use the same abstract ideas of color and shape combined with simplicity for the new script. The stage from curtain line to cyc was divided into one-foot planes, twenty-six planes on the main stage and fourteen planes on each of the side stages.

On the main stage, the Barnhill home was a structure made of two-inch-by-six-inch boards with one-inch pipes forming a series of ladders reaching from the floor at curtain line to the catwalk twenty feet above using only the third plane. The spacing of the pipes on the ladders, painted in primary colors or black, made different rectangular shapes reminiscent of a painting by Mondrian. The deceased Reverend Barnhill entered the stage from the catwalk down the Barnhill ladder. His figure, emerging from on high, clearly defined his domination of his family, even after his death.

Movement up or down a level was used for character emphasis. In another instance, stage lighting portrayed the growth of Royal's friend, Nelda Lou. While she told the story of her child-hood, her shadow grew from two feet to twelve feet as she moved from upstage to downstage. A night scene played by the towns-people ensemble used all four jungle gym units. The audience watched as each household shut down for the night, their evening routines etched against the cyc on each of the three stages.

The stage lighting was designed to light only one plane at a time. The Barnhill home changed in color through the use of three ellipsoidal lighting instruments directly overhead, three more from stage left and stage right, and three from the orchestra pit. The lights could make the actors seem to move in space as

A *Different Drummer*, Baylor Theater

A *Different Drummer*, Dallas Theater Center

A Different Drummer, Baylor Theater

colors and directions played across their faces. The reflections of the jungle gyms made colorful and effective designs on the cyclorama of each stage. Color, line, pattern, choral speaking, and vertical planes merged to catch the emotions and images of the town in *A Different Drummer*. It remains one of the most loved and remembered Baylor productions.

When we began planning the 1956 production of Shakespeare's *Hamlet*, the faculty and student body had been experimenting for four productive years with the revolutionary ideas gleaned from the discoveries made in the Paris art galleries, the French theater, and French architecture. The still-life paintings of Braque and Picasso showed not only the object but the surface on which it sat, the image of the object against its base. Why not do that in theater? If we tilted the stage up, it would give the actor and the director an entirely new dimension. The audience could see the patterns of movement across the stage. Instead of losing depth perception as happened when the audience saw the stage floor at eye level, the audience could see the actor and the floor with depth perspective.

For the *Hamlet* production, the tabletops of the Picasso and Braque canvases grew into a huge ramp, fifty-five feet wide by twenty-eight feet deep, covering most of the stage floor of Studio One. It was raked at a forty-five-degree angle from curtain line to back cyclorama. The ramp was covered with carpet and painted like a Jackson Pollack canvas with different colored paint dripped onto the ramped surface.

For scenes like the one in the queen's bedroom or the banquet scene, a large door was cut in the ramp, hinged from the upstage side, and propped open from the interior of the ramp. Drapes and scenery pieces were flown from the gridiron to establish locale. Due to the severely raked floor, every movement on the ramp was dramatic and full of energy. The impact of every actor's pattern through space was translated to the audience with crystal clarity. Gravity became a player as each actor's body was energized to maintain balance. The entire figure was seen against the floor surface, amplifying every movement, projecting every emotion, every nuance with dynamic force.

Hamlet, Baylor Theater, Burgess Meredith far right

Hamlet, Baylor Theater, Burgess Meredith

Burgess Meredith dropped out of his leading role of a Chicago production of *Teahouse of the August Moon* in order to rehearse for the Baylor Theater *Hamlet*, a multisided *Hamlet* on a multisided stage. I decided to clarify the complex character of the prince of Denmark by presenting four figures in the Hamlet role—three representing different aspects of Hamlet's personality or egos and a fourth, played by Meredith, as a composite of all three. The three Hamlet egos spoke only to repeat or to anticipate a significant passage, while Meredith carried the major portion of the lines.

Virgil Beavers' sets made full use of Studio One's three stages and its two connecting stages for the "play within a play" scene that *Hamlet* created as a scheme to "catch the conscience of the King." The play within the play was enacted on the center stage with Hamlet cheering the actors from the audience level. On one side stage the courtiers were assembled, and on the other side stage, the king and queen. At the moment of unraveling, the entire cast echoed and reechoed King Claudius' line, "Give me some light!" as they swirled in dizzying motion across the ramp, over the side stages and back again, setting the entire acting space ablaze in the horror of discovery.[5]

Another experimental *Hamlet* was staged in Studio One during the spring of 1957. This was to be the last of the experiments with a Shakespearian play until *Hamlet ESP* was produced at the Dallas Theater Center in 1970. The 1957 production featured additional experiments with sound and movement and an all-student cast. Three actors portrayed all the leading characters; three actors speaking in unison portrayed those characters with only a few lines. The producers of George Bernard Shaw's *Major Barbara* canceled a Broadway performance, and the cast flew to Waco to see the Baylor *Hamlet*. Burgess Meredith, Charles Laughton, and other members of the *Major Barbara* cast declared that in some ways this *Hamlet* was better than the 1956 version.

Hamlet, Baylor Theater, Burgess Meredith center

After watching the exciting Woodstock Festival for several nights on TV in 1969, I was thrilled by the energy and professional acumen of the musicians and the aliveness of the audience. The sound developed by the musicians and amplified by the electronic equipment was at times overpowering, the message conveyed to the audience by body movement, vocal power, electronic shock, and almost every method of communication the performers could envision. The message was so overpowering, so multifaceted that there was no way an audience could evade hearing and seeing it.

Could a theater production be developed using many of the techniques of the Woodstock Festival? I immediately thought of *Hamlet* as appropriate for the Woodstock treatment because the main action of play is inside his mind and the excitement for the audience would be to be able to see Hamlet's mind—his imagination, his emotions, his intellect, his senses—

71

as he grappled with the tragic events and conniving characters he encountered during the course of the play.

We cast three actors as *Hamlet*. Each of these three Hamlets was a complete character; in prior productions I divided the Hamlet character into three psychological parts. The *ESP* production began with the first great soliloquy, "O, that this too, too solid flesh should melt. . . ." As the soliloquy referred to various parts of the preceding scenes—to the emotional, physical, imaginative relationships in those scenes—I let Hamlet enact the scene as he, in his mind, saw those characters. While doing this, one of the characters remained Hamlet while the other two took on the character of the king,

Hamlet, ESP; Dallas Theater Center

queen, Ophelia, Laertes, or Polonius, and said those lines as Hamlet, with his sensitivity and insight, saw them when the line had happened in its original sequence. Each soliloquy became a centerpiece summarizing a sizable area of the preceding action so that as the actors spoke the soliloquy, they flashed back to the action to which the soliloquy referred.

Hamlet, ESP; Dallas Theater Center

In this way Hamlet's extrasensory perception came into full play. As Charles Laughton declared, "Hamlet is a genius in his own right." He had the rare ability to read minds. He had associated with many of the main characters and the king's court since he was a teenager. It seemed natural for Hamlet to impersonate and mimic some of the characters he encountered, particularly as he had the terrible burden of trying to discover the truth concerning the death of his father.

In order to highlight every movement made during the unfolding of the tragedy, the setting for *Hamlet ESP* was a large ramp measuring thirty-six feet at the widest point by twenty-eight feet deep and pitched from curtain line to ten feet at the cyclorama. There was an entrance at top and bottom of the ramp both stage left and right. There was also a level platform on the back part of the ramp.[6] At the extreme upstage right of the ramp a gaming booth held cutouts of the king, queen, Polonius, and Laertes. At side stages right and left were huge graffiti boards six feet high on which brown drawing paper was attached. Members of the cast and crew used brushes, colored chalk, pots of paint to write important lines and draw caricatures, movement, rhythms of the characters.

Keeping the Woodstock Festival in mind, an orchestra played rock music on electric guitar with large amplifier, flutes, drums, and the string section of an old piano. The rock band improvised sound and composed music for the production.

We tried to capture the impromptu quality of Woodstock by having the prop girl onstage at all times wearing simple mod clothing. She generally sat at the top of the ramp with her props laid out on the walkway. She handed those props to the actors as required by the play. The production started in a relaxed way with the cast coming out and warming up by throwing a football. The football was painted like a ghost head with hair glued on one end. Upstage left was a fencing warm-up between Laertes and Hamlet. Several of the characters—player king, gravedigger, prop girl—warmed up by throwing bean bags at the cutout figures of the king, queen, and Laertes in the gaming booth. Two of the Hamlets wrote a key line on the graffiti boards.

The lighting in the first act was a strong white light that changed only once, when the ghost came in, to a harder and stronger white light from one direction. Dramatic lighting was used in Act II and Act III. Mike girls controlled and handled seven microphones—three for the Hamlets and three to five other mikes—from a sound console placed down center stage. Generally the sound control required two mike girls. To make sure the sound, both vocal and instrumental, would not escape a single member of the audience and could be as overpowering as the sound produced at Woodstock, we placed small speakers under every fifth seat in the auditorium. These were hooked up to the sound control on the main stage. I wanted the audience to hear and feel every word.

Those productions are a part of my past. Today, I have no theater where I can realize my ideas onstage. Nevertheless, I continue to explore plays and ways to give fresh meaning to them. For a long time I have been fascinated with the idea of presenting Henrik Ibsen's *Peer Gynt*. This interest dates back to the time I memorized most of Peer Gynt's lines for my acting final at the Yale department of drama in 1939. In 1981, Kitty and I traveled to Paris to see a two-day production of *Peer Gynt* at the Sarah Bernhardt Theatre. Later we attended an experimental production of *Peer Gynt* Off Broadway and a stunning production of the play by the Houston Ballet Company.

I made an in-depth study of the interpretation and critical comments on *Peer Gynt* by Rolf Fjeldis, Michael Myers' excellent biography of Henrik Ibsen, and dozens of other books and

74

articles. I have been challenged ever since to present a staging concept that would simplify and clarify this mammoth classic.

Ibsen was fascinated with puppets, and he wrote several puppet plays and staged them. He wrote, "To draw a clear distinction between what one has merely experienced and what one has spiritually lived through for only the latter is proper matter for creative writing." How do those apply to directing *Peer Gynt*?

The main thrust of Act V must be felt, must be kept present. Peer is at the end of his life. He remembers the high points. He sits down and peels himself layer by layer. He goes to an auction of his belongings. Each item evokes a memory, dream, or nightmare. These should move fast, change tempos, enlarge, diminish, overlap, telescope, and somehow keep the image of the old man who is both Peer and Ibsen.

Perhaps we play lots of scenes with only mouths or feet or hands, a series of tableaux cut out of canvas with places for heads painted in grotesque shapes. Perhaps we rely on sound to make the transition; it would be simple. The shipwreck should be highly stylized, a board and two figures. The evil forces and the few good forces should be lined up on either side of the stage, the auxiliary actors in the center.

Work slowly over and over each statement until it is down to its spiritual essence, very clear, very simple. Peer is drowning. He becomes an animal, clinging. Another body, the cook, tries to board. The essence is Peer's fear and determination to live, casting off religion and dull human rights.

I must see Act V through the eyes of a man of sixty-nine or seventy years. I must see the events of Act V through a view of life that encompasses the end of life, the falling away of unnecessary barnacles that usually keep a younger man from seeing the simple truths. Peer wants to live. He is focused on living or making a bargain with the Devil, the best bargain possible. He finds that only one person, Solveig, has the true image of his potential in her heart. It never tarnished. He realizes that he has spent his life going round about, not straight through. He relives the moments of his life that were high points, moments that he lived through spiritually.

The director must find spiritual moments in his own life that correspond to those moments that Ibsen selected. Certainly, I have experienced the tug of evil forces, the trolls and goblins. We have all experienced nightmares and dreams that are a conglomerate of special events in our lives put together in startling contrast. We have all had deeply spiritual relationships with our mothers or other members of our family, been jeered by callous colleagues. We have run away with an Ingrid; have had the Victorians say grace over us just as Peer was prayed over by Solveig's father and mother.

Simplify. Keep it honest. Make it new. ■

End Notes

[1] Work with lighting became so important at Baylor Theater that Eliot Elisofon, an artist whose paintings were in permanent collections of the Museum of Modern Art in New York, the Philadelphia Museum of Art, and the Pennsylvania Academy of Fine Arts, took leave of absence as staff photographer for *Life* magazine to work on the Baylor Theater production *Of Time and the River* as associate director of visual effects in lighting. Elisofon wrote in the theater program, "I have been here two weeks, and I have had perhaps the most exhilarating experience of my life."

[2] In *New Dimensions in Sound and Form*, the three of us (Mary Sue Jones, Luanne Klaras, Ruth Byers) presented an interpretation of Psalm I. Our work that summer led to an appearance on the Dave Garroway *Today Show*, a thirty-minute program on NBC's "Frontiers of Faith," opening Houston's "Bible in the Arts Festival" at Temple Emmanuel, a radio tape made for the Southern Baptist Convention Radio-Television Commission for its Christmas broadcast, and the recording of an album for Word Records titled *The Speak 4 Trio*. . . . One night in New Jersey the creative director for Proctor and Gamble . . . heard a local disc jockey play something from *The Speak 4 Trio* album that had just received the Billboard Award as the outstanding religious recording of the year. For almost four years we made the soundtrack for Prell Shampoo commercials and were introduced to residual income. *Ruth Byers*

[3] As sound grew in importance in the Baker productions, a unique rhythm to each play developed, the haunting sound of words which suggested feelings that could re-create the memory of my experience. Even now I can revive the experience by restoring the sound memories to my imagination and so bring into focus a play that was produced many years ago . . . as distinctive and clear as though the lights had just faded into darkness. This was the cause for the chorus in *A Different Drummer*: creating the sounds of children's voices at play; the sounds of the different times of the night and day . . . . there was nothing quite like the magic of it. *Ruth Byers*

[4] The outdoor production of *A Cloud of Witnesses* for the San Antonio Conservation Society was produced against the wall of the old San Jose Mission. I had the assignment of checking the exact time of the first appearance of the moon each evening, its location, and its movement in the sky. The play began with its characters behind a scrim covering the skeleton of the Alamo, and Baker did

not want the moon to preview the characters before the cyc lights did.
Ruth Byers

5 I have hundreds of vivid memories to remind me of Prof's directorial skills. But I feel the best example occurred in the 1956 production of *Hamlet* starring Burgess Meredith. Both Meredith and Charles Laughton, who was there for a sizable part of the rehearsals, had difficulty at times keeping their hands off of the directorial reins. One afternoon both attempted to stage the plain of Denmark scene, trying various ideas, none of which worked successfully while Prof watched in frustration. The two admitted defeat and left for dinner. Prof kept the cast and started working. An hour and a half later, Meredith and Laughton returned. Prof said he had something to show them. They sat stunned and awed watching that scene exploding around them on all stages, with heads and bodies suddenly appearing from behind a series of giant shields. Though a minor and brief scene in the play, it is imprinted indelibly in my mind as my favorite sequence in that production.
Eugene McKinney

6 As Ophelia in *Hamlet ESP*, the movement, line and texture of the character I portrayed changed progressively as the plot developed. Ophelia wore a contemporary costume adorned with a short, crisp, white scarf shifting quickly behind me. As the play progressed, the shorter scarf was replaced with a longer and more flowing one, causing me to move in a different way, floating across the stage. After the drowning scene, the huge white scarf covered the stage, Ophelia lying in the middle of the cloth. The cast encircled the cloth, picked it up, and lowered it and me into the grave. What a picture that painted for the audience.
Pam Gorham Iorio

7 Eliot Elisofon was a renowned *Time/Life* photographer, a master at multitasking, fearless whether playing the role of artist, photographer, lighting designer, gourmet cook, or general entertainment chairman. The set for *Of Time and the River* was a combination of scrim and scaffold. The main stage was cut from side to side by two large scrims. Upstage of the second scrim was a scaffold covering most of the cyc. Lights positioned from the sides and above illuminated action between the scrims, from the front to opaque the scrim and from behind to shine through both layers of scrim, casting sequences of shadows.

The lighting for *Of Time and the River* flowed from one visual effect to another in a unique dance of its own, a series of award-winning photographs. In a scene called "The City," actors took places on the upstage scaffolding. Side, down, and cyc lights caught them in space, creating a cubistic painting effect of city apartments. As intensities of the down and sidelights shifted, a sense of motion was created that seemed to bring the city dwellers to life.

As Thomas Wolfe walked between the two scrims observing the pulse of the city, stage lighting transformed the front scrim from opaque to translucent. At times Wolfe was surrounded by figures larger than life, an effect created by the footlights

Once more have the dramatic forces of Baylor, under Baker, revealed some of the most thoughtful and creative play-making in Texas, amateur or professional, educational or recreational.

John Rosenfield
review of *The Long Gallery*

77

at the rear of the stage projecting the shadows of the city dwellers in medium size against the back scrim and larger than life size against the front scrim. Light shapes and patterns were projected on the front scrim along with film footage, and at the edges of the stages, pools of magenta dramatically accentuated the silhouettes of the senses.

Elisofon was a passionate headmaster. He taught us the process of painting with light, to love saturated color, and gave us a glimpse of the world through the photographer's eye, inspiring several of us to pursue lighting design ourselves.

As a lighting designer, Eliot taught me to be bold, to seek harsh angle, to love saturated color. He showed me how to use lighting as a point of origin, as poetic statement. The lighting layout for *Of Time and the River* remains a template in my mind even today. After forty years in professional theater, my experience in lighting serves as a cornerstone for my creative process. As a director, I seek the poetry of pattern and light across a face or object. I think of the play as a series of photographs, which I hope will be memorable. When lights make a production soar, I often hear the echoes of Eliot's instructions and recall the images of the visual feasts he created for *Of Time and the River*. *Robyn Baker Flatt*

Work Cited

Elizabeth Wear, "The Method of Work of the Baylor Theater with a Critical Analysis of the Production of *Othello*," unpublished master's thesis, Baylor University, 1956.

Hope Springs Eternal: A Different Drummer Times Six

Darrel Baergen

If a man does not keep pace with his companions, perhaps it is because he hears a different drummer. Let him step to the music he hears, however measured or far away.

Henry David Thoreau

I heard a different drummer at the Baylor Theater in 1957 and listened intently. It changed my life. That "drummer" was Paul Baker. Never had I been challenged so consistently to introspection. Never had I been challenged so absolutely to respect my creative process. Indeed, I had never been challenged to define a creative process; I really never knew any process other than rote learning. I had memorized lines for play production. I had memorized in preparation for exams. It was easier to memorize than to assimilate. Paul Baker taught me to assimilate, to absorb, to experience osmosis all within the framework of self-discovery. He encouraged. He did not spoon-feed. He expected the best, and his students responded.

I did not see the 1955 Baylor Theater stage production of Eugene McKinney's *A Different Drummer*. John Rosenfield, drama critic and reviewer for the *Dallas Morning News*, wrote in his review of the play:

> The Baylor University Theater, still famous for its schizogenetic *Othello* two years ago, has done it again. Friday night it began a run of Gene McKinney's *A Different Drummer* which will challenge, enthrall, and divide playgoers at home and from afar. . . . Students and faculty are experimenting with the theatrical vocabulary, hoping to find a phrase or a shape of enrichment. It is a tribute to the soundness of the aims and achievements that such laboratory work has turned out four times to be a whopping good show also. . . . From the two-hour spectacle in Baylor's Studio One you can reach estimates that McKinney never wastes a speech, has a vein of gentle but inexorable satire, can limn character of dimensions with a couple of thrifty speeches and can deploy a large cast easily through his staging resources.

Since I will be dealing with different directorial approaches to this play, perhaps this synopsis of the plot will be helpful: Royal Barnhill, son of the Reverend Franklin Barnhill, deceased, lives with his mother, Grace. He is trying to discover who he is. His girlfriend, Nelda Lou, patiently waits for him to find himself. His father comes back to counsel him. Royal is a frustrated trumpet player who meets a jazz musician through a has-been publicist who tries to take advantage of Royal's insecurity. Royal's adventures are as imaginary as his real life is bland. He stages a fight with a bank president. He allows himself to become a part of a fake wrestling match. He tries out for a jazz band and can't cut it. His mother does not understand him but loves him all the same. Nelda Lou loves him and believes her love can help Royal become more than he is. He finds his hope in the awakening love for her and the dawning discovery of his worth as an individual.

In the play, McKinney uses two choral groups: the Royal Chorus, a group of three or four actors, who speak Royal's thoughts and stay with him throughout the play, "invisible" to all but Royal; and the Objective Chorus, a group of five to ten actors who make comments on the action. The scheme is similar to the Greek chorus of old. Their poses, sometimes frozen in space, give the audience focus as if time can be suspended and they can reflect on the moment.

I directed the play for the first time in 1960, in the Dorland Theatre on the campus of Oklahoma Baptist University. I had been hired as an instructor in the speech and drama department. The stage was a proscenium type with two small side stages outside the main stage but with adjacent access. It had served the campus for many years.

The previous year we had produced the musical *Carousel* for which the college physical plant built a revolving stage. The decision to produce A *Different Drummer* allowed considerable latitude in staging options. I wanted space, and I wanted to use the space. When Royal runs away and when he walks sadly back home, the revolve allowed us to create the image of movement while leaving the actor essentially downstage center. It is similar to the image of Marcel Marceau walking in place yet seemingly moving through space. Master-mime Etienne Decroux, Marcel Marceau's mentor, had been brought to Baylor by Baker to conduct a two-week workshop and to demonstrate basic mime precepts. It was an effect that added to the use of space: a figure alone—at one time elated to be leaving, at another time dejected to be returning—walking, as it were, in place, as the world around him moved on.

80

The set was a simple skeletal representation of Royal's home, principally a front porch, a porch railing, and a straw rocker. It gave us a level to use and the suggestion of a house in comparatively open space. The skeletal design for the house would become specific in later productions.

Virgil Beavers' design for *A Cloud of Witnesses*—a play about the Alamo—left a distinct impression on me as to the viability and poetry of skeletal design. Beavers used linear design. Horizontal levels accentuated and supported by vertical two-inch-by-four-inch lumber, open step units, with the option of seeing through the set allowed the director to place and move the actors in space without traditional solid walls, in and out of areas of light. The lumber allowed unique and creative body positions and gave actors potential for physical characterization. I have turned to that staging idea several times during my career.

The open space was critical to the presentational approach. Space allows for unencumbered movement—strategic for Royal and the Royal Chorus and the Objective Chorus as they filled the space with interpretative dance, movement, and poses.

Four actors formed the Royal Chorus and employed vocal techniques reminiscent of the Baylor Theater's use of choral readings. The makeup for that group was influenced by that theater's use of contemporary art techniques in past productions. That approach provided a remarkable visual effect as the four accompanied Royal, speaking his innermost thoughts, desires, and reactions. The abstract makeup on the faces matched the abstract in the mind.

I taught in the department of speech and drama at Hardin-Simmons University following graduate work at the University of

A Different Drummer
Dallas Theater Center

81

Iowa and at the University of Denver. At Hardin-Simmons, I chose to direct *A Different Drummer* for the second time.

The theater was similar in design to the original Studio One theater at Baylor. (The theater director at Hardin-Simmons, Harry Thompson, designed the Hardin-Simmons theater.) The architectural concept allowed considerable creativity in staging choices. The set I used evolved somewhat from the previous production at OBU. Royal's house became a two-story skeletal structure with an open staircase for Royal to ascend to his room. The idea was to allow for levels and to provide Royal a place alone to practice his trumpet and to think Royal-type thoughts. Mother and Royal could use the porch—another level—and move into and out of the screen door. Mood and atmosphere were enhanced, and blocking options abounded. The entire skeletal set gave the Royal Chorus room to move, sit, stand, and generally surround Royal. The lumber and levels were painted with a bright variety of vibrant colors. The set became an artistic expression of the play in color, texture, and size framed by space.

We used a jungle gym unit with its tubular look and feel. The nostalgia of the set piece was not lost on the audience. It gave our actors more intricate space in which to move and pose. While it may be a stretch of memory to impose a Baylor Theater experiential carryover to the Hardin-Simmons production, nonetheless the effect of the tubular set design Virgil Beavers created for Ramsey Yelvington's *The Golden Stairs* at the Baylor Theater was another profound influence in my directing and design choices.

The presence of Royal's deceased father is a significant motivation for Royal. To emphasize the idea, we lowered a small platform with Royal's father standing behind a pulpit, stage left of

The Golden Stairs, Baylor Theater

82

the jungle gym. The action between father and son needed spatial relationships: father higher, son lower; father stiffer and locked in, son looser and free to shuffle. The contrast was provided by the platform.

When Royal confronted the bank president in a flashback, all we needed was a desk chair on wheels for the actor playing the banker, a limbo lighting effect, and Royal. The simplicity of the atmosphere was complemented by the large darkened space around it. The focus thus achieved gave significance to the scene.

My second production of McKinney's play grew out of the first. The see-through skeletal structure of the house became more involved and usable with the addition of a small square second floor, a chair on the second level to represent Royal's room, and a porch swing below on the front porch. The revolve was gone. The jungle gym stood alone in space and became a symbol of Royal's childhood. His formative years had occurred in and out of his house, on and off the jungle gym, and in the yard between. His romance with Nelda Lou blossomed in the same space. It was home.

When Nelda Lou came to visit Royal her movements were tentative in a secretive, introspective way as she tried to develop a relationship of some kind with him. She sat and moved about on the jungle gym, dreaming about Royal, and rendered a speech about her past youthful fantasies and her present love for Royal. The singular tubular set piece was cold and immovable in contrast to Nelda Lou's warmth and affection. It was her space when she used it.

When Royal chose to run away, the set designer, Robert Scales, placed the train station on the audience-right side stage. The sign announcing the town's name, Hope Springs, hung over a ticket window suspended from a batten representing a train station. The stationmaster faced Royal through the window bars. Royal bought the ticket and then turned downstage and faced the audience in an obvious presentational style. The audience swiveled in their chairs to look at the side stage and Royal. Royal looked out over the audience, first hearing the train, then turning to his left, waiting as the train sounds became louder and passed from speaker to speaker to give the impression of the train speeding by, and then he looked to his right. The saddened walk home was a good use of space—because the space was available and uncluttered. It was another defeat in his life: he could not run away with any success.

We used three actors in the Royal Chorus and divided the lines accordingly. I have attempted during my career in educational theater to use as many actors as come to tryouts, if at all possible. A budding talent may be in the casting call, and I would hate to discourage that person. It might take more intense personal coaching on my part, but I always felt it was worth it. The cast list for *Drummer* allows for some flexibility in numbers, e.g., in the Objective Chorus and the townspeople.

The makeup created for the previous production at OBU worked for the new production. The actors in the Royal Chorus wore black in both productions so the emphasis could be on the makeup and the body movements.

While I was at the Baylor Theater Baker, McKinney, and Beavers had inspired me to use slides and film in stage productions. In my thesis production, *The Emperor Jones*, I used motion picture film of the actor playing Brutus Jones, Ron Wilcox, projected onto a black scrim in a small-space theater called The Sidewalk Theater.

Baker had refurbished a café next door to the Baylor Theater and changed it into a small space for experimental theater. He called it "camera theater" and suggested it be used to create closer interactions between actors and audience than could happen in traditional theaters. The stage space was small as was the backstage area. There was no room for offstage areas right or left. The house would seat about fifty people. A small light booth was located behind the audience.

The actor could work behind the scrim as if inside his own mind thus enhancing the expressionism of the Eugene O'Neill masterpiece. Slides were also used. Using exposed and unprocessed 35mm slide film, each slide was etched on the emulsion side to create jagged, uneven lines. One slide had four square holes cut into it for actors to use the light thus created to show parts of their bodies and four jagged lines scraped on the film and colored red to create lightning effects. Another slide used vertical strips scraped on the emulsion side. When projected, the slides cast green on the stage except where the light was directly exposed. That limited perception to the back of a prisoner in one square of light and a hand holding a whip in another. It was a stunning effect. The use of green to create the effect of a forest when actors moved, cutting through the light from the jagged green lines. Another slide was created with three square holes colored with pastel shades to show the back of a prisoner with a striped jacket in one hole and a hand with a whip in another hole and feet dragging in the third hole. The process allowed us a high level of selectivity in interpretation of the play's theme and story.

I decided to use 16mm motion picture film with the Hardin-Simmons production of *A Different Drummer*. The designer, the actor playing Royal, and I went to Roscoe—west of Abilene—to film a particularly barren landscape with a lonely train track for Royal to walk. Royal would be walking home, along the tracks, providing atmosphere. The visual emphasis at OBU was provided by the revolve which became a viable set piece giving unique staging options. The set at Hardin-Simmons, on the other hand, allowed us to think of film to incorporate into the production. The designer and I came up with the idea of using motion picture film as a prologue to the play and opened Act I with Royal walking into the scene and to his house.

A unique feature of this production was the use of an original music score composed by Mary Truly, an instructor in music theory and piano at the university, and Mike Moseley, a senior

A Different Drummer, Dallas Theater Center

music education student. The *Abilene Reporter-News* said, "Using thematic arrangements for principal characters in the story, the two composers are writing a score to run the full length of the production. The music and improvisation on various themes will be taped for playing during the presentation."

Conferences between the composers and the director brought a special quality to the play's production because of the score—a combination of contemporary jazz and musical comedy. Speed Patterpeck, a character in *A Different Drummer*, is a somewhat inept jazz musician whose influence over Royal creates dramatic conflict. Royal practices his trumpet endlessly—and does it badly. But it is jazz, and our score used the musical medium as an effective interpretation of theme. The synthesis of artists and art forms once again proved the intrinsic value of theater: a gathering of the arts to communicate an idea.

San Marcos Baptist Academy, a private elementary-through-high school affiliated with the Baptist General Convention of Texas, serves students from around the world. My wife, Judy Baergen, taught at the academy, first in the elementary grades and then in the high school. She decided to direct a play, asking me to assist. Judy chose *A Different Drummer*. Experience during the first two productions had been with college students. Now the cast would be made up of high school students.

The creation of characters older than the actual age of the actors meant special coaching in line delivery and body use. Words needed to be spoken more slowly and with more clarity. Gestures and walking had to be consistent with the ages of the characters. It was important for Royal's mother, for example, to be his mother, not a high school girl playing as if she were a mother. The play is a comedy of sorts, but the actors had to be reminded that the warmth and humor were in the lines, action, and characterizations, not forced on top of the character.

A good play will reach any audience, and *Drummer* proved its enduring value once again. The cast did well, and the audiences responded with understanding and empathy. Royal—accident prone, frustrated with home, unable to escape, living in the shadow of someone else—became a recognizable character to the students and faculty of the San Marcos Baptist Academy.

At the San Marcos Baptist Academy Judy and I decided to create the image of filmic movement by using slides. It was a choice determined by budgetary and equipment limitations, but the adaptation became a critical part of the production.

We took slides of Royal alone and of Royal and Nelda Lou from various distances to the lens: close up, medium shot, long shot, keeping the camera in a fixed position. The slides were then used at the opening of the play; two projectors and a dissolve unit created the effect of Royal coming from a distance, getting closer to the house, then appearing on the stage. At the end of the play we saw Royal and Nelda Lou, backs to the camera, holding hands, walking away from his house as the slides dissolved one into the other to give the illusion of the two actors walking into their future.

The use of space, the creation of mood and atmosphere, the elements of storytelling such as conflict, resolution, and characterization are not determined by large budgets and the newest in technological developments. A good story can be told with a minimum of accoutrements.

The production of *A Different Drummer* at San Marcos Baptist Academy gave testimony to the universality of drama. Produced in an older building, using lighting instruments from another era, and working within a limited budget contributed to the creative process we call educational theater. I have believed in and taught that in play production, after the significance of the script has been determined, that the next most important production aspect should be lighting. Lighting can create mood and atmosphere, with or without a complicated or involved set design. This staging concept has served me well in school and church productions where the funds are limited. The temptation when large budgets are available is to do more technical wonders and effects to the play than the play needs. Lighting instruments need not be the newest design. I have used tin cans with parabolic (household spot and flood) lights, although I prefer somewhat higher quality choices. Limbo lighting, backlight, key light, silhouette lighting, side lighting, low light to accentuate mood—it is all available when lighting becomes a predominant design feature for stage production.

Royal Barnhill appeared again on May 27 and 28, 1977. This time Hope Springs took up residence at the Harbor Playhouse in Corpus Christi, Texas. I had taken a leave of absence from Southwest Texas State University and become the founding director of Christian Community Productions of Corpus Christi, Inc. The dream of the founders was to put together a community theater group that would produce good theater, most of which would be produced at the Harbor Playhouse, a stage home for a variety of performances with community appeal. Our 1977–1978 season included *Our Town*, *A Different Drummer*, the "After Dinner Players" from Houston, *A Day in the Life of Jot*, a multimedia play for children,[1] and *Amahl and the Night Visitors*.

The cast for *A Different Drummer* represented a cross-section of Corpus Christi residents—an announcer with KSIX and KZTV, a data processor, an office manager, a student at the Dallas Theater Center, another student from a junior high school, a chemical engineer, a physician, a mother of three, a salesman, an account executive for a TV station, and the wife of the play's director. Judy, who had directed the play at the San Marcos Baptist Academy, was cast as the super-pious Mrs. Buxley whose hypercritical attitude brought humor and meaning to the play.

This was the first time I had worked with a cast of different ages in the production of *Drummer*. The majority of the actors were close to the ages of the characters and had experience and knowledge not yet gained by college or high school actors. The bodies moved in rhythms similar to the characters' ages. The thought processes were more mature when applied to the characters. There was, however, a comparative lack of willingness to follow directions. Not that the attitudes were wrong, but some of the actors could not re-create what I had asked in blocking or line interpretation from rehearsal to rehearsal. They had other priorities: work, family, travel, schedules. One actor in particular was so inconsistent that I was never sure where or when he might move and how he might read his lines, sometimes improvising the words rather than quoting the actual words. He apparently did not worry about it—in rehearsal or performance. Fortunately the other actors around him could compensate.

Since the Harbor Playhouse was a community house, the rehearsal, set-up, and performance times were a significant part of the budget. The space had to be rented whenever it was used. The times available for rehearsals presented a scheduling challenge. Fortunately, the play could be divided along McKinney's use of French scene outlines and not everyone was called all of the time.

Some rehearsals were held at other locations. We used the recreation area at First Baptist Church for "extracurricular" rehearsals. Substitute props and furniture were placed in approximately the same position in the rehearsal hall as in the theater. Vocal projection changed and had to be corrected in the theater space.

The set was a skeletal representation of Royal's house. The space was unencumbered to add to the play's thematic elements. All that space, and Royal was still locked in his own small world:

house, playground, friends, critical townspeople, a doting mother. While space was the consistent facet of all the productions of *Drummer*, the area on the Corpus Christi stage was larger than the previous stages. Lighting and placement of set pieces were adjusted while the proscenium curtain and the tormentors were closed a bit to accentuate the horizontal space.

Expense, a significant part of community theater production, precluded the use of slides or film. Projection equipment was not readily available and costly. The previous use of projection had added a dimension of design interest and integration to the staging of *Drummer*. I missed it in Corpus Christi, but the play carried itself on the strength of the story and the characterizations. Since the initial concept did not include slides or film, other production ideas came into focus. The cast and audience did not miss filmic images because they had never been a consideration.

The use of a Royal Chorus presented a casting and logistical challenge. I chose to pre-record the Royal Chorus as a single voice—Royal's voice. The intention was to give the effect of Royal's thoughts verbalized, as it were, in space. I prefer the actual stage presence of the Royal Chorus, but the prerecorded idea worked, nonetheless. As with the filmic projections, the cast and audience accepted the recorded single vocal thoughts for Royal since there was no other option available due to casting and rehearsal needs. I felt we lost the design effect created by the contemporary art in the Royal Chorus makeup, the wonderful potential for body movements and postures, and the unique vocal textures of previous productions.

The presentation became a challenging mix of elements uncommon to those of us conditioned to college production. Within academic theater class assignments and programs of study predetermined certain expectations. Outside of the collegiate atmosphere, however, schedules and levels of commitment were less likely to be taken as seriously and thus not necessarily under the director's control. All in all, the experience was valid: a good play provided good theater.

In the summer of 1980 I became the chair of the department of communication and the director of the Center for Christian Communication Studies at Southwestern Baptist Theological Seminary in Fort Worth. I went there to begin a new academic program, the master of arts degree in communication, using the personnel and facilities of both institutions to train graduate students in the use of radio and television for denominational and church production. A part of the assignment was the development of new courses to complement the new M.A.

degree. Drama was an element in the construction of the new program. One of the first plays I chose to direct was *A Different Drummer*.

The playwright's father had been a longtime member of the seminary's music faculty. The author was literally raised in the shadow of the seminary since the McKinney home was adjacent to the campus. When I moved to Fort Worth that house was still standing. I decided to make the author's boyhood home a major scenic symbol in the production. Gene McKinney. Son of Baptists' favorite hymn writer. His home right there at the campus. It was an ideal time to produce *A Different Drummer*.

We chose once again to design the set as a skeletal structure useful for levels and acting positions. The use of stage space took precedence as a design choice but was modified from past productions. The "house" was downstage right, as it had been in the other productions. It had a porch on a platform, a porch railing, a working screen door to the left and upstage of the railing. Behind the two-by-four-foot structure was a step unit going from stage left to a platform above the screen door where Royal could sit or stand and blow his horn. Suspended from battens we used an angled two-by-four-inch board matching the angle of the step unit and a window frame above Royal's "room" or platform. Another batten was devoted to a sign that was used in each production: "My name is Jack Dempsey. If you don't believe it, I'll punch you in the eye." (This was used while Royal was trying to exert himself as the winner of a fake wrestling match.) A third batten flew the name of the town for the train station scene: "Hope Springs." The jungle gym was replaced by a swing set, giving interesting physical interactions for the actors. The actors climbed on the bars, sat on the swings, and generally used the set piece with childlike reminiscence. We chose the swing set because it was available without cost. A jungle gym was not available. We added five ladders stage left of the swing set. Each ladder was a different height—eighteen feet, sixteen, twelve, ten, and three—arranged so that the tallest ladder was upstage of the others and the smallest downstage, creating a small grouping of ladders. Limbo light accentuated the variety of heights. The Objective Chorus, numbering five, used the ladders for posing and line reading some of the time. The effect combined with the swing set and the skeletal house gave the stage design visual interest and a variety of space for body positions in three specific areas.

An added feature was filmic. We took a single slide of the front of the boyhood home of the playwright. A projector mounted immediately above the proscenium arch focused the picture on the back wall or cyc. We projected the McKinney home on the wall for the entire production. It was a good effect: the ever-present Fort Worth home of McKinney as a design element. When the downstage lights dimmed, the projected house remained.

The actors were all graduate students. Here was a third group of actors used in my productions of this play: undergraduate, community, graduate. Their level of expertise had developed over the years, and they brought a heightened sense of commitment to the play and its production. The actors were motivated by more than their interest in theater, although that was a significant ingredient. They were students at a religious graduate institution, and their intent was to communicate their beliefs using the medium of drama. A *Different Drummer* did just that—with warmth and humor. The crew was made up of students in a class in set design, a part of the newly fashioned curriculum in communication at the seminary. Several of the actors worked as interns at the Baptist Radio-Television Commission, a production house in Fort Worth. Others worked in church dramatics. The actor playing Jessie Miller, Royal's sometime-friend and other-time nemesis, became a faculty member in the department of communication at the seminary.

The rehearsal schedule precluded work on Sundays and Wednesdays—"sacred" in Baptist life. The actors brought homework to rehearsals, and rehearsal schedules took advantage of the easy division of scenes in the play. Several Saturday rehearsals were scheduled.

The stage was a proscenium type with very little space off right or left. We used area lighting with minimal props to create some of the scenes. A particularly important scene to show Royal's insecurity occurs when he accidentally knocks a flowerpot off the porch railing. His mother starts to scold him and then excuses him. The lighting focused on the porch and the two actors. The rest of the set and stage was dark except for the cyclorama on which the picture of the McKinney home was seen. The audience juxtaposed the scene on the porch and the picture on the wall. The atmosphere and mood were remarkable. Later, after the mother's exit into the house and out of the light, Royal knocks over a garden rake. His closing line for the act gave continuing insight into his character: "Nothing fell." And the singular limbo light faded to black. The larger space allowed for movement and freedom. Lighting assisted atmosphere and mood.

My son, Jeffrey Baergen, directed A *Different Drummer* at the San Marcos Baptist Academy in April 1996, forty-one years after the play was first produced at the Baylor in 1955. A new generation has been introduced to Royal Barnhill. Perhaps they, too, will hear a different drummer.

The director used yet another approach to set design. No one design is the final and only design for any play. Jeffrey built a wall on a platform that rolled on casters. One half of the platform was the Barnhill front porch with a railing and two chairs. The other half, which could be revolved to face the audience, was the bank president's office and the train depot. The Objective Chorus revolved the set, and the stage crew changed the sets while the front porch was facing downstage. To the right and left edges of the dividing wall the director placed tall ladders for the Royal Chorus to climb and pose and speak their lines. A two-inch-by-six-inch board was placed on top of the wall for another acting area for the Royal Chorus.

The play was produced in the Robinson Chapel. Upstage center is a large and beautiful stained glass window. Drapes can be pulled to cover the window or opened to reveal the window. When Jeff wanted a background for the Reverend Franklin Barnhill, the drapes were opened revealing Royal's father on a platform in front of the stained glass window.

Royal, his mother, Grace Barnhill, Nelda Lou, Norma Buxley, and the other inhabitants of Hope Springs have appeared on different stages to diverse audiences performed by actors in and out of academic theater. The play has withstood the test of time.

In "Theater of Faith," an essay written for *The Talents of the American Theater* (David H. Stevens, ed. Norman: University of Oklahoma Press, 1970), Baker wrote:

> The raw material of the theater is each play. This raw material must be brought to life to make its own statement through the use of space, direction, silhouette, sound, silence, light and dark—each receiving the emphasis and the importance that the director and actors have discovered through experimentation and work."[2]

The experiences of that marvelously mind-expanding year at the Baylor Theater in 1957–1958 cannot be summarized in a sentence or two. Those experiences continue to offer new horizons even after a teaching and directing career of forty-two years. Most people work for results rather than discovery. The concept of the integration of abilities has had a profound effect on my teaching and directing. In classes in acting, directing, scene design, or creative dramatics, the various techniques and approaches to learning must be in process rather that an effort to reach some kind of predicted end result. The creative process is a never-ending continuum, renewed with each teaching and/or directing effort, with each new semester, with each new student, with each new idea. And there is still room for growth. ■

Some of the seed fell on rocky places with no soil. Some grew too quickly with no roots. Some growth was choked out by thorns. But, some fell on good soil and it produced and reproduced again and again. He who has ears to hear, let him hear.

Luke 8:6–8

Every young actor or theater artist needs someone like Paul Baker in his life: he needs to crash into an ego and a talent much bigger than his own.

Edward Herrmann

End Notes

[1] When Paul Stevens, director of the Southern Baptist Radio and TV Commission in Fort Worth, decided to begin children's programming for television, he turned to one who had a background with children and theater and with whom he had worked before (*The Speak 4 Trio* tapings and other random assignments). I was to work with Ted Perry, a writer for the commission who had studied under both Paul Baker and Gene McKinney.

[2] We applied Baker's concepts to our work, viewing the television screen as a combination of empty space and silence. We created in that space and silence an animated character that was a circle, a dot that could become anything and move any way, enter or exit at any place on the screen. Once the dot stopped moving, he sprouted legs, arms and became a little boy, a dot named Jot, a happy, well-balanced child until he did something wrong. At that point he changed color and shape to show how he felt on the inside. Once he righted the wrong, he changed again into the happy character and face of Jot. *JOT* went on the air in 1963 and has been translated into nineteen languages. Outside the United States, Jot's greatest popularity was in Japan and Mexico. Jot inspired T-shirts, books, puppets, puzzles, activity books, buttons, dolls, stories, and a Vacation Bible School format.
Ruth Byers

93

A Different Drummer, Hardin Simmons University

Playwrights Are Made, Not Born

Eugene McKinney

Paul Baker has produced more bad plays than any theater director in America. He invested in raw young talent by putting onstage their callow scripts in the belief that playwrights, like all theater artists, learn by doing, or in the writers' cases, learn by their works being done. As a result of that investment, Baker's program has spawned hundreds of writers. That has resulted in a multitude of produced and published plays and dozens of published novels.

Theater is a collaborative art form in which individuals bring their specialized talents to a group effort in evolving a stage production of a script. I use the word "script" since I believe in a way that the playwright's work exists only as text—a piece of literature, good or bad—until it is brought to life onstage. After a show closes, the play reverts to being text, and returns to its place on library shelves, in Samuel French catalogs, or back in the author's filing cabinet.

In many drama programs, neophyte actors, directors, and designers are given ample chances to develop their talents, but young playwrights are ignored and their early works remain unproduced scripts. Not so in Paul Baker's theaters. He considered the playwright as an essential part of his program, and writers were given opportunities equal to those offered other participants. He invested in inexperienced playwrights just as he did in inexperienced actors, directors, and designers.

I did not know of Baker's admiration, bordering on adoration, for playwrights when I started my circuitous journey trying to find what I wanted to do with my life. Serendipity played a large part in my decision to become a writer.

The journey began in 1940 when I was a sophomore ministerial student at Baylor. I knew little about the arts. And I had seen only one stage play in my life. Being Baptist I had felt guilty the whole time I was watching it.

My status was secure; my destiny was preordained. My horizons were so close to me that I could almost touch them. I felt secure. And safe. And satisfied.

All of that changed because of Paul Baker. One day on my way to class, a burly, black-haired man stopped me in front of a classroom building. He introduced himself and said he was directing a play. He asked me if I wanted to be in it. My mind said no. But my lips said yes. This was a pattern I was to follow throughout my relationship with Baker.

The play was *Abe Lincoln in Illinois*. Somehow, from my conversation with Baker I thought I was going to star in it. I did not. My total lines were "Stand back!! Stand back!" Two lines. Or, four words. And I shared them with five other Union soldiers. But it was so exciting. Again, I felt guilty. I also felt strangely invigorated. I did not know it at the time, but I had found a home.

The next semester, at registration I tripped over a professor's leg extending from his desk into the aisle. To this day I claim that Paul Baker tripped me deliberately. However, he apologized, asked me what I was looking for, and I said I wanted to sign up for a religion course. He said he could take care of me. When he handed back the materials, I glanced down and saw that he had signed me up for a drama course with a strange title, Integration of Abilities.

He then laughed and said he was just joking, and pointed me in the right direction. I stood there for a moment, and then made a snap decision, one that would cause a monumental change in my life. This audacious and unconventional man intrigued me. Perhaps I was influenced by my introduction to him and to show business the preceding semester. For whatever reason, I decided to stay in the course with the strange title.

I didn't know it at the time, but because of that decision my life would soon leave its safe orbit around its predictable future and shoot off into uncharted territory. If I had known beforehand, I do not think I would have given up my secure status, my preordained destiny, or my horizons that I could almost touch.

That course and that home I had found at the Baylor Theater challenged me, compelled me, to give up my security and establish new and ever-receding horizons that I not only could not touch but indeed could barely see. The arts (not just drama) became not simply important but essential and gave me a new and constantly changing view of myself and my place in the world.

Although I had found a home, I struggled to find my "room" in that home. I tried acting, and although I was cast in a number of plays, I felt insecure onstage and found little gratification as an actor. Being nearly color-blind, I knew that designing was not for me. I had just returned to college from a stint in the army where I learned that I did not like to be in charge of people, so I had no desire to be a director.

However, in high school I had developed a love for writing—not research papers—but fiction.

Although at that time the Baylor Theater did not have a playwriting program, I decided to write a play. So I wrote a first draft and loved the result so much that I didn't want to change one word of it. I was gratified, but at the same time I yearned to see it onstage so that others could share my delight. Instinctively, I was beginning to feel like a playwright.

Again serendipity: I got lucky. Shortly after finishing the script, I became a student member of the 1947 Southwest Summer Theater at Baylor. For that summer, Baker decided that the company would be run on a totally democratic basis. Each member had one vote, and all major decisions would be voted on.

We had already selected two short plays and needed another one-act to fill out the bill for the second show of the summer. I submitted my short play, *How Are the Mighty Fallen*. The title was as pretentious as the play turned out to be. After the company heard me read it aloud, the vote was taken. The only ones in favor of doing the play were Baker, Treysa Seely (who soon was to become my wife), and the play's author. Baker announced that it was time to break for lunch. And then he said, "When we get back we'll start tryouts for McKinney's play." So much for democracy.

My script was given a full-scale production. The audience response was underwhelming. I sat there slowly realizing I had written an abysmally bad play. But at the same time I was enthralled by hearing the words I had written and by seeing the characters I had set down on paper come at least partially alive. It was the most exciting experience of my young life. I was hooked. I had found my role in the theater. For better or worse, I had become a playwright. Baker made that investment in me (and continued to do so) because he saw that potential in me.

Encouraged by his faith in me and goaded by him during encounters in the lobby and after class ("McKinney, where's your next script?"), I wrote a one-act play, a comedy, for my directing class project. When he critiqued my production, he heaped scorn on my directing but poured balm on that wound by reminding me that he had laughed all the way through the show. I then wrote and directed another short play. Both productions were toured to WBAP-TV in Fort Worth as a part of the first live drama telecasts in the Southwest.

By this time, Baker had initiated a playwriting program on a continuing basis and had added a series of writing courses, taught by a local writer, to the drama curriculum. The beginning course would be required of all drama majors. Baker believed that students, no matter what they later

"Wide, Wide World", NBC-TV, Baylor

wanted to specialize in, needed a hands-on experience in all areas of theater. And that included writing a play.

To further encourage neophyte playwrights, Baker stipulated that the short plays written in the beginning and advanced classes would form a script pool from which the beginning members of the directing class could choose their production projects. Thus, the writer was given the invaluable experience of working with the director and the chance to revise the script during rehearsals. Even an experienced playwright does not know the merit of his or her script until a director attempts to "bring it alive" onstage. Even then, it may be a stillbirth.

I received my M.A. degree in drama in 1950. Almost simultaneously, the playwriting instructor resigned. Again, serendipity. Baker asked me to take over the playwriting program. I accepted his offer, with more fear than elation. That started me on a journey of thirty-five uninterrupted years as a creative writing teacher and playwright-in-residence under the aegis of Baker.

98

The year before, I had decided to try writing my first full-length play. I had been stimulated to do so by watching the rehearsals and performances of a new play by Ramsey Yelvington, another Baker protégé from earlier years. That production inspired me to continue with my project despite the pressure of my new teaching duties. I knew I could not match Yelvington's writing skills with my first full-length work and, in retrospect, I certainly did not match his prolificacy—over the next decade Baker directed new scripts by Yelvington on an almost annual basis.[1]

I wanted my first long play to be a learning experience for me, an attempt to master the fundamental structure of an orthodox play. I wanted to learn how to walk so that with more experience I might learn how to fly. So I set out certain parameters as restrictions: single set, a minimum of time breaks, guaranteeing long stretches of continuous action.

It was a difficult task I undertook—devising motivations for the characters' entrances and exits in a way that the audience would accept the action taking place onstage as plausible. The entire time I felt like I was writing while wearing a straitjacket.

After I finished several revisions of the script, I gave it to Baker with fear and trepidation. The next day he pulled me aside and said he wanted to do the play. He said further that 1952 was the silver anniversary of the Baylor Theater, and he wanted the production of my play to be the centerpiece of the celebration. I felt honored, and the trepidation was suddenly replaced by elation. But the fear remained.

That fear was dispelled when the show opened. The production of *The Answer Is Two* was beautifully staged and wel-received by the audience. I learned a lot about structuring a play into a solid orthodox piece, with every element efficiently in place. However, I did resolve that I would never again impose such severe restrictions on my writing process.

That decision was reinforced the next year when the production of *Othello* broke all bonds of traditional staging, and freedom did indeed reign. It was truly a revolutionary work that explored unknown territory. Amazingly for an "experiment," it brought national attention to the Baylor Theater, which in turn provided the catalyst for subsequent theater adventures. As a playwright, I now felt liberated, and I wanted to be a part of that journey.

The success of *Othello* triggered Baker's decision to use the summer of 1953 as a workshop devoted to experimentation, with the emphasis more on process (exploration) than on product

Choral Reading, "Speak 4 Trio"

(eventual public performance). The students and faculty were encouraged to go beyond the boundaries of orthodoxy and to let the group's collective imagination run free.

New discoveries were made in the use of the human voice, either collectively as a large ensemble or in small groups. As a springboard, we used selected passages from the Bible plus a few poems.

In addition, I devised an experiment in comedy, exploring techniques common to stage humor—repetition, sudden violation of the norm, abrupt changes in pattern, etc. But I did not want to focus primarily on the human body, nor did I want to write literal gags that would be spoken by two actors.

From time to time, I had been amused by observing an unseen student sliding a stage flat across empty space. That rectangular object appeared to assume a life of its own. How could I use that object in an abstract way to create comedy and at the same to time convey, albeit obscurely, some specific in the human condition? So flats became my primary tool, although I did not limit myself to that. Stealing ideas from members of the group, I developed a piece called *Three Zeros and One One*.

My agent had been expecting a play from me during that summer and queried me about its progress. I replied that I had set it aside to write a short piece for the summer company. The agent shot back a note: "Be sure to send me a copy of your one-act as soon as it's finished." I replied: "I will as soon as I figure out a way to put it down on paper." I never did. It remained in outline form, with each segment represented by one or two words.

For example, "Rope Pull." The rope being pulled started out the size of hawser for towing a ship. The more the actor pulled, the smaller the rope became until finally it was dental floss. The actor picked his teeth with it, looked at the audience, and walked offstage.

In "Flats Mating," two flats, one blue and the other pink, were flirtatiously moved together while the unseen actors sliding the flats made masculine and feminine abstract courting sounds. The larger blue flat covered the pink flat, and when the two flats separated, a small blue and pink striped flat was revealed.

Finally we opened the theater doors to test our work before an audience. The response was strong. Theatergoers had never witnessed such an audacious performance. They were moved by the Bible readings and found delight in the poetry. They howled laughter in response to my comedic presentation. I felt a little guilty for having used the audience members as guinea pigs in my experiment, but the results were so positive and I had learned so much that I forgave myself.

At that time, NBC-TV carried *Wide Wide World*, a weekly cultural documentary hosted by Dave Garroway. The show was done live with no film footage. Although studio-based in New York, most of the program was devoted to live remotes around the United States that were beamed back to the studio and almost simultaneously shown on TV sets across the nation.

The show's producers had been planning a documentary on the state of Texas. Having seen the national coverage of *Othello*, they made further inquiries and then flew to Waco to audition the Baylor Theater. Baker staged an excerpt from *Othello*, and they sat through a private performance of our summer production.

The producers were so excited by our work that they decided on the spot that we would represent Texas theater on their show. In addition, they commissioned me to write a special three-minute script about Texas that would end the Baylor Theater segment. They had only four requirements: "You must use devices from your comedy, it must be funny, it must be fast moving, and it must end with a bang."

I hastily wrote the script, a satire on Texas, but could not come up with the required "bang" ending. Then I recalled an incident a few months earlier that showed that Baker's sense of humor was as imaginative as his directorial approach. For some reason, the Baylor marching band had changed from its normal practice field and had begun rehearsing its halftime show on the vacant field to the side of the Baylor Theater. The sound was extremely loud and was proving to be an aggravating distraction to our afternoon classes and rehearsals. One day, Baker rigged up a public address system, with turntable, and positioned large loudspeakers atop the theater and facing the field. He also sent a dozen drama students, dressed in motley costumes, to the roof.

In the middle of the band's rehearsal, the loudspeakers blared forth marching music and shouted absurd instructions, and the drama students performed a savage parody of halftime shows. Needless to say, the band rehearsal was disrupted. In fact, the rehearsal was through for the day, since some of the band members were lying on the field totally exhausted from laughter. The band director left the field looking defeated.

The next afternoon the band director sent the hundred-member Baylor band marching through the front doors of the theater playing the "Baylor Fight Song." The band marched through rehearsals and classes and departed the building leaving reverberations and damaged eardrums.

It was *Wide Wide World* showtime at Baylor. The TV director was in his mobile control unit outside. The cameras were in place in Studio One, as was an audience. Our performance went smoothly, including my short comedy. At the moment of the last stage action, the cameras picked up the Baylor band, instruments blaring, invading the theater and engulfing the stages, actors, and startled audience. That was, indeed, a big "bang." After the show, the unseen host spoke to us from New York and pronounced it the most exciting segment that *Wide Wide World* had ever done.

My writer's mind returned to the script I had been working on before the summer production. Heavily influenced by the *Othello* production and now enriched by the summer's experimental work, I revised what I had written and plunged forward into heretofore unknown territory. Unlike the church-building set of my first full-length play, my setting was a general one: a small town. And, for the first time, in a major way I was drawing on my own background, depicting a shy young man struggling to break away from the constraints of his religious upbringing.

From the *Othello* experiment, I used the device of having the protagonist played by more than one actor—in my case presenting an onstage alter ego. And choral reading, as in the summer show, was also used.

I finished the play in 1954 and named it *Royal Barnhill*. During rehearsals, I changed the name to *A Different Drummer*. That was not the only change. It entered the rehearsal period as a two-act play. By opening night it had become a three-act play. This growth was primarily the result of the play's adventurous director opening up new vistas in the mind of the playwright.

Before casting the show and starting rehearsals, the faculty held the customary "brain-storming" sessions. Baker's creed for these meeting was: "Stretch your imagination to its limits. No idea is too wild to be considered." Our resident designer, Virgil Beavers, was a key figure in those discussions. Baker had a special working relationship with him. He knew that Beavers would design a set that would allow his directorial dreams to be realized onstage. He often said, "I can't direct the play until Virgil designs the set."

After the final brainstorming session, Baker took me aside and said, "Virgil and I have decided to stage your play vertically." By this time, I should have become accustomed to Baker's strange ideas. But I was momentarily stunned. In writing the play, naturally I had envisioned the action taking place horizontally—on the stage floor.

However, Baker showed me some preliminary sketches by Virgil. I immediately saw the possibilities in the Mondrian-like jungle gyms with minimum set pieces to be carried onstage in order to establish specific locales. Yes, a great deal of the play could be staged vertically, especially the townspeople sequences. I could see that the rectangular spaces formed by the bars could be used as a stage equivalent of the cinema's close-up, framing and making more important a character's face. This play could soar!

Tryouts were held, followed by a group discussion with the cast, and it was time for the first rehearsal. I was eager to hear the first words I had written being spoken aloud from the stage. But I wasn't surprised when Baker informed the cast that they should

A Different Drummer, Baylor Theater

103

get onstage without their scripts. He told them, "We are going to create the small town of Hope Springs." And he and the cast spent the evening doing just that.

I went home afterward and wrote a new opening for the play, based on what I had observed from that long exercise. I also stole a number of lines that had been ad-libbed by the actors. This new sequence required the creation of another choral reading group, the Objective Chorus.

The play continued to grow as a result of rehearsals and sometimes from an outside stimulus. One day, Baker had attended the Waco City Council meeting to plead for some cause. He came back indignant because the meeting had gone overlong due to

A Different Drummer,
Dallas Theater Center

the squabbling among the council members, and he hadn't had a chance to speak. He told me they would take up an issue and argue over it but never reach an agreement and then go on to another problem. He said that each time, it would end with someone saying, "Well, we don't want to decide anything today. We'll take that under advisement." I had wanted to develop a sequence showing the disparate and petty problems of the Hope Springs citizens. Inspired by Baker's experience, I wrote a city council scene. It played well.

As rehearsals went on, I started searching for one additional complication to flesh out the play. I couldn't come up with one that would produce a crisis. Then Beavers showed me some sketches he had made for the carry-on stylized pieces that would establish a new locale. One sketch caught my eye. It was just a door frame. Across the header was a sign: Train Station. I said, "Virgil, there's no train station scene in my play." He replied, "Every small town wants the train to stop there."

That conversation provided me with the complication I needed. My protagonist, Royal, desperate to escape his problems, decides to run away. That led to my writing two of my favorite sequences: the "going to sleep" scene, with the townspeople scattered all over the jungle gym; and Royal, in the early morning, saying good-bye to his home, engendering a remembrance sequence in which he recalls, in movement and sound, the outdoor games he played as a child. However, the stationmaster thwarts his escape from the town, and he is thrown back into his problem cauldron. With those additions, I now had a three-act play.

Revising and enlarging ended as opening night drew nearer. Baker continued to solve minor problems and also focused on pacing. It was entirely in his hands now, and I was a bystander.

On opening night, I sat in an end-row seat in the rear, so that if something went wrong I could slip away in the darkness of the night, never to return. Instead, everything went right. I quickly lost my fear as I became transfigured by something I had started and Baker had finished. The production, indeed, soared and went higher than my most optimistic expectation, and far beyond the limits of my talent. That's the magic of the collaborative art form called theater.

The production was a huge success, the reviews were ecstatic, and once again the Baylor Theater received national attention. Recent history repeated itself when the producer of *Omnibus*, a CBS television program, flew to Waco to see a private performance of the first act of *A Different*

Drummer. He was excited about what he saw and commissioned me to revise the play into a much shorter television script that would be performed live, originating in their New York studio. In addition, he would bring director Baker and his assistant director, Mary Sue Jones, to New York to supervise the rehearsals. He also decided to import the two student leads, Clu and Miriam Gulager, to duplicate their stage roles, with the rest of the cast being supplied by Equity actors. In addition, a portion of Beavers' stylized set would be replicated in the studio.

All of that happened. Although my experience in TV had been limited to the *Wide Wide World* brief segment and the two short plays performed in a regional TV station, and even though I didn't own a TV set, I set out to carve the play down to a forty-three-minute television script. It was a painful process, but I did it, agonizing over each cut. I flew to New York two weeks before the date it was scheduled to air and did additional work on the script, supervised by the production staff. I was joined a week later by Baker and Jones and the two students. It was a hectic and at times nightmarish experience for all the Texans involved.

Although the live performance went well, I left New York feeling dissatisfied with the result. I had gone from living on the mountaintop (the stage production) to existing on a molehill (the *Omnibus* truncated show). What had appeared excitingly innovative in the stage production appeared arty on television. The simple warmth of the staged play turned cold on TV. Because this was pre-color TV, the staging seemed stark compared to the stage production.

The major weakness, I feel in retrospect, was my inexperience as a writer for this medium. The *Omnibus* producer insisted on the inclusion of the play's most daring sequences, which meant I had to cut a great deal of characterization and sacrifice all nuances in order to meet the time restriction. I returned to Waco and, as a consolation present to myself, used most of my writer's fee on a TV set.

There was an unexpected benefit from having the show performed on national TV. The ratings system showed that over nineteen million people saw the production. Some of those were theater directors who tracked me down wanting a copy of the stage play. I sent a dozen of the scripts left over from our production. Most of the directors to whom I sent the play scheduled it for production. Those productions around the country started a chain reaction of requests.

Encouraged by the response, I had my agent submit the play to Samuel French for possible publication. It was summarily rejected—too experimental, too large a cast, too difficult to stage. By now I was running out of copies and requested that any theater doing my play run off ten extra mimeographed copies in lieu of one night's royalty. That way, I kept up with the demand.

A year later, Baker was in New York and encountered the owner of Samuel French at a party. Baker chastised him for rejecting my play, citing its young but burgeoning track record of productions. The owner gave Baker his home address to bypass the editors who had given short shrift to my work. I sent him the play and soon received a contract. After it was published, the volume of productions increased rapidly, and the play remained popular for years. By 2002, the play had been staged over nine hundred times. That is a remarkable record, especially since the play was never done on Broadway, Off Broadway, or even Off Off Broadway.

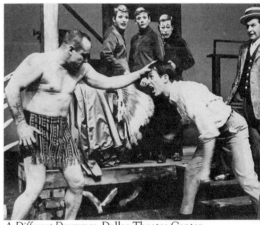

A Different Drummer, Dallas Theater Center

Through the years, I was able to attend a number of those productions. Some were bad, a number were excellent, a few were superb. But none of them matched the magic of that first production.

My next writing task as Baylor's playwright-in-residence was easier. In 1958, Baker decided to work on a new project, the staging of Thomas Wolfe's massive novel, *Of Time and the River*. A number of copies of that 912-page book were purchased, and their covers and bindings were ripped off, leaving only the printed text. The student company was divided into nine groups. Each group had a leader, a director, and a playwright.

Different segments of the book were given to the groups, and they were told to develop a script from their assigned section of printed text. They were to look for important scenes that could

Of Time and the River
Dallas Theater Center

be staged. But they also should find narrative passages that were important to the progression of the plot, established locale and seasons, or were rich in lyrical writing typical of Wolfe's style.

In most stage adaptations of novels, some of the narrative can be translated into dialogue but most of it is eliminated due to lack of onstage action. However, the students knew that Baker was planning to use choral reading techniques combined with motion picture footage especially filmed for this production. That would prevent the lack of onstage character movement from becoming a liability. The students could cut or compress the text, but they had to conform to one rule: The purity of Wolfe's writing should not be violated by paraphrasing or inventing new lines. For the most part, we complied with this rule. The groups set to work, both off and onstage. Several weeks later, the faculty gathered to see this work in progress. For one weekend, we sat through eight hours of Wolfe onstage. We emerged exhausted but thrilled by what we had witnessed.

After some more work by the student playwrights, all nine scripts were handed over to me. I had the job of condensing this sprawling play from eight hours of performance time to a script that could be played in three hours. I made truly painful decisions, but I did tighten the script drastically. I accepted the rule the students had to follow: it must be Wolfe's writing, not mine. I admit that I did fudge a little here and there. But what I did add or change was Wolfean in style!

Eventually, we ended up with a script that was ninety-nine percent Wolfe.[2]

The production opened in the spring of 1959. It was our most complex staging, involving innovative use of scrims, special lighting effects, twenty minutes of film footage using three projectors simultaneously, and a cast of 115. Once again, the production received national attention. This success led to the play being chosen by Baker to inaugurate the new Dallas Theater Center's first season beginning in late December 1959.

Prior to the Wolfe experience, I had been working on a full-length comedy, *The Cross-Eyed Bear*, and had completed a draft of a play that would include some film. I was so intrigued at the combination of film with live action in the Wolfe drama that I revised my script to exploit that idea. That decision liberated me from the tight stricture of limited stage space. Using film, I could violate space and time easily. However, I also wanted to use lip-synchronized sound film, integrating stage action with filmed action. The soliloquy, normally given as a monologue by a live actor, could be turned into a dialogue between the character onstage and his filmed image on the screen. That concept was the driving force behind my final revision.

I had shown my early draft to Baker, and he decided to schedule it for production at the Dallas Theater Center. Since I also taught a film production course, using excellent equipment, we could shoot all the silent film footage at Baylor. But the lip-synchronized footage would have to be filmed in Dallas using the cast members there.

With the construction of the Theater Center's building nearly completed and company members already being recruited,

The Cross-Eyed Bear, Baylor Theater

Baker, as managing director of the DTC (while retaining his position at Baylor), was already commuting between Dallas and Waco.

Baylor's graduate drama program had been transferred to the DTC but retained its ties to the university's graduate school. When the 1959 fall semester began, I also started weekly trips to Dallas to teach the graduate playwriting courses. This gave me the opportunity to help with the inaugural production and to attend the tryouts and many rehearsals for the second show, *The Cross-Eyed Bear*.

The just-finished DTC building opened its doors to the public on December 27, 1959, with its first production, *Of Time and the River*. It was a gala occasion; the show was received enthusiastically by the audience and had a highly successful run. Since the two plays had been cast and rehearsed simultaneously, *The Cross-Eyed Bear* followed the Wolfe show quickly on January 14. The national media praised it. The two local papers panned it, but I was mollified by the enthusiastic response of audiences throughout its run. I was also delighted that my experiment with film integrated so well with the onstage action.

By doing a second production of a new script and then a premiere of another one during its first season, the DTC set a benchmark for its strong support of developing playwrights. In the following two years, eleven new plays were given full production—six by DTC playwrights and the others submitted from outside.

In 1962, the DTC produced on its main stage a full-length script written as a master's thesis by a graduate student. The play, *Sister*, by Glenn Allen Smith, was one of the first of these plays to be staged, but it was followed by many others. In addition, new

Sister, Dallas Theater Center

110

plays were being performed in the DTC's Magic Turtle series, popular Saturday performances for children. We were developing a cadre of resident playwrights!

All graduate students were required to take the basic course in playwriting, as was the policy at Baylor. But there had been only a handful of Baylor graduate students. Our first year at the DTC we had forty-eight students, several of them specializing in playwriting. Also, our eagerness to produce new plays quickly attracted neophyte playwrights to our program. My teaching load increased dramatically and, although two DTC resident playwrights helped carry that load, the time I would ordinarily devote to my own writing was shifted to helping students develop their scripts. I started living vicariously through the writing projects of young playwrights.

A small fifty-five-seat theater was built in the DTC basement. Over the years, it was devoted almost totally to the staging of new scripts. In addition, "Dark Night" readings were held of works in progress, with critiques given afterward by the audience and staff.

Meantime, in 1963 our graduate academic program left its alliance with Baylor and accepted the sponsorship of Trinity University. Baker became chairman of Trinity's speech and drama department, bringing with him his Baylor faculty and its undergraduate academic curriculum. There, in contrast to the DTC enrollment, we started over again with less than a dozen drama majors.

However, our academic program and our production schedule thrived, and the number of majors increased dramatically. We started in a third-floor classroom transformed into a temporary theater. Three years later we inaugurated our new home, the magnificent Ruth Taylor Theater building, with a production of A Different Drummer.[3] Three DTC resident company actors—Edward Herrmann, James Harrell, and Ella Mae Brainard—were imported to join the cast of undergraduates, a valuable experience for both groups. This kind of cooperation between Trinity and the DTC continued over the years. Each Trinity theater season included one or two DTC productions transported to the campus in San Antonio. A number of these shows were new plays that had premiered in Dallas.

Our undergraduate playwriting program mushroomed along with the increase in majors. Student directors staged student-written plays. "Dark Night" readings were held, and new play workshops were conducted. Another instructor conducted evening playwriting classes for the community. Writers' experimental projects were tested in a Happening production staged toward the end of each school year.

As had been our practice, all students majoring in drama were required to take the beginning playwriting course. A growing number of them chose to enroll in elective advanced writing classes. Some of those writers, having discovered their life focus, finished their undergraduate degrees and moved on to the DTC to further hone their talents.

If such students enrolled in the DTC graduate program in the fall of 1973, they would be involved in one of Baker's most daring experiments. Baker had believed for some time that he wanted the playwrights' new works to be seen by a wider audience than the regional one. He was thinking of nationally recognized directors, producers, agents, critics, and leaders of various professional theater organizations.

Baker decided that most of the 1973–1974 season would be devoted to the production of eight new scripts using both theaters. At the end of the season, he would revive all of those productions, to be seen by an invited audience, over a four-day period. He named the event New Playmarket.

After each show had completed its run during the season, a space in a warehouse was allocated to that production's sets, costumes, props, furniture, etc. Even so, staging the New Playmarket turned out to be a logistical nightmare. Not only would sets for both theaters have to be replaced quickly with other sets, but also the scheduling had to be reconciled with the multiple uses of actors and technical crews. Baker had always demanded that his resident company members be versatile theater craftsmen. For example, one playwright who had two works presented would also perform in three productions.

A miracle happened in May 1974. The New Playmarket opened to an audience of distinguished theater professionals from across the country and a number of critics, including two from England.[4] Surprisingly, there were few noticeable hitches in the shows, and the response of our special audience was enthusiastic. The viewers left four days later, weary-eyed and seat-sore but excited by what they had experienced. The New Playmarket had been a spectacular success, causing widespread press coverage but, more importantly, creating interest in individual plays that resulted in a number of subsequent productions.

The DTC staged two more Playmarkets. In 1976, eight new plays were presented, followed by nine in 1979.[5] The results were similar to those of the first Playmarket—additional recognition for some of the playwrights and new productions of their scripts by regional and Off-Broadway theaters.[6]

Those New Playmarkets represented the peak of my professional career. I had watched and counseled those young writers in their growth from would-be dramatists to experienced and talent-tested playwrights. I treasure my memories of their struggling to master the craft of structuring a play, to realize, finally, that a first draft is not immortal and must be rewritten again and again, and that any merit a script may have must be proven in a good production.

My long journey with Paul Baker was almost over. It had been a strange and wondrous adventure resulting in many memories of events, some triumphant, some painful, some poignant. I recall an incident that happened after we resigned from Baylor and were about to leave for San Antonio and Trinity. Baker suggested to me that we tour through the empty Baylor Theater for one last look. The building was deserted, and we walked in silence through the theater—Studio One, the green room, the workshop, Weston Studio, and the lobby. We ended our tour in Baker's office.

He looked around at the bare space, still not saying a word. Then he hawked up a good one and spat on the floor. I was stunned by the drama of it. I was greatly appreciative of the comment. And we left. Several years later that remarkably innovative theater was razed, and a new orthodox playhouse was built elsewhere on the campus. I have repeated that tradition, alone, in saying good-bye to two other theaters. Except for the spitting.

In 1976, Baker reluctantly retired from Trinity, but at that time it was mandatory for a professor of his age to do so. A new administration arrived on the scene, one that wanted the focus of the drama program to be on theater history and not on play production. For several years, I hung like a tenured albatross around the neck of the administration. Finally I was offered a golden parachute and gladly took early retirement. At the end of my last day there, I toured through all areas of the Ruth Taylor Theater, spending much of the time in multistage Theater One. Years later, that theater's interior was ripped out and replaced by a traditional proscenium-arch theater.

In 1982, Baker bitterly resigned from the Dallas Theater Center when its board of directors decided to close the graduate program and release the permanent resident company so that they could bring in individual actors from outside for each production. When the graduate program was being phased out, I made my last commute. Just before leaving for my San Antonio home, I said good-bye to my Dallas theater home. The theater was almost empty when I walked through the building. I saved for my last stop the Stecker Library, where I had held playwriting classes for twenty-five rewarding years.

I walked through the door, expecting the room to be crowded with memories. Instead, I found Robyn Baker Flatt and a cohort hunched over a paper-filled table. They were planning the birth of the Dallas Children's Theater. Suddenly I felt all right about leaving. Because I saw a continuum taking place. An enlargement of one man's vision was happening in that room. And I knew that in so many places it had happened, was happening, and that it would continue to happen.

Buildings can be destroyed or disastrously reshaped. Successful programs can be dissolved abruptly. But the individuals who spent years creatively working in those buildings and whose lives those programs changed do survive and prosper. The playwrights to whom I gave my support can still write dramas. They are an integral part of that continuum, through whom the Paul Baker concepts still flourish. ∎

Children's Theater
Dallas Theater Center

114

End Notes

1 Yelvington's most dynamic play, *A Cloud of Witnesses*, a poetic drama about the Alamo, premiered in the Baylor Theater in 1954. It received rave reviews and great regional attention. In 1955 the San Antonio Conservation Society sponsored an outdoor presentation of the production, staged against the walls of the San Jose Mission. It was so well received that a permanent amphitheater was constructed at the mission for a return presentation in 1958. A double-page spread of Eliot Elisofon's photo of the production was the most prominent display in *Life* magazine's entertainment issue of December 1958.

A Cloud of Witnesses, BaylorTheater

2 After the first production, an attempt was made by Baker and the Baylor Theater to copyright the play version of *Of Time and The River*. The Wolfe estate thwarted that attempt on the grounds that the great majority of the play's narrative and dialogue had been drawn directly from the novel. Selection and arrangement of the scenes was discounted and preserving the integrity of the novel was viewed as a negative rather than a positive effect.

3 I had the good fortune to be cast in the Ruth Taylor Theater's opening production of *A Different Drummer*. We rehearsed in what we were told would one day be the theater, waiting for our next scenes seated on sheets of cardboard on the still-drying cement floor as we leaned away from the damp walls. During one rehearsal Baker wrung from the chorus and from that dark overwhelming space the most profound moment of theater I've ever experienced. Royal's "farewell" scene began quietly. Then we were all—actors, director, spectators—transformed, weightless, without form, all enveloped in the magic. The scene over, no one spoke. No one asked nor was there a reason to explain the tears on my cheeks. *Mary McCullough*

4 Theater professionals attending Playmarket included Lee Richardson, representing the National Endowment for the Arts; Kim Friedman of the New York Shakespeare Festival; Adrian Hall of Trinity Square Theater; Larry Mirkin of the Mark Taper Forum; Richmond Crinkley of the Kennedy Center; Arthur Ballet of the Office for Advanced Drama Research; Jules Weiss, representing Cafe LaMama; Rosemary Tichler, Theater Communication group; Jack Larsen, Rockefeller Foundation; playwright Jerome Lawrence; producer/author David Ayres; director Alan Schneider; agents Audrey Wood and Kay Brown; critics Bruce Cook, Henry Hewes, William Glover, Suzanne Shelton; and, from England, John Lahr and Irving Wardle of the *London Times*.

5 New Playmarket Plays/Authors 1974
    Getting to Know the Natives, by Daniel Turner
    A Midsummer Night's Dream (Musical), by William Shakespeare, music and
        lyrics by Randolph Tallman and Steven Mackenroth
    The Last Meeting of the Knights of the White Magnolias, by Preston Jones
    Dear Luger, by Kerry Newcomb
    Lu Ann Hampton Laverty Oberlander, by Preston Jones

Lu Ann Hampton Laverty Oberlander, Dallas Theater Center

Curious in L.A., by Glenn Allen Smith
Fuse, by Sally Netzel

Playmarket 1976
Jack Ruby, All-American Boy, by John Logan with Paul Baker
StillSong, by Sallie Baker Laurie
A Place on the Magdalena Flats, by Preston Jones
A Marvelous War, by Charles Beachley
Manny, music by Randolph Tallman and Steven Mackenroth;
        words by Glenn Allen Smith
Standoff at Beaver and Pine, by Sally Netzel
Canzada and the Boys, by Sam Havens
Faces of U.S., developed by DTC MimeAct

Playmarket 1979
Remember, by Preston Jones
Years in the Making, by Glenn Allen Smith
Lady Bug, Lady Bug, Fly Away Home, Mary Rohde
Firekeeper, Mark Medoff
Blood Money, words/lyrics by M. G. Johnson; music by Jim Abbott
Door Play, by Sallie Baker Laurie
Attic Aphrodite, by Sally Netzel
Interweave, developed by DTC MimeAct
The Squires and the Golden King, Paul Munger

[6] Of all the DTC playwrights, Preston Jones benefited most from the New
Playmarkets. Two of his plays, *The Last Meeting of the Knights of the White Magnolias*
and *Lu Ann Hampton Laverty Oberlander*, were produced at the first Playmarket. As
a result, the legendary literary agent, Audrey Wood, who attended the event,
agreed to represent him. In addition, representatives of the American Playwrights
Theater loved one of his plays so much that they recommended his script for production by the membership of that organization. The first to do so, in April 1975,
was the Arena Stage in Washington, D.C. Alan Schneider, who also had attended
the Playmarket, directed the production. By April of the next year, seven other
member theaters had also produced the play.

The second Playmarket introduced a new play by Jones, *The Oldest Living
Graduate*, and the last year's production of his two plays were redesigned to join the
new play on the DTC large stage. This completed the trilogy Jones called *The
Bradleyville Trilogy*. Noted producer Robert Whitehead was in attendance and
optioned the three plays. He also changed the title of the combined plays to
A Texas Trilogy.

A Texas Trilogy opened at the Kennedy Theater, Washington, D.C., on April 29,
1976. The three plays were presented in repertory style. The collective shows
received ecstatic local reviews and had a great run. As had been planned, the
production was moved to New York and opened on Broadway September 21, 1976.

Despite the great advance publicity created by the Kennedy Center shows, or

116

possibly because of it, the two most powerful New York critics did not like the plays, although most of the other critics gave the shows highly positive reviews. The trilogy had a brief but respectable run. Jones returned to Dallas, had several new plays produced by the DTC, and then died far too young.

Bad reviews may kill a production, just as a sudden illness can cause the death of a writer. But those events can't kill the printed text. Those plays that Jones put down on paper came alive again on other stages and will continue to be produced. His works will endure as a part of that great body of dramatic literature.

Stillsong, by Sallie Baker Laurie (Playmarket 1976)

Sam

118

Chester, Grace, and Me

Glenn Allen Smith

I'm stuck.

I need a scene.

I need a scene to end this play I've been working on for the past year. Just a short scene. A scene to show two people trapped together forever in the heavenly limbo of eternity. But what does "eternity" look like? What does "eternity" feel like? Sound like?

I'm stuck.

Maybe if I look back through what I've written so far something will come to me . . . an image, a feeling, something to express. . . .

On July 12, 1906, the pregnant body of Grace Brown (age twenty) was discovered floating next to an overturned rowboat on Big Moose Lake in upper New York State. Her companion, Chester Gillette, who had been seen with her rowing away from shore, was nowhere to be found. Two days later, however, he was located at a nearby resort hotel on another lake, charming the other guests and acting like a free spirit on holiday. He was arrested for Grace's murder.

There were no witnesses to the alleged crime, yet Chester eventually would be convicted (on circumstantial evidence) and executed—March 30, 1908, age twenty-four—always professing his innocence, swearing he had not been responsible for his lover's death. Did Grace actually commit suicide as he claimed?

A fascinating story. A story filled with all the elements needed for compelling drama. Theodore Dreiser certainly thought so when he used some of the incidents and characters for his novel, *An American Tragedy*, fictionalizing and updating the period to his own mid-1920s. George Stevens thought so, too, reworking and updating Dreiser decades later to reflect the early 1950s in his film, *A Place in the Sun*. Now I'm writing a play, because the Cortland Repertory Theatre (in Cortland, New York, where much of the story took place) has asked me to, only this time keeping the narrative in its original period, staying as close to the facts as possible.

And there are plenty of facts. Newspapers of the era chronicled the affair in graphic details that rival any tabloid of today for salaciousness. Yet facts in and of themselves are not necessarily dramatic; what makes for intriguing reading on the printed page doesn't always make for strong drama on stage. What's more, many of the supposed "facts" of the story were and still are in dispute. This means that I, as the playwright, have had to sift through what is known to find what I can use for my play, relying on my "mother wit" to fill in many of the personal moments that went unrecorded, especially the intimate encounters between Chester and Grace. In truth, the uncertain elements of so much of the story, the conflicting perceptions of what actually happened, give it its greatest resonance and have attracted me so strongly to the material.

I knew very little of Chester Gillette and Grace Brown when I began the research that would eventually take four months to complete. In fact, I had heard of neither until a friend, who worked at Cortland Rep and was visiting me, handed me a few old newspaper clippings to read (referring to the trial of a young man for murder in the early part of the twentieth century) and asked if I might be interested in dramatizing the story. The story is of legendary proportion in that part of the country, and the theater wanted to include the play as part of its twentieth season.

I live in Dallas, Texas—had never been to upper New York State. Despite a topographical undulation or two, the land around here can best be described as "flat." The land where Chester and Grace lived? I didn't know. But I do believe the land where we live affects us deeply, for good or ill; because of this, from the moment I decided this play was something I wanted to write, I knew there was no way I was going to even have a chance of understanding the two central characters in the drama unless I went to New York and walked through the very spaces they had walked through, sensed the nature of their surroundings.

Space. When I think of eternity I think of space . . . endless, empty space. So maybe that's how I'll begin the scene. I'll start with a bare stage . . . empty of any set pieces. And yet, no matter what illusion I propose to conjure up, I can't escape reality: this is still a stage, and we are all— actors and audience—still earthbound. So how to achieve an image that translates as "endless" space without the aid of costly special effects? No choice; I'll have to rely on two of the best friends a playwright has, light and imagination. The right lighting and the audience's imagination will go a long way in helping to create my "heavenly limbo of eternity," and from there. . . .

I stood in Valley View Cemetery in the tiny village of South Otselic, just outside Cortland, looking down at the upright, granite gravestone that read, "Grace M. Brown, 1886–1906, At Rest." Rolling, tree-dotted farmland rose and fell in gentle hills all around me. To my right, the other side of one hill, past fields of ripening corn, was the farm where Grace had lived with her family before moving to nearby Cortland to work in the skirt factory where she met the young man who would become her obsession and be her undoing. It was from the white frame house of that farm (where she had returned to pick up a few clothes, telling no one of her plan) that she set out on her ill-fated secret journey to meet Chester and travel north with him by train to Big Moose Lake in the Adirondack Mountains. The road she went down, in the buckboard driven by her father, curved through the valley nearby, paved now instead of the dirt lane it was then. Some of the oak trees in the cemetery were old enough to have been there when Grace passed by that Sunday, three days before she died. They saw her disappear over the hill as she went with the expectation that Chester was about to marry her, was about to make her his wife before her condition started to show, before she had to face the shame of everyone knowing she was already carrying his child. Now the trees looked down at the weedy patch of grass, beneath which what was left of Grace rested through eternity, the silence of the cemetery broken only at times by the chirping of a bird or the rustling of leaves.

Silence. No sound. An empty stage. For a moment, only stillness. And then, offstage, a sound to break the silence . . . a sound to break the peaceful nothingness of eternity . . . the sound of laughter, a lilting laugh. Grace laughing—but not the voice of the Grace we saw in the last moments of her life . . . not the doomed Grace . . . frantic . . . in despair. This is the laughter of the Grace we first knew, when she was first in love with Chester . . . when she was still full of joy . . . before Chester seduced her, taking her virginity . . . before Chester. . . .

The walls of Auburn State Prison, where Chester died, towered above me to a menacing height, grim in their starkness, exactly as they were all those years ago, looking the very cliché of every prison wall in every prison movie I've ever seen. Only this was no Hollywood set; this was real, depressingly real. And just on the other side of those grayish stone walls Chester literally "fried" in the electric chair—eighteen hundred volts, seven and a half amperes, shot through his body for thirty seconds...then, the voltage gradually reduced to two hundred . . . then, the voltage back up to eighteen hundred for another minute (his body temperature reaching 140 degrees Fahrenheit) and it was over. I'd have to get that on stage, the feel and horror of his death . . . and before his death, his days in prison . . . days in which Chester experienced every emotion there is, from hope to fear to resignation. There was so much of the story I'd have to get on stage.

Therein lay my problem, a big problem. I wouldn't have the verbiage a novel allows for extended narrative and description. I wouldn't have the visuals of a film to focus the eye of reality on tiny detail or provide epic sweep. There's great complexity and depth to the tale but only so much time and so much space on stage to tell it. Even as I visited the places where Chester and Grace had lived and died, even as I scoured the local libraries and historical societies for the minutiae of their lives, I was trying to resolve one of the most difficult decisions a dramatist must make—how to tell the story. No matter how wonderful the material, it won't be effective if it isn't presented in the right way. For me, writing for theater, the telling of any story begins with how I will use the space in which it must be told.

And yet, the use of space is ultimately determined by what I have to put in that space. Few characters confronting each other in a compressed time period might lead me to place those characters in a single room. I had done that in *Land of Fire*, in which a husband and wife (the only characters) come together in the kitchen of their home for a few hours in the middle of the night to thrash out a family crisis. The details and furnishings of a real kitchen were important, even to the ability to prepare food and drink. The space of this story needed to hold the characters in, to contain them tightly in a pressured atmosphere. Furthermore, the space had to provide the characters immediate access to a variety of props, giving them a chance to support the torrent of dialogue with business stemming from the use of the myriad objects that might clutter a kitchen.

With *Chester and Grace* (the title I'd decided on) I would have more than a dozen characters involved in events that spanned a three-year period, events that took place in numerous locales. But which characters? Which events? I couldn't possibly tell the whole story. I would have to choose carefully. Chester's death . . . Grace and Chester on the lake . . . those scenes for certain . . . their first meeting . . . the trial, of course, but only moments, since I didn't want this to turn into a "trial play." What else? Who else? Grace's mother, the prosecutor, the defense attorney, the preacher who counseled Chester, Chester's younger sister—these characters were of particular importance, with excellent dramatic possibilities. Next to the two lovers, the most important person in the entire account was Chester's mother, Louise Gillette, an officer in the Salvation Army. It was she who made the long journey from Denver to be at Chester's side through the agonizing ordeal, never giving up hope, even to the end, that she would somehow find a way to save her son. It was she who stood before gatherings across the state—in churches, theaters, and social halls—trying to rally public support, trying to raise funds for Chester's defense. I'd have to include that. And I'd have to include her confrontation with the governor when she begged for clemency. And the moment when Grace told Chester she was pregnant and expected him to marry her. And of course I'd have to include the moment just before Grace steps into the boat for the last time, when she and Chester . . .

Grace. She runs into the scene . . . into the empty space, breaking the nothingness suddenly, radiant in the light . . . light that cuts and shapes a glowing place of haven in the midst of the dark nothingness . . . an exuberant smile on her face, for now she and Chester are together as she always had hoped they would be . . . together forever. This is a strong physical image, the movement of her body into the space, and yet, the image needs something else. The image needs something to articulate poetically for the audience this feeling of endless time as well as Grace's joy . . . time that goes on and on. The scene needs another element, a specific, visual element, a visual texture that can help express the feeling . . . help create the feeling. Yes, a texture that gives the feeling of time flowing on and on . . . and movement, movement that has the rhythm of . . .

Fluidity. That word says most clearly what would be required of the stage space needed for the telling of this story. There would have to be several playing areas. To accomplish this I saw simple platforms, platforms of several heights (for visual variety), with ramps or steps connecting the platforms. The areas created could be whatever locale I needed, areas that would allow for movement from scene to scene with maximum fluidity and ease.

Through experience I have learned not to write a play for any particular type of theater space. There was a time when the proscenium stage dictated how a play was written. For years, plays were set in picture frames. Playwrights spoke of "upstage," "downstage," "stage left," and "stage right" in their directions. Now, however, besides the classic proscenium stage, we have "the arena," in which the audience surrounds the stage completely; "the thrust," with the audience on three sides of the stage; the inverse of "the thrust," in which the stage is on three sides of the audience; "the black box," with the audience here, there, and everywhere—and, of course, endless variations on these spatial themes. With such a multiplicity of spaces possible, therefore, it's best to keep stage directions neutral. State the basic set requirements, indicate where the actors enter and exit, and leave it to each particular theater to visualize the play in its own particular space. In the case of *Chester and Grace*, I believed that in whatever type of space it was presented, a minimum of scenery should be used to define the locale of each scene. In the interests of (again, that word) fluidity, perhaps as little as a single piece of furniture or a prop could tell the audience where the action was taking place. A rowboat on a lake, a courtroom, the prison, the skirt factory—these and other locations would have to be merely indicated, to keep the pace and flow of the play from bogging down under the weight of too much scenery being carted on and off. This simplification of the scenic requirements, however, meant that costuming would take on even more importance than usual. With the actor left with so few physical trappings on the set, the actor's physical shape and line or silhouette would be especially prominent in the overall design of the scene.

I believe firmly in the dramatic statement that is made by the physical placement of one actor in relationship to another. How close or far apart are they? Is one elevated above the other? Are they facing or turned away? Seated, standing, kneeling, lying down? These positionings of the body are more than mere blocking problems to be left for a director to solve. These concerns for the silhouette of the actor, though admittedly not as great in importance, are as much a part of the writing process as is the creation of dialogue and plot. An enormous amount can be said dramatically by the way in which characters are placed in a space, by the visual tension their bodies create in that space.

To take advantage of the visual power that can be achieved with actors in silhouette, I knew that one area, higher than the rest, would be needed, an area where characters could be presented with particular strength and focus at needed moments.

Grace is in this area, the space I'm using for "the heavenly limbo of eternity." She spins around, smiling in delight, arms uplifted, holding with both hands a length of fabric a yard wide and eight feet long that circles in the air above her head as she turns, looking almost like a large halo. This is the element I've decided to use, this piece of fabric, to help in visualizing the endless flow of time and Grace's ecstasy. Fabric has been an important element for Grace throughout the play: she was sewing on a pink blouse when Chester seduced her; she wore a black veil when she appeared to him in his jail cell after her death. Fabric was also an element present in the moment Grace met Chester in the skirt factory—she carried several bolts of woolen material as she walked by the stock room and saw him asleep in a chair:

GRACE

You'll get fired for sleeping on the job.
  (She pokes him and Chester sits up)

CHESTER

  (Groggy)
What?

GRACE

Sleeping on the job'll get you canned.

CHESTER

  (standing)
I wasn't sleeping.

GRACE

Sure.

CHESTER

I was praying.

GRACE

And I'm the Queen of the May.

But this fabric she holds now, I've decided, must be almost ethereal in its texture . . . not of this earth but of the heavens . . . the lightest chiffon . . . fabric that ripples lightly in the air, seeming almost weightless. And the color should be . . .

CHESTER

(A bit too much to be sincere)
I come from a very religious family—praying is an important part of my life—finding a moment to be still—to be one with God and my inner thoughts is the only way I can find peace in a world that's nothing but turmoil—but I guess if you don't believe in God, if you don't know what joy can come from daily meditation in the presence of Our Savior, then you couldn't possibly understand.

GRACE

Oh . . . gee . . . I didn't mean . . . I'm sorry . . . I was only trying to keep you from getting in trouble.

CHESTER

My uncle owns the factory. I can't possibly get in trouble.

Blue? That's a possibility . . . pale blue, sky blue, the color of a heaven free of tempest or turmoil. But it isn't the sky I want to represent in this bit of cloth. It's Grace herself . . . a reflection of Grace's inner self.

GRACE

My name's Grace—I work in "White Goods"—but everybody calls me Billy.

CHESTER

I know.

GRACE

You do?

CHESTER

I've had my eye on you.

GRACE

Really?

CHESTER

Is that such a surprise?

GRACE

Well—

Yellow? That's bright and cheery. But Grace is feeling something beyond "bright and cheery." She is feeling something that is almost beyond any recognizable happiness.

CHESTER

You're the kind of girl a guy would notice even in a crowd because you're not like the other girls around here—not always giggling and worrying about their looks like they do—you're more serious, I can tell.

GRACE

I do like to read.
(Chester grabs her hand)

CHESTER

(Reading her palm)
Sure, it's all here. You're a kind person. Very thoughtful. You're the sort of girl who makes a fella feel good. Your love line's very long. And there . . . that little line, straight as can be, says you're a virgin. The line would be broken if you weren't.
(Grace pulls her hand away)

GRACE

I think you're awful fresh.

CHESTER

Do you like that?

GRACE

You better get back to the stock room.
(She turns to go)

127

CHESTER

(Savoring the word)
Grace.

(She stops and looks back at him)
Your Mama sure knew what she was doing when she named you Grace.

The color . . . the color . . . more thought as the entire color spectrum flashes through my mind. Finally I decide there's only one possibility—the color must be white, pure white, the classic hue that's used to represent a soul without blemish, a soul that has transcended beyond all other earthly color. In this case, it would represent the inner state of Grace. As she whirls about, the fabric moves through a shaft of light that accentuates its movement and hers. Rippling though the light . . . rippling through the light. . . .

The small stone I tossed into Big Moose Lake broke through the water's surface with a plopping sound, sending out ripples that gently rocked the white pond lilies growing near the bank. Grace had picked some of these same lilies shortly before her death—however it occurred—there in the lake not far from where I stood. The evergreen trees that rose up tall around me were old enough to have seen what really happened that hot, humid summer afternoon. They saw the rowboat with the two people drift into the secluded inlet of the lake, saw the boat touch shore and its passengers get out to sit for a while in the shade. The trees heard and saw the truth . . . when Chester and Grace talked of the frightening dilemma that faced them both . . . when Chester and Grace got back into the boat . . . when Chester rowed a few feet off shore, Grace reaching out to pluck the lilies—and for certain, the trees saw the moment when. . . .

As I stood there I knew what is known of that day. The hours when Chester and Grace were alone comes only from Chester's testimony, testimony that contradicts itself. At first, he said that Grace's death was an accident. She had stood up in the boat, causing it to tip over. The boat hit her on the head, and she drowned. Later, he changed his story, saying that she purposely killed herself. Becoming distraught at the idea of returning home and telling her family she was pregnant—and believing Chester wouldn't marry her, despite his protestations that he would—she decided to take her own life. Before he could do anything she threw herself into the lake. In trying to save her, he overturned the boat. In no way, however, did he have a hand in her death. When her body didn't surface, he fled out of fear. Or so he claimed. Because the trees, who knew which version was correct, were not about to tell me much, I realized that I was free—no, obligated—to find my own truth when the time came to write the scene. I also realized that it was time for me to decide how I was going to set out the events of the story. Would it be a linear or non-linear telling? Would I relate things in chronological order or move freely back and forth in time and place?

The advantage of a chronological telling would be the orderly presentation of events, unfolding in a logical progression. But, because I couldn't deal with all that happened and was going to have to make jumps in time and the action, there were sure to be awkward bumps in the narrative flow. Furthermore, I did want to deal with some of Chester's time in prison, his trial and execution, as well as the eventual effect of all that happened on the other major characters in the story. This meant that Grace, by virtue of her death, would disappear from the narrative well before the end of the play if told chronologically.

There was something else, however, that was an even more important influence on the decision I had to make. The single most dramatically arresting aspect of the entire story is whether Chester did or did not kill Grace. This was a moment with which I was going to have to deal, and, because of its climactic quality, it was a scene I believed had to be saved for placement as near to the end of the play as possible, in order to build and sustain audience interest.

Telling the events out of order, leaping back and forth in time and place, meant that I could choose which moments I felt were most vital to the drama. More importantly, by the arrangement of these moments —"the orchestration"—I could shape more carefully the dramatic rise and fall of the action. I could begin the play at a particularly potent moment—to capture audience interest— and proceed from there. I could begin each scene at the emotional pitch I felt was needed to propel the action forward. I could interweave the various dramatic themes, much as a composer does with music. In other words, I could control the tempo and rhythm of the piece.

Rhythm. There isn't a moment in the writing process that I'm not aware of the importance of rhythm. The rhythm of each word . . . of each line of dialogue . . . the rhythm of each speech . . . each scene . . . the rhythm with which a character enters or leaves a scene . . . the rhythm of each act . . . of the entire play. Each play I write has its own rhythm, rooted in the rhythms of the characters themselves.

(Grace stops spinning, the white chiffon sinking gently down. She looks at Chester, who enters, glancing about, a bit disoriented)

GRACE

Didn't I tell you it'd be fun? No day or night . . . just endless time . . . and you'll never get tired and you'll never get angry and you'll never tell any more lies . . . isn't it wonderful?

CHESTER

Somehow . . . I thought I'd wind up in that other place.

GRACE

(Billowing the cloth)

There's only one place—in the end it's all the same.

(Stopping)

You weren't really a bad person, Chester. You just . . .

CHESTER

Really wasn't very good.

GRACE

I can't judge.

So, I had worked out how I would use the stage space, and I had decided on a nonlinear telling of the narrative. Two sides of my "compositional triangle." The third side, if you will, involved the theatrical style of the play. I had to decide how realistic or nonrealistic the presentation would be.

This decision was affected by my decision to use as little scenery as possible. Already I called upon the audience to use its imagination in visualizing the setting of a scene. It was just a step from there to call upon the audience's imagination even further, by breaking the "fourth wall," i.e., by removing the audience as mere spectator of the drama, thus enhancing the ritualistic, the participatory aspect of the play. Allowing the characters to acknowledge the existence of the audience

130

would accomplish this, having them address it from time to time, commenting on the action or their inner thoughts and feelings. Even using this time-honored theatrical device, though, I still needed to find a way to get across a great deal of narrative information without the major characters' having the burden of relating such details themselves. A single narrator could do the job, of course; that's a storytelling tradition as old as theater itself. But I didn't want a single narrator. I wanted something a little more interesting, a little more . . . I wasn't sure. But if I thought about it a while . . .

I believe it is the wise playwright who is aware of the drama that has come before, all styles of drama, especially the crafting of that drama. When one is stuck on a technical writing problem, it's foolish to try to "reinvent the wheel." Someone before has probably faced and solved the problem already. By studying the technique of past masters, much as painters or composers do, one's own dramaturgical skills are greatly enriched. Each theater artist is influenced in some degree by others; this is a reality of theater. It goes for actors, designers, and directors, as well as playwrights. How had other playwrights dealt with the narrative problem I faced in *Chester and Grace*? I'd think about it . . . see what I could find . . . and at the same time I would work on something else . . . knowing that eventually . . .

CHESTER

Have you forgiven me, Billy?

GRACE

There's nothing to forgive.

CHESTER

That's awful decent of you.

GRACE

That's just the way I am now. No more crying. No trying to make you feel guilty, and I'm never jealous.

Grace had been jealous, from the very beginning. Chester was the nephew of the factory owner; she, a lowly employee. He could move freely in Cortland society, invited into the finest homes; she spent hours alone in the little room she rented. She didn't have the education, fancy clothes, or the social graces of so many of the other girls that Chester courted.

Girls. Chester loved them, and they loved him. He wasn't tall, only five feet seven inches. But he was muscular, athletic, had a full head of dark hair, and, no matter which way you turned him, front-on or profile, he had a sullen cuteness and cocky personality that charmed. Because he had bounced around the United States doing nothing in particular—until he wound up in Cortland—he also had a certain "bad boy" reputation. Before the event that made him famous, he was the "object of interest" of many of the local females, all ages. After his arrest and imprisonment, he became more than a local "object of interest"—he was transformed into an "object of sexual adoration"—statewide and nationwide. Flowers, candy, love letters arrived daily in his jail cell. And proposals of marriage every day from females of all ages—women, girls, wanting to marry him, wanting to mother him. Outside the prison walls . . . a chorus of voices calling . . . all ages . . . hoping . . . wanting . . .

CHESTER

Billy . . .

GRACE

I know what you're going to say and you don't have to.

CHESTER

I'm sorry . . . for everything.

GRACE

So am I. We didn't treat each other as good as we should have.

CHESTER

I did worse than that.

GRACE

Well . . . maybe just a little.

Women . . . voices . . . all ages . . . maybe . . . maybe that was it. Yes, that's what they were like . . . the chorus of women clamoring for Chester, like a chorus from a play by Aeschylus or Euripides. That's what it seemed like when I thought of the masses of women who gathered to see Chester as he was transferred from jail cell to courthouse and back again during the trial—a Greek

132

chorus commenting to each other and to us, interrelating and relating, telling and foretelling Chester's fate . . . the fates of all the characters. Sometimes the oldest solutions are the best—a chorus commenting on the fates of all, almost like The Three Fates or The Three Graces of mythology . . . perhaps a combination of both. Three . . . a chorus of three women. But not just women . . . women of different ages—an old woman, a young woman, and a little girl . . . the chorus . . . Cora, Corinne, and Corie. Yes. I had found my narrative device:

CORA

. . . we saw it . . . we see it all . . . then,

CORINNE

now,

CORIE

and forever.

I used them throughout the play—moving in and out of the action, observing, commenting, singing, playing parts, placing and removing props and set pieces. They were able to be anywhere at any time. They were there to strap Chester into the electric chair and witness his death. They were here, to witness "the moment of truth."

CORA

The rowboat was seventeen feet long, made of wood. Chester sat in the front where he could reach the oars and Grace in the rear, where it was a little more comfortable, and they drifted their way languidly through the waters of Big Moose Lake that hot July afternoon.

The scene in which I had believed, since first undertaking the project, I would have to make the decision: Did he or did he not kill Grace?

CORINNE

Shortly after one o'clock, in a remote inlet of the lake, far from any other people, the rowboat touched shore.

In getting to this point in the play I had made a long, emotional journey with Chester and Grace . . .

CORIE

Chester and Grace got out of the boat.

and, in making that journey over the months it had taken me to write, I had moved deeper and deeper into the heart and mind of each.

They walked away from the water's edge, the grass still damp in the shade under the trees.

What I had discovered was this: neither was all good or all bad; each had virtues and flaws. But most importantly, I had come to believe that each had participated in creating the tragedy that ultimately occurred, each was to blame in some way, each a victim.

And when I realized that, I realized that the climax of the drama did not lie in depicting the moment when Chester did or did not kill Grace . . . when Grace did or did not commit suicide. The climax was in those moments just before the final calamity on the lake . . . in the final emotional confrontation between them—creating a scene in which either outcome (murder or suicide) would be a reasonable possibility.

The scene begins with both on edge as they step out of the boat, Chester carrying a small suitcase, Grace with a few lilies in her hand. No sooner are they ashore than Chester tries to impress her with his athleticism, boastfully trying to climb one of the trees blindfolded. Grace stares at the lilies in her hand, lost in thought. When she sees the foolhardy thing he is trying to do, she stops him, now angry and upset:

GRACE

(Batting away bugs)
So many flies—and mosquitoes—and the heat's just unbearable even here in the shade—I wish we'd never come.

CHESTER

It was your idea.

GRACE

Was it?

CHESTER

We should go back to Cortland.

GRACE

We can't.

CHESTER

We got no money, we got no chance of making any up here in the boondocks—

GRACE

(Suddenly faint)

Chester . . . .

CHESTER

and I think you should go to that doctor outside of town and have the operation.

GRACE

Chester . . . I don't feel . . .

CHESTER

(Seeing her)

Christ Almighty.

GRACE

I think I'm going to throw . . .

CHESTER

(Rushing to support her)

Take it easy.

GRACE

Nauseous . . .

CHESTER

(Guiding her to the suitcase)

I told you to eat breakfast.

135

GRACE

and dizzy . . .

> *(He lowers her onto the suitcase)*

CHESTER

When we're married you gotta start doing like I tell you and stop being so hardheaded. You think everything has to be your way only—there. Now you'll be more comfortable.

GRACE

Are you really going to marry me?

CHESTER

I said I am.

> *(She looks into his face a moment before continuing)*

GRACE

Words . . . only words to shut me up . . . just another one of your lies so I won't suspect what you're really up to.

CHESTER

And what the hell is that supposed to mean?

GRACE

You know very well.

CHESTER

Can you stop talking in riddles for once?

GRACE

You think I don't know why you've brought me up here?

CHESTER

I thought this was supposed to be—

GRACE

You think I'm so dumb?

CHESTER

Billy, just calm down and—

GRACE

You're gonna kill me!

CHESTER

(Starting to laugh)
Are you out of your head?

GRACE

(Starting to sniffle)
I know you are.

CHESTER

(Moving to comfort her)
Billy, honey, don't say such things.

GRACE

(Stopping him)
Why wouldn't you let me tell anyone we were coming on this trip together?

CHESTER

Because we're not married. Because it would·look bad for you.

GRACE

Because you don't want anyone to know you were even here when my body is found!

CHESTER

(A weary sigh)
Oh, Lord. I heard pregnant women act weird . . . but I never expected anything like this.

GRACE

In my heart I know you'll never marry me.

CHESTER

There's an orange in the suitcase.

GRACE

In the year you've known me you've never even said you love me.

CHESTER

Want it?

GRACE

Do you?

CHESTER

Or some crackers?

GRACE

Do you love me, Chester? Have you ever?

CHESTER

What a damned question.

GRACE

Say it . . . say it now . . . say, "Billy, I love you with all my heart."

CHESTER

Sounds like something out of a novel.

GRACE

I don't care . . . I want to hear it.

CHESTER

You should stop reading all those sappy women's stories.

GRACE

Tell me you love me!

> *(Chester looks at her a moment)*

CHESTER

Sure I do.

> *(She gives a sad little laugh)*

Time to start back if we're going to get the train tonight.

GRACE

I . . . I don't want to go in the rowboat.

CHESTER

What?

GRACE

I'm afraid to go in the rowboat.

138

CHESTER

What are you talking about? You've been in the rowboat all morning . . . you came here in the rowboat.

GRACE

But it scares me. You know I can't swim. We should have taken a ride on the lake in that little steamer boat. It's safer.

CHESTER

We wanted to be alone.

GRACE

You wanted to be alone.

CHESTER

Oh, now, just wait a minute. I said, "Wouldn't it be fun to go out on the lake?" And you said a lot of people made you nervous, which is when I—

GRACE

I won't go in it anymore.

CHESTER

Then how are we going to get back?

GRACE

We . . . can walk.

CHESTER

It's miles. There's no road.

GRACE

I'll walk.

CHESTER

They'll charge me extra if I don't bring the boat back.

GRACE

(Suddenly near hysteria)

I'm not going in the boat!

Rhythm, silhouette, texture, color, sound. I called upon all of these elements as I wrote this scene.

GRACE

(On edge; fidgeting with the flowers)

. . . that last day at home I was near crazy . . . not knowing if you'd meet me . . . believing all those hateful things the girls at the factory had written me about you. I wandered around the farm hardly able to breathe. Going to each and every little nook I've known nearly all my life. All of them so dear to me— the spring house with its great masses of green moss. I said goodbye to it. I said goodbye to the beehives in the orchard. I was frantic . . . trying to see everything one last time. Because I knew . . . knew I'd never see any of them again. And Mama! Hardest of all to say goodbye to her. Because I love her. Because I don't know what I'll do without her. Never cross. Always helping me so much. If I could just tell Mama. If I could just—but I can't. I couldn't break her heart like that. Maybe if I come back dead . . . maybe if she doesn't know . . . she won't be angry. I . . . wish . . . I could die.

CHESTER

Kid, don't talk like that.

GRACE

I wish I could die.

CHESTER

Jesus Christ, Billy—

GRACE

(Looking at him)

Wouldn't you be glad to be rid of the burden I've become to you?

CHESTER

Let's just go catch the train back to Cortland.

GRACE

(Rising)

Haven't you wished every second since we started this journey that I was dead and gone?

CHESTER

(Going to gather up the suitcase)

And no more talk about not getting in the boat—

140

Haven't you wished I was dead?

CHESTER

It's just plain silly to act the way . . .

GRACE

(*Grabbing him*)

Haven't you?

CHESTER

(*Trying to pull loose*)

you're acting when—

GRACE

(*Holding on*)

Haven't you?

CHESTER

Yes!

(*He throws the suitcase down*)

Yes, goddamit! Yes!

(*She lets go of him*)

How do you expect me to feel? I've got a crummy job. No money. No prospects. The little I've got going for me I've hustled with bullshit and a smile—but finally I'm rising up there with the cream. Rising to the top. Respectability. And then suddenly the goddam sky falls in. A wife. A kid. What do any of those people care about another dumb son-of-a-bitch with a wife and a kid?

GRACE

We'll have each other, Chester. I'll be a good wife to you. Better than any of those society girls. You'll see. Together we can still get where you want to go.

CHESTER

(*Near tears*)

It won't be the same if I'm tied down. The chances that come when you're . . . when you're free to move any way you want . . . those chances won't come to a guy who's . . . trapped . . . who's not free to . . . who's not free. . . .

(He drops down onto the ground)

GRACE

(Going to him)

I won't tie you down, Chester. I swear. I won't mistrust you. I'll believe anything you tell me.

CHESTER

You don't understand. People in Cortland . . . finally, I belong somewhere.

GRACE

You'll still belong somewhere.

CHESTER

People that matter . . . they like me . . . for the first time in my life.

GRACE

(Touching him gently)

They'll still like you.

CHESTER

(Looking at her)

Please, Billy. Don't let me lose my chance. Get rid of the baby.

(He is weeping softly, lying on his back)

GRACE

I can't.

CHESTER

Don't make me marry you.

GRACE

I love you, Chester. You're all I want in this world. All I want forever.

CHESTER

I'll stop loving you.

GRACE

I won't let you.

142

CHESTER

(Looking away)

Please . . .

GRACE

I'll make you happy. I swear I will. So happy.

> *(She lies on the ground next to him, her head on his shoulder.*
>
> *There is a moment of silence between them. Only the sounds of the woods and the lake)*

The truth, Chester. No one can hear you. Only you and me now. Alone. You brought me here to kill me, didn't you? Didn't you?

> *(A pause)*

CHESTER

Yes.

GRACE

How?

CHESTER

Doesn't matter.

GRACE

Are you going to?

CHESTER

No. I'm too afraid. Too much of a coward.

GRACE

Are you sure?

> *(A pause)*

I knew that's what was on your mind. I knew all along. From the minute I met you at the train in DeRuyter. It was in your eyes. I suppose I knew even before then.

CHESTER

And you came anyway?

GRACE

I love you, Chester. I love you so much. Sometimes it frightens me how much I love you.

143

(A pause)

CHESTER

Well, I guess . . . I guess we better get back.
     (He stands)
We got a long way to go.
     (He reaches down to help her up)
The woods are so thick. It'll take hours to walk.

GRACE

     (After she stands)
We can go in the boat.

CHESTER

No . . . it scares you.

GRACE

I don't mind.

CHESTER

No.

GRACE

We'll go in the boat, Chester. I won't be afraid. I'll pretend we're . . . rowing on a lake in paradise . . . where the waters are always calm. I guess that's the only place we'll ever be happy together . . . so I'll pretend we're drifting through paradise.

Rhythm, silhouette, texture, color, sound—an immutable part of my creative process.

When I first began my training in theater I tended to think of each element in an individual way: Rhythm. Silhouette. Texture. Color. Sound. But as time passed, as I started writing for the stage and my sense of these elements developed and deepened, the words themselves began to blend together, as if in reality they were but one element: rhythm-silhouette-texture-color-sound. Now, I no longer think of them separately. When I write a scene they are united, influencing each other constantly in varying degrees. Rhythm-silhouette-texture-color-sound . . . like a mantra . . . instinctive . . . indispensable—indispensable to every play I've written in the past, indispensable now to this play as I write this final scene, the final image of eternity for Chester and Grace.

(She is billowing the chiffon, all business, avoiding the kiss he tries to give her)

GRACE

Now grab the other end of this.

CHESTER

Do I have to?

GRACE

Well of course you don't have to, Chester, not if you don't want. I just thought you'd like to do something nice with me for a change.

CHESTER

(Giving in)

O.K.

GRACE

You can always say "no."

CHESTER

(Taking the end of the chiffon)

What are we doing?

GRACE

Making clouds.

(They billow the chiffon up above their heads, watching it flutter and swell like a cloud)

Isn't this fun?

CHESTER

I guess.

GRACE

Again!

(The chiffon billows up above their heads, puffing out again like a cloud)

CHESTER

How long do we do this?

Forever if we want.

CHESTER

Oh.

GRACE

Remember how I always said I'd love you forever?

> *(Chester says nothing)*

Chester?

CHESTER

> *(Without much spirit)*

I remember.

GRACE

This is forever, Chester.

CHESTER

> *(A weary sigh)*

Oh, Lord.

> *(They continue to billow the chiffon as the lights slowly fade . . . the fabric rising and falling . . . making clouds . . . on and on and on and . . . .)* ∎

Roots and Wings

Irene Corey

The time was the evening of February 9, 1962. Our show was opening Off Broadway—and we didn't wait up for the reviews! Not that we weren't excited. It was just that we were confident in the talent of our cast, in the imagery of mosaic icons, and the sound and beauty of the language. This was a production of *The Book of Job*, a play arranged and directed by Orlin Corey; I had designed the production—set, costumes, and makeup

The next morning the reviews came in. Lewis Funke of *The New York Times* wrote:

> For some years now there has been word of an unusual production of *The Book of Job* taking place, first in Georgetown College, Kentucky, later during summers in Pine Mountain State Park. . . . Last night it was performed in the nave of Christ Church Methodist . . . and there is, happily, no need to quarrel with reports. *The Book of Job* is an awesome and most majestic rendition, to be remembered both for the adapter's concept as well as for the costumes and makeup of the participants . . . there is a sound to all this that is bound to linger for a long time in memory. The imagination is stirred, the eye magnetized. (February 10, 1962)

How had we two arrived at this point of confidence, this place of recognition? A reminder was there that night in the ebullient personage of Sammy Leve, noted Broadway designer. We had met him when Paul Baker brought him to the Baylor Theater as a guest artist. It was there at the Baylor Theater that we got our training. It was there that we were given roots and wings!

I consider it a miracle that I went to college in the fall of 1943. I was born on a farm in Iowa, and I attended first through the sixth grades in a one-room school. My father endured seven years of drought, many blizzards, and the Great Depression before he put his family into a car and headed south, armed only with a sixth-grade education, a license from the Sweeney Automobile School, and a Houston newspaper. Although "college" had not been in our family's vocabulary, our young pastor, a recent graduate of Baylor University, convinced my father that I should go to college and study art.

Ignorant of the registration process, when I arrived on campus I looked until I saw a sign that said Art. Under it sat a gentleman who spoke with a strong German accent. I told him that I wanted to major in art, so he filled my afternoons with art classes. Thanks to our combined disregard for

The Skin of Our Teeth, Trinity Theater

the custom of waiting two years before declaring a major, my art training was off to an early start. I did not realize at the time that I had the good fortune to be studying under Dr. Edmond Kinzinger, an eminent German artist who had fled Hitler's Germany. He armed me with a thorough understanding of the universal principles of design. Equally important, he instilled in me confidence in my ability as an artist.

One evening during my junior year I wandered into final rehearsals for *The Skin of Our Teeth*. Although there was a policy of closed rehearsals, Paul Baker noticed that I was entranced and allowed me to stay. Doors opened upon undreamed possibilities . . . such as opening a show Off Broadway!

Orlin Corey came to Baylor intent on pursuing a degree in history. His father, a rural route mail carrier for a small Oklahoma town, had gifted him with a love of history. Orlin had vowed that as soon as World War II was over he would travel the United States and see a part of every state. His fascination with the history of places and the recurrent themes of history became an integral part of his theatrical work.

Orlin loved language, and his exploration of choral work had its beginning when he used a strong choral treatment of R. H. Wards' *The Prodigal Son* as his undergraduate directing project in 1950. The following year, the play was used as a project for Baker's advanced acting class to further develop vocal experiments. Respect for the material at hand, and a sensitivity for the sound growing out of it, marked subsequent works of both Baker and Corey.

Baylor Theater had an atmosphere of possibilities, discoveries, dreams we didn't know we had as Baker challenged us to do honest, thorough work, to apply "head, heart, and hands" to whatever we undertook. He gave us space for self-discovery and permission to think. He told us,

148

"You can do anything you want to do, wherever you are."

Baker enriched those who worked with him by inviting exciting artists, architects, actors, designers, dancers, and writers to interact with us. Integration of abilities in action. And he arranged the pivotal trip, "Baylor in Paris, 1952"—a summer of new impressions filled with daily lectures by Louvre historian Marthe Arnould, introductions to contemporary art by painter Reynold Arnould, evenings at the theater, visits to cathedrals. It was a new world to most of us.

Upon returning to Waco, Baker explored dynamic new ways of making and of seeing theater, and Orlin and I left for our first teaching jobs at Georgetown College, Georgetown, Kentucky. I was chair of the art department, and Orlin was director of drama. Thus began a twenty-year collaboration in play making, plumbing the script for ideas that would best illuminate the playwright's intention and point us toward the research necessary to give those ideas form.

Our work progressed under the patronage of two colleges, first in Kentucky and ten years later at Centenary College in Shreveport, Louisiana. It also grew within the structure of an ensemble repertory company we called Everyman Players. In his book, *An Odyssey of Masquers: The Everyman Players*, Orlin described The Everyman Players as "an indigenous regional theater troupe in origin."

We moved about the world with our repertoire of classics for nearly a quarter of a century. In twenty-four seasons we traveled a million miles on four continents and were featured at two world's fairs and many international festivals. What we chose to lend our energy to was not goal oriented. We aimed toward the greater satisfaction suggested by the test offered by Paul Baker, that "saints, dogs, and children should have found something of wonder and of worth in our offerings."

In our working partnership, Orlin and I enjoyed a free flow of artistic input. In many ways, as designer, I codirected and Corey as director codesigned. My costumes sometimes dictated his staging and lighting; his staging influenced my designs. Frequently, at the end of a production, we could not remember who first thought of what idea. It was more important that we visualize the same goal, and engage the imagination of the young people who would bring it life.

Paul Baker did not work from a set of rules. When he discovered a fresh way to illuminate the author's intent, that spark of innovation ignited the imagination of director, designers, cast,

The Tempest, Georgetown College

and crew. Everyone participated. Together, we worked to realize the vision. That was the pattern that was implanted in those who studied with him.

The creative path takes many directions. People who left the Baylor Theater, sparked by Baker's imagination, found their own path, grew, evolved, and touched others who grew and evolved, creating an ever expanding ripple. As part of that ripple, I offer summaries of some of the work Orlin and I did together, its reception, and suggest that it is a reflection of insights received from Paul Baker.

In our production of Shakespeare's *The Tempest*, Orlin established the directorial concept: to stage Prospero's magic domain as though it were the sunken island of Atlantis. Into this watery world would come those who drowned in the shipwreck. The lines, "Nothing of him that doth fade / But doth suffer a sea-change / Into something rich and strange" gave origin to the concept and sparked the direction of research: Everything was to be derived from underwater sea life.

Our company, The Everyman Players, was on tour as I designed *The Tempest*. A stop in Chicago allowed us to visit that city's superb aquarium. I observed that as the water became deeper it became darker and more mysterious, providing a perfect backdrop for the luminous fish and underwater creatures. I looked through books of photographs of coral reefs and underwater life forms, flagging pictures that suggested mystery. I was excited to find an elegant, transparent jellyfish, dome shaped, glowing with inner lights. When combined with the potential suggested by a cluster of brain coral, I had found the vision for Prospero's magic costume! Continuing through the books, I marked creatures that

150

suggested qualities such as comic, malevolent, innocent, fragile, or noble, noting line, color, and silhouette. This was the period of incubation, of "mulling," a time for allowing imagery to flow freely. Only after that were characters matched to creatures.

The curtain opened on a dark stage, except for lights glowing inside Prospero's domed headdress. As he conjured the storm, a tiny ship was buffeted and then sank into silken waves. When the lights came up, people from the ship emerged onto the island, moving slowly as against the currents, costumed in shiny, wet-looking fabrics. Schools of fishes shimmered on black silk as they were whisked across the stage by anemone spirits with black tentacles. Caliban merged into the white and black coral of the setting. Ariel bore the marks of the tree in which he had been imprisoned and now had the wings of the winged fish. Prospero and Miranda's costumes were encrusted with coral. The "sea change" had taken place!

> In a shimmering but darkened world, set symbolically in the formative sea, (this) production of *The Tempest* builds a play to prove Prospero's contention that mercy is a rarer and finer experience than vengeance. . . . Last night it proved that point beautifully . . . in poetry, visual richness, fun, music, and a compassionate point of view"
>
> (*The [Nashville] Tennessean*, October 25, 1972, 12).

For a specially commissioned version of the biblical book of Romans, we turned to the sculptural figures at the entrances to Chartres Cathedral. My designs for Orlin's adaptation, *Romans by St. Paul*, sought to match the dynamic intensity of late gothic sculpture with the passion and affirmation of the faith of St. Paul. These figures had begun to move out of their niches, reaching out into the world, questioning, just as St. Paul questioned and affirmed.

To achieve the verticality of the figures, we used heightened foreheads, elongated fingers, and built-up shoes. Robes were weighted at intervals along the hemline to maintain the sculptural folds. In chant and in song, a chorus of accompanying saints echoed St. Paul's rhetorical questions.

Romans by St. Paul toured to many venues of varied sizes and shapes. During a tour to cathedrals in England, we had an opportunity to see how the architectural spaces in which we performed affected the audience's perception. At Bristol Cathedral, built in the more rational

151

classical style, the discussions afterward focused on St. Paul's lawyer-like logic. However, in Gothic cathedrals, the audience responded to the vision of St. Paul standing tall in his faith. We found that the Liverpool Cathedral, Gothic in inspiration, was vast enough that Gordon Craig himself would have been awed by the lighting possibilities. As the figure of St. Paul approached the transept, the light split, casting his shadow 140 feet upward to the spine of the vaulted ceiling.

With incredulity we saw men as trees walking—and truly awesome. The cadences of the Authorized Version rose and fell with a compelling power that positively made the scalp prickle. . . . There were giants in the earth.

(*London Tablet*, November 5, 1966).

This was not only quite unlike any theater one has seen, but . . . it has tremendous and, at times, almost frightening power.

(*Liverpool Daily Post*, October 15, 1966).

In harnessing art forms to serve the theater, the designs for *Job* and *Romans* were relatively straightforward adaptations from the original Byzantine mosaics and Gothic sculpture. However, Sophocles' *Electra* led me into many diverse areas of research. We found that the script contained two concurrent themes: the power of past evil and the presence of a divine justice that rights wrongs. This correlates with the surrealist view that recognizes the world of the visible while being aware of the shadowy subconscious. The play was to be staged as a memory play, with the events of the past and the events of the present linked in the mind of Electra. The raw brutality of past events caused me to explore the primitive roots of many cultures. With no particular characters in mind, I dug and sketched my way through books on the arts of Africa, Assyria, Sumeria, the Mayans, and the exotic designs of Indonesia.

After these images simmered in my mind, a selection process began. An Indonesian snake necklace was placed around Clytemnestra's neck. Her crown was inspired from a Sumerian queen's headdress. She walked under an Assyrian umbrella. The old tutor carried a staff fashioned after a Mayan scepter and wore a headdress shaped like a gnarled tree stump, found on a Sumerian statue.

I turned to the pre-Greek Minoan culture for elements of the setting. A raked, marble-white stage with diminishing perspective lines was overhung with a coarse net, symbolizing a woven web of the past. It cradled the severed head of Agamemnon. Hal Proske, who played the old tutor, described the setting from the actor's point of view:

> Here I would like to witness to the very sensible influence on the actors of the physical envelope of space created for the tragedy. The great net of doom hung above, all pervading. . . . Perspective lines raced up the massive, triangular rake, toward their vanishing point in infinity, where fate is ordained and divine mysteries resolved. The lines drew the eye and the mind of both actor and spectator from the altar of Apollo, sole bright symbol of hope and justice, past the dreaded gates of Agamemnon's palace—gates that periodically disgorged its demented inhabitants, malicious or pitiable, each by turn to dominate the chorus or to challenge Electra.
>
> (*The Mask of Reality*, New Orleans: Anchorage Press, 1968).

Electra, Georgetown College

As the complexity of the characters increased, so did the makeup stylization. Stylized realism indicated the suffering of Electra and the grave resolve of Orestes to right the wrong done to his father. The use of white makeup underlined the surreal theme and suggested the futility of trying to cover up the underlying evil. Thus whitened, Clytemnestra and members of the corrupt court stood in stark contrast to the mourning Electra, robed in black. Aegisthus, an ominous presence, felt and feared throughout, brought a visage of cruel decadence, when he finally made his appearance. Again, in the words of Proske: "I recall . . . watching my fellow actor torturously assume the visage of my enemy, Aegisthus. Covered with the white of hypocrisy, he slowly adorned himself with the marks and lines of cruelty, lust, and cowardice. He wore them like jewels."

There was a metamorphosis of mysterious forms from the past mingling with the needs of the characters, and magnifying their presence. Ceremonially thrust within a surrealistic setting evocative of infinity, they succeeded in presenting the once and present horror as one.

Everyman Players create a riveting, primitive, gods-filled world by the use of terrifying bird cries, distant gongs, and horns . . . and a marvelous Dali-like raked stage.
(*Fort Wayne News Sentinel*, October 16, 1971, 7).

. . . . a brilliantly created and arresting *Electra*, mounted with haunting impact—so highly styled as to be almost liturgical in effect, yet moving to a crushingly powerful climax.
(*Peoria Journal Star*, October 12, 1971, B-6).

There is no way to establish the true course of the creative process. Somehow in the depths of experience that exist in all of us, images combine, surface, and are united to serve the undertakings of the moment. First you find a vision—then you find a way to do it!

Through the years I have become known for my makeup designs. Who knows—perhaps my interest started in the little Iowa schoolhouse the day I traded my treasured set of Prang watercolors for a tube of Blue Waltz lipstick. More likely it was kindled by Alexander Koriansky, a Russian director Paul Baker invited to serve as visiting professor. Instead of using natural skin tones to describe the facial contours, he created shadows with a tracery of fine lines using pure colors—like the Expressionist painters.

My first use of stylized makeup was in the analysis of *Macbeth* at Georgetown College. The directorial premise was to stress the superhuman, evil qualities of the three witches, paralleling the emergence of evil in Macbeth's life. Out of the text arose malevolent images of the three witches, as cat, bat, and toad. Makeup was painted in patterns of green and gray and looked " . . . not like the inhabitants of the earth." As an artist, I was familiar with creating dimensional illusions on a blank paper or canvas. It seemed a natural step to assume the same privilege on the human face—to treat it as a canvas.

In 1959, I spoke of the validity of unified makeup and costume to a small group of people attending a southeastern theater conference at Berea, Kentucky. Student actors were made up as Job and various characters from *A Midsummer Night's Dream*. At the finish of the presentation, a gentleman at the back of the room asked, "Have you ever thought of writing a book?" From the front row came the voice of Sara Spencer, owner of Anchorage Press and champion of children's theater. "If you write it, I'll print it." Although many plays and many years intervened, *The Mask of Reality: An Approach to Design for the Theater*, was published in 1968. This was followed in 1990 by *The Face Is a Canvas: The Design and Technique of Theatrical Makeup*.

In the intervening years, Sara asked me to provide costume designs to accompany a play script based on the fable of the hare and the tortoise. These included complete "how to" instructions for making the costumes, and applying the makeup. By the time Orlin and I got around to producing it, I found myself following my own instructions! The first time we combined makeup with costume on an actor, there was an excited, somewhat incredulous shout of, "It works!" And so it did. The play continues in popularity and has been produced over a forty-year period, both here and abroad. That unleashed the designs into public domain. From time to time, I recognize a familiar whisker, among the *Cats* and *The Wiz's* of the world.

My concept of the makeup mask reached a national audience when *Horizon Magazine*, January 1963, featured "A Pair of Modern Masquers," showing full-color photographs of animals from *Reynard the Fox* and the cast of *The Book of Job*. *Horizon* wrote, "Irene Corey demonstrated that costume and makeup can be a single design element, and so add visual force to verbal drama."

Everyone who studied with Paul Baker recalls taking his famous integration of abilities class and the fearsome day we had to walk across the stage twice as two different characters. My characters were vague and unsuccessful, but they were not failures. I learned an important lesson—go to the source. Be specific. Be observant. I had assumed information I did not have. This experience defined my absolute belief in research as it relates to designing. It precedes finding the vision.

Designing *The Hare and the Tortoise* serves as an example of the research process as it relates to costume and makeup and the unification of the two. When Sara Spencer requested the costume designs, I went directly to the zoo. There I studied the slow, lumbering pace of the tortoise, encased and encumbered by his heavy shell, the wrinkled skin of his mouth and neck, and the almost human slant of his eyes. The contrast with the sleek, streamlined, fast-paced hare was immediate. The fluffy marmot, the prickly hedgehog, and the rotund badger presented other textures and shapes. I turned to the script and found human characteristics: a faithful, honest tortoise; a sneaky, tricky hare; a lovable hedgehog; and an officious badger. I chose not to use hard masks but designed the animal features as a continuation of the costume. Makeup painted directly onto the actor's face provided a "flexible" mask. The designs were finalized when all these elements were wedded. Now I had the vision!

Once the vision was set down on paper, a second challenge appeared—find a way to do it. I could rely on known methods of construction or explore new methods and techniques. The tortoise's shell, for example, presented several problems. It had to be light enough for the actor to carry on his back throughout the play; large enough for him to retract inside it, and strong enough to support the ample weight of the badger, who sat upon it, thinking it a stone. I turned to screen wire to form the basic shape of the shell. When pulled diagonally, it had a bias that helped create a convex shape. Fiberglass solidified it. Painted and hooped fabric over arms and legs added cumbersome bulk. Makeup was styled to suggest the protruding beak and the wide, wrinkled mouth. The fluffy marmot became a cocoon of several layers of net; a prickly hedgehog was suggested by rows of gathered net stuck with white pipe cleaners and a cocoon of black organdy over hoops shaped the rotund badger.

In 1970, *The Hare and the Tortoise* joined the venerable *Job* for a two-month tour of the United States, then played at the Biennale Festival in Venice, before touring to Holland and Britain. While it was playing in Yorkshire, the playwright Alan Broadhurst first saw The Everyman Player's version of his play, *The Hare and the Tortoise*, evoking this comment: "You made a better show, a truer show than I wrote or staged myself. You have even made me a better playwright than I am, and I like that!"

As *Job* continued to "go to and fro in the earth," one of his most successful touring companions was the universally appealing fable, *Reynard the Fox*, by Arthur Fauquez. Our goal was to reveal the foibles in man through the antics of animals. It was usual to turn to critical reviews to verify whether we had reached our production goals. It was equally enlightening to turn to the voice of some of the actors, speaking from inside their costume/makeup.

The *Reynard* cast had made their trip to the zoo and studied their animal counterparts. Hal Proske, who played Brun the bear noted:

> . . . bear's hindquarters operate independently of his headquarters. That final observation was my key to the bear's basic mime. Hips roll and surge into the mass of the stomach as the hind legs push and thrust to move the bear forward. Such motion is absorbed by the tremendous belly. . . . So it went: arms akimbo, body heaving and rolling—in grumbling frustration, in pained hunger, in gleeful pursuit of honey or revenge, in gluttonous stupor. . . . The final element was the gift of the designer: the costume-makeup mask. My eyebrows were gone. The bridge of my nose spread from cheek to cheek. My eyes were reduced to two small circles of black . . . the day-to-day me was imprisoned but the burgeoning bear within came slowly to realize that . . . the actor within was protected from physical and emotional attack by the size and density of his outer self. Brun rushed into the forest . . . and possessed it. He was finally free to be a bear.

Reynard the Fox, Georgetown College

157

Gay Farley described her experience of playing Tiecelin the crow:

> For days I had observed the sleek, intense bird called the crow. The sharp action, the quick run, and the keen look in the eye with the head cocked at an angle, all became part of my character. . . . Although I felt confident that my movements were precise, I knew that I was too conscious of myself acting as a crow. And, to be honest, I did not look too much like a bird. The week before the show opened, the costumes were completed and that exciting time of concealment came. I grabbed my scepter and dashed to the mirror. The reflection was shocking. There stood the largest crow I'd ever seen. I looked at it for some time—at its large yellow feet, sleek body, glistening breast, and small black face. Suddenly I cocked my head to one side. The transformation was complete. I was still the actress, but the image in the mirror was an extension of myself.

The critics agreed.

> Children will leap for joy from their seats at the antics of Reynard. When I try to recall Gay Farley's officious crow, all that comes to mind is the image of a strutting, pecking, cawing, cocked-head black bird. I can still see the shambling gait of Harold Proske's bear, the loopy-loo walk of Donald Farley's highly comical wolf, and the proud stroll of Allen Shaffer's lion. Randolph Tallman (Job last week—what virtuosity!) catches the quick scamper of Reynard to the last wisp of his flying tail. The player's keen edge slices the satire one moment, and then, in the next . . . the fox nicks the laughter of children. This is a fine family show if ever there was one.
>
> (*Durban [South Africa] Daily News*, November 17, 1964).

Inevitably, the visual appeal of the iconic figures and the animals attracted the attention of photographers. The characters led the way, opening doors to television. *The Book of Job, Romans by St. Paul*, and *The Hare and the Tortoise* were shown on BBC. *The Book of Job* was presented on Latin American television, and *Romans by St. Paul* was televised by CBS. Images of the mosaic

158

Job appeared in hundreds of magazines and newspapers, including *Life, Paris-Match, Newsweek,* and the Italian magazine *OGGI.*

It was back in 1969 at Georgetown College that we had first realized the visual power of the *Job* designs. Costumes and makeup were combined for dress rehearsal. When ten life-sized Byzantine figures in shimmering mosaics made their entrance, Orlin and I gasped! Gone were the students we knew so well. In their place were larger-than-life personages. "Have we gone too far? Is it too strong?" The answer was no. The power that resulted from the merging of the timeless beauty of mosaics with the ritual enactment of the ancient poem of Job's passion propelled *The Book of Job* onto the world's stage.

Although *Reynard the Fox* was highly popular everywhere it traveled, it was the majestic *Job* that created its own aura, led the way, and took command of whatever space was encountered. That was true even at the Brussels World Fair where the sun shone through the clear glass walls of the Protestant pavilion and glittered off ten mosaic figures. Or in great contrast, as it appeared at Laurel Cove in a natural amphitheater as described by Clara Hieronymous, critic with the *Nashville Tennessean:*

An eighty-foot sandstone cliff whose craggy face is softened with a luxurious spill of rhododendron, forms a backdrop . . . Jewel colors of living mosaics are reflected in a pool stretched between the players and the audience. As Job . . . stands with arms outstretched, his shadow is projected like a giant crucifix against the rock behind him, the frogs and the whippoorwills, as if on cue, take up the refrain . . . "I know that my Redeemer liveth . . . and in my flesh shall I see God!" (July 31, 1960, F-1)

So it was, that opening night in New York that *Job* had already made its pilgrimage from Georgetown, Kentucky, to England, to the Southern Governors Conference, and to Pineville, Kentucky, where it had begun a twenty-year run in the outdoor theater. The words of Paul Baker were verified. "You can do anything you want to do—wherever you are." There where we got our training was the beginning. Paul Baker gave us roots and wings. ■

Further Reading

Broadhurst, Alan. *The Hare and the Tortoise*. Costume and makeup designs, Irene Corey. Louisville, KY: Anchorage Press Plays, Inc., 1968.

Corey, Irene. *The Mask of Reality: An Approach to Design for the Theater*. Louisville, KY: Anchorage Press Plays, Inc., 1968.

———. *The Face Is a Canvas: The Design and Technique of Theatrical Makeup*. Louisville, KY: Anchorage Press Plays, Inc., 1968.

Corey, Orlin. *An Odyssey of Masquers: The Everyman Players*. New Orleans: Rivendell House, Ltd., 1988.

Fauquez, Alan. *Reynard the Fox*. Costume and makeup designs, Irene Corey. Louisville, KY: Anchorage Press Plays, Inc., 1962.

The Tempest
Georgetown College

160

Find Your Own Path: An Actor's Journey

Claudia Sullivan

I first heard of Paul Baker during my days at the Casa Mañana Theater School in Fort Worth, Texas. Sharon Benge, director of the Children's Theater Program, had been a student of Baker's, and she passed along his passion for creativity and desire for new energy in the program that covered acting, theater games, voice and diction, and theater movement and pantomime. Even then there were rumors that Baker's approach was unconventional, but what did I know? I was fourteen and had neither experience nor education to compare one approach with another.

After high school and four years working on my undergraduate degree in Indiana, I returned to Texas to study with the legendary (and somewhat infamous) director himself. When I entered the Dallas Theater Center's graduate program I expected my studies to follow the pattern from undergraduate work. Voice and diction. Dance training. Character study. History of the theater. The Baker approach was different. The Baker approach began with a discussion and workshop in *landscape*.

Theater training in the United States, especially in the professional acting schools of the 1930s and 1940s, was a tired rehash of an American interpretation of European acting styles. All that changed when Stanislavski and the actors of the Moscow Art Theater toured America and introduced to American audiences an electrifying style of acting based on realism, ensemble playing, and natural unaffected manners of speech and movement. Stanislavski encouraged actors to study roles using personal memory (what he called sense memory or emotion memory) as a point of departure. He suggested that actors and other artists study behavior patterns, speech patterns, mannerisms, and facial expressions of people in a variety of situations. He also advocated extensive study by students of their own personal habits, feelings, and behaviors.

By the 1950s the Stanislavski style of acting and his formula for character development were labeled "the Method." During the fifties and sixties followers and devotees of "the Method" flocked to theater schools to learn this new and exciting way to act with more conviction, honesty, and creativity.

Baker synthesized artistic theories from Stanislavski and other theorists working in Europe and the United States, and with his book, *Integration of Abilities: Exercises for Creative Growth* (1972), Baker solidified for all theater practitioners and followers of the creative spirit

161

the importance of creative integrity. He expanded the theories of master artists—Diderot, Stanislavski, Artaud, Grotowski, and others—to reach beyond theater and the study of the arts. He found a central component that spoke to all interested in the unique and sacred part of each individual—the creative expression of one's own view of the world.[1] His theories were relevant to educators, writers, city planners, business managers, theologians, and, especially, artists.[2]

The Dallas Theater Center was a place to test one's process of working, and, more importantly, it was a place of learning *how* to work. Many of us who were first-year students at the DTC had been educated in the program of, "do what I tell you . . . follow my directions . . . think like *this* . . . do it like it has been done before . . . and . . . as director I don't have time to work with you individually, so figure it out on your own." This led to what I later called "sheep acting"—following the director, doing what the director said, and never following one's own instincts or discovering one's own process.

I had grown comfortable with that program during my college years. It was not until I came to the DTC that I discovered that there was another way of approaching creative work. The first day of acting class Baker walked into the large, empty space that was our classroom. He asked us to think of someone we knew well and to imagine a rhythm that expressed that person. *Rhythm,* I thought, *What rhythm? Why is rhythm important?* Then he asked for volunteers to stand and clap out the rhythm of that person. Reluctantly, one student did, clapping quietly at first, then louder, then harder, then a slow one-two-three clap. Baker gave a detailed description of the person, including the fact that the person had had a traumatic event in late childhood. We sat silently. "Yes," the student replied. "You are right." Was this some kind of carnival trick? No. This was a demonstration of awareness of character, of rhythm, and of intense focus on the exercise.

After this first demonstration Baker asked us to walk a rhythm across the floor to express a person, even ourselves. It seemed too easy, but as it came my turn I realized how difficult it was to simplify a character, a person, myself into a pure physical exercise. This was the beginning of my education in simplicity, in abstraction, in focus, and ultimately, in myself . . . to trust myself, my own process for discovery, my own personal landscape that connected me to my artistic and creative roots. That, of course, required a risk. It required courageous action on the part of the artist and the artistic community supporting the work.

162

The heart of the Baker philosophy involves an understanding of the basic elements of theater. These elements include rhythm, space, sound and silence, movement, line and direction, silhouette, and texture and color. These basic elements are common in all works of art, but are of special consideration for the actor. They provide an integrated approach to the study of acting, an approach that does not offer a quick fix, that forces the actor into a pattern of acting styles or development of personal idiosyncrasies.

Acting Class, Dallas Theater Center

In our acting classes at the DTC each student chose a character and explored that character through each of the elements, in sequence. What is the character's rhythm? Speech rhythm? Walking rhythm? Emotional rhythm? These questions lead to a deeper understanding of the character, his or her responses to others in the play, motivations for action. How does the character respond to space? Does she fill a room or hide in the background? Does he gesture broadly or remain rigid and physically quiet? What sounds accompany the day of Linda Loman, the wife and mother in Arthur Miller's *Death of a Salesman*? Kitchen sounds: slicing, chopping, washing, mopping, the squeak of an old screen door. What is the sound of her breathing? The tone of her voice?

How has the playwright used silence? What does the character think during pauses and silences? How does the character move, sit, stand? How does he or she eat and drink and smoke? Does she play with her hair? Does he have a nervous gesture of the hands? Movement is the key to the inner life of the character as expressed in an outward manner. Modern dance choreographer and dancer Martha Graham once said, "The body doesn't know

163

how to lie." Line, direction, and silhouette contribute also to the outer manifestation of the character. Texture and color can refer to color choices by the character, but in a broader sense they refer to sound, mood, clothing choice, and environment.

Aspects of this work should not be confused with similar work done in acting programs such as Lee Strasberg's Actors Studio where psychological introspection is a requirement of acting students. Baker's exercises were devised to promote creative responses, not psychotherapy. Many of the exercises promoted through the Stanislavski Method use *sense memory*. *Emotion memory* exercises encourage the actor to recall the physical *sense* and/or the emotional feelings at particular moments in one's life. What was the physical sense you recall when you broke your leg? Did you express the pain in your face, your hands, through your voice? These remembered responses were used to affect similar situations in the life of the character.

The art of acting resides in a world of words and actions, but the inner realm of acting, portraying a character, exists within the world that is beyond words and actions. The actor must carve out and shape a character that is composed of more than words and stage movements. The character must reveal emotions, feelings, psychological dispositions, body awareness, and an environmental context. The actor creates a role that has a life visible onstage to the audience and other actors, but one that also lives outside of the context of the play. "Where were you five minutes before you entered the stage?" a director might probe.

Often the playwright offers little background information for the actor. Temperament, attitude, and self-concept are revealed by what the character says about himself, what others say about him, and his motivation. How can an actor know other important aspects of the character? Through an investigation of his own responses to the stimuli offered in the play and the creation of the character's biography. What kind of childhood did the character have? Who were the important people in his past life? Did he have a dog, did he enjoy school, how did he get that scar on his knee? What sounds were and are present in the life of the character? Describe his silhouette, movement patterns, and color of clothing. Baker's integration of abilities begins with these basic questions that lead the actor on a road of self-discovery as well as character development.

Movement and sound are important to the character of Laura Wingfield from Tennessee Williams' *The Glass Menagerie* because of her physical challenge and the sound the leg brace makes as she walks. In the play Laura refers to the painful memory of the sound of her walking up the stairs at her school. To her the sound must have been deafening, because it brought unwanted attention to her awkward movements. Laura lives in a world of tension between her desire to be left alone and her yearning for a social life like others girls in her high school. There is silence as she plays with her glass figures, yet she also plays old records on the Victrola, evoking the sounds of another time and age. Texture plays a role in the environmental sounds through the scratchy records that she plays over and over.

Shakespeare's Juliet is young and innocent like Laura Wingfield, but she is more confident, open to romance, and confident in her love for Romeo. Her movements are quick, light, and graceful because of the culture and class in which she was born. An actor portraying Juliet must come to terms with the language of Shakespeare but must also master the elegant, classical movement style of the Italian Renaissance. Clap the rhythm of Shakespeare's language from a particular scene or soliloquy. Walk the rhythm of Juliet before she meets Romeo and after. What is the texture of emotions, of voice quality during the final suicide scene? Each element can play a part in each character's development from the actor's investigation of those elements.

To understand the elements is to grasp the core of all artistic work.

Rhythm: Rhythm begins when life begins. There is the rhythm of breath, the heartbeat, motor rhythm, and emotional rhythm. Breathing dictates a subconscious and often conscious timing to our movements, speech, and thinking. Each person has a unique manner of walking, gesturing, and expressing physical as well as emotional states of being. As the emotional rhythm rises or subsides, verbal, vocal, and physical manners are manifested.

Perform a simple breathing exercise for a character, perhaps Laura Wingfield. Close your eyes and breathe as Laura would in the opening moments of the play. How does her breathing change when her brother Tom comes in drunk? When her mother, Amanda, scolds her for lying about attending business school? Breathe the final moments of the play as Laura blows out her candles and faces the future alone.

Beyond personal rhythms, the body encounters auditory rhythms within the environment. City rhythms, waves breaking against the shore. The different rhythms of historical periods, seasons, or times of the day can affect the character in a play. Baker, like Stanislavski, always indicated "begin first with rhythm." Dancer and choreographer Doris Humphrey stated in her book, *The Art of Making Dances*, "Rhythm so permeates every aspect of human beings, and indeed, of the known world, that it might be compared to the ambiance of existence, like the water in which a fish moves. . . . Rhythm is the great organizer" (Princeton Book Co., 1991, 104). Every individual is faced at one time or another with the choice of abiding by a pattern or breaking away from its monotony and creating something unique and rhythmically inventive. This decision is particularly important to the actor on the modern stage.

Summer and Smoke, Dallas Theater Center

In the years that I have taught acting to college students many were reluctant to approach dramatic characters through the elements exercises. They were more comfortable with "Learn your lines and do your blocking." Asking a student to clap a rhythm or walk a line or make an abstract sound study of the character puts him or her in a position of taking a risk and making his own unique statement about his interpretation of the character and the scene. Preliminary work must be completed before students can feel confident in their own abilities and bold enough to attempt personal expression. Exercises must be judged as work in progress. Students must be taught that while "there are no wrong answers . . . there may be better choices."

Not only must the actor analyze the rhythm of his character but the rhythm of each scene and the play as a whole. The opening act of *Our Town* is very different in rhythm from the final act. The rapid-fire, one-liner comedy style of many of Neil Simon's plays contrasts with the lyrical and poetic rhythm of Tennessee Williams' works. Rhythm does not exist in emptiness. Rhythm fills space.

166

Space: All characters exist within some sort of space. All actors portraying characters must enter into the theatrical space. Physical spaces vary from the tiny space within a matchbox to the closeness of a prison cell or the immensity of the Grand Canyon. Mental space encompasses concepts, ideas, philosophies, and emotions. People may protect their own intimate space in a variety of ways depending on their background, their culture, and their personal responses to strangers invading their space. Watch people in a crowded elevator or in a crowded subway or movie line. In certain situations we must allow strangers to enter into our "space," but some may feel more threatened than others; some may refuse to allow physical contact. Likewise each of us fills our personal living spaces with clutter, openness, or a flair for the eclectic. Consider how a character fills his space. If you were a designer for a play how would you enter into the mind and life of the character and construct a home or an apartment? How would you decorate a desk or choose bedroom accessories?

Individual responses occur as awareness to space is developed, its color, its texture, its mood, and its effect on an individual's overall mood. Baker suggested that in the initial stages of character work the actor should work in an empty or blank space. Trappings of other scenes or plays might add unnecessary or distracting factors that would only serve to weaken the actor's concentration.

Sound: Sound and silence are inseparable from space. The various kinds of space are constantly being filled with differing sounds and atmospherically changeable silences. There are natural sounds, environmental sounds, nonverbal human sounds, and vocal sounds.[3] Silence can be as powerful as any sound. An exercise that was used often at the DTC had each actor express

There is no one quite like Paul Baker. . . . He shattered my brittle, Anglo-oriented view of theater and film and gave me to understand that there is a power beneath the lines of a play that can overwhelm both a performer and an audience.

Edward Herrmann

167

an emotion or attitudes such as anger, physical pain, passionate love, or impatience using only breathing. Although students might exhibit the same emotion it was amazing how the quality of the sound differed.

Experiments in modern psychology show that sounds and smells can evoke memories of one's past, often with extremely emotional results, proving Stanislavski's *emotion memory* and *sense memory* exercises. By recalling such specific sounds and the reactions to those sounds and silences the actor can better determine the role that sound has played in the character's life. Sound and silence hold secret powers that make them a useful tool in the dramatic arts. The actor commands attention and fills the space of the theater with the application and intermingling of sound and silence.

People don't talk continually. They take time to think, to respond, to sip coffee or stare at the other person in anger, disbelief, confusion, or astonishment. Too often actors rush from one line to another, and most playwrights fail to note in the text opportunities for short or long periods of silence. The director constructs the timing and rhythm of lines, scenes, and acts. Actors should study the text themselves to use appropriate breaks and silences and understand the meaning of particular sounds in the play.

When I directed *Crimes of the Heart*, a play revolving around three sisters in the Deep South, I insisted that we have a squeaky screen door. My experience growing up in the South recalled a specific feeling and recollection of place whenever I heard that screen door open and slam shut. I wanted the actresses to associate similar memories with the South, with summer breezes, with a house open to outside noises, as they portrayed those women.

Through an awareness of these related elements the actor is better equipped to recall events of similar consequence and reproduce them on the stage. The actor now has a space in which to perform, a space to fill with rhythms, sounds, and dramatic silences.

Movement: The actor embodies the character through movement. Movement carries inner impressions to the outer world, and it is our most unique and personal manifestation. Researchers in the areas of body language and nonverbal behavior have long associated certain styles of movement with personality types. Someone who walks with head or forehead forward is said to be cerebral, intellectual, an egghead, someone with his or her thoughts in the clouds. Those who walk with chest out appear to be overly confident, boastful, egotistical, even arrogant. When hips or pelvis lead the body, the person is overtly sexual, sensual, usually feminine, and sometimes blatantly on the prowl. Emotions, and psychological attitudes and concepts constitute inner movements. These inner movements, in turn, change and affect the outer movements of those more commonly referred to as body movements or bodily actions.

Many of Baker's exercises focused on aspects of movements. At times he asked students to walk through the space as the character. How does the character enter the space? What pattern of movement is expressed? The actor was reminded that many factors can affect movement: style of costume, style of production, customs or manners of the day in which the play was set, size of the stage space, physical attributes of the character, contrasting or complimenting physical attributes of the actor, and the emotional state of the character.[4]

Prior to my DTC training I had some concept of the importance of movement, space, and rhythm. Baker made his greatest impact on me with his understanding of line and direction, silhouette, and texture and color. These lesser elements (my words) were taken from the visual arts vocabulary, and I thought had little meaning to me.

Line: Line is the intangible path cut in space between the beginning and end of a movement. Direction is the course that line pursues. These elements form a skeletal foundation for an actor's blocking—pattern of movement on stage and psychophysical extension of character. In acting classes Baker asked us to walk the pattern of our character across the space. "Trace your footsteps," he encouraged, mindful of the straight path, the meandering shuffle,

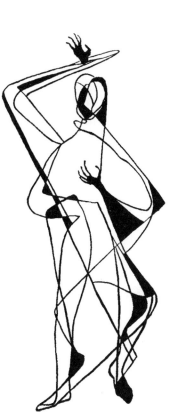

by Virgil Beavers

169

and the strident pace. These insights into character helped those student actors who were more comfortable with body interpretations of their characters than psychological ones. In addition to walking the path of our characters, we were asked to do abstract line drawings for each character. Some drawings were of movement patterns on the floor. Others were of movement patterns of gestures, posture, or body stance. These drawings provided an objective picture whereby actors could study and analyze their characters overall movements.

Silhouette: Silhouette is an ingredient of line. As line pursues a direction in space it forms outlines of shapes that compose silhouette. This silhouette points out emotional qualities; certain postures may represent suppressed rage; height may be a sign of dominance; physical peculiarities may signify deeper emotional conflicts. Baker's explanation of silhouette recalled my undergraduate reading of Michael Chekhov's *To the Actor*. Chekhov explained *psychological gesture* this way: "To assume a PG [psychological gesture] means, then, to prepare the entire part in its essence, after which it will become an easy task to work out all the details in actual rehearsals on the stage. . . . It is the shortest, easiest and the most artistic way of transforming a literary creation into a theatrical piece of art" (Chekov 1953, 75).

Texture: Texture may refer to a visually perceived tactile stimulus or texture (and color, for they seldom exist singularly) may be expressed emotionally. Humans not only see color and texture; we experience them—green envy, red anger, and blue mood. Vocal traits can be gruff, sensuous, gravelly, smooth, or satiny. Likewise, physical patterns may be sluggish, hypertensive, elongated, catlike, or strident.

The Latent Heterosexual
Burgess Meredith, Chris Richard, Zero
Mostel, Randy Moore, Jules Munshin

Once we had a visiting professional from the Broadway stage speak to our acting class. She admitted that there were those in professional circles, on and Off Broadway, who were familiar with Baker's theories, or thought they were, who sometimes referred to acting through the elements as *voodoo acting*. She confessed that she thought so, too . . . until she tried it. To her surprise she discovered that this approach provided an understanding of theater, of all the arts, that were connected by a common vocabulary and common foundation.

In our graduate theater history classes at the DTC, Professor Anne Bromberg referred often to the writings of mythologist and teacher Joseph Campbell. *The Hero with a Thousand Faces* (1994) was required reading. One of Campbell's favorite myths, one of the Grail romances, has particular meaning to me and is reminiscent of Paul Baker and his gift to us. Gawain, the young hero, begins his journey as many of us did at the DTC . . . afraid, unsure, but committed to the quest.

The adventure, in this case, is that the Grail appears, carried by angelic messengers and covered with a veil, and it hovers above the company. Everyone sits there in rapture, and then Gawain . . . stands up and says, "I propose a quest. I propose that we now should go in quest of that Grail, each to behold it unveiled. . . . of that grail, each to behold it unveiled."

They agreed that all would go on the quest . . . but they thought it would be a disgrace to go forth in a group, so each entered the forest "at a point that he, himself, had chosen, where it was darkest and there was no path."

If there is a path, it is someone else's path, and you are not on the adventure . . . This is a wonderful story: that which we intend, that which is the journey, that which is the goal, is the fulfillment of something that never was on earth before—namely, your own potentiality. Every thumbprint is different from every other. Every cell and structure in your body is different from that of anyone who has ever been on earth before, so you have to work it out yourself, taking your clues from here and there (211–212).

Campbell's mythic story illustrates Baker's message—find your own way. My journey took me on a path of discovery that ultimately led to my own version of the Baker theory, *The Actor Alone: Exercises for Creative Growth*. I could not have developed these exercises and taught theater at the university level for more than twenty-five years without the support of Baker and the DTC faculty. Sally Netzel provided the framework for these exercises in her graduate acting class.

She suggested that actors often find themselves working without needed assistance from directors. There may be a lack of rehearsal time; not all directors are skilled or experienced; fellow actors and directors may be incompatible; actors with few lines seldom get help with character development. As a solution to these problems and as a pathway for individualized work, Netzel, Juana Laban, Baker, and others assisted me in developing the ten-line exercise, a series of six exercises designed to promote the creative growth of the actor during a work in progress. The first five studies or exercises culminate in a final study called the ten-line study. This final step is completed after the actor has fleshed out all the necessary experiences. The exercises include word study, sound study, visual study, movement study, the choice exercise, and, finally, the ten-line exercise.

Word study is an inventory of impressions, associations, and ideas that the actor has noted upon the initial reading of the play—likes and dislikes of the character, physical or vocal traits, and background information. The word list should be updated throughout rehearsal; it helps actors explore facets of the life of the character that are not in the script. Word study grew from Baker's suggestion of writing about the color, the texture, the line or mass of an object in an effort to explore fully the rhythm and spatial character of the object.

172

Sound study was a soundtrack of the character performed live or with the use of a tape recorder. Rather than dialogue, sounds and intonations were used that evoked emotional and psychological responses. Environmental sounds, breathing, vocalizations, rhythmic sounds, and a minimum of musical sounds made up many of the students' sound studies. The purpose of the sound study was to expand the actor's knowledge of the character's audible traits and rhythms and, more importantly, to expand sound in both abstract and real sense of communication. The actors often discovered personal reactions to specific sounds, and those reactions were applied to the character. The sound study was linked to the Stanislavski *emotion memory* and *sense memory* exercises.

Visual study was productive for those actors who were more visually oriented than verbally. It allowed the actor to express character through painting, collage, a three-dimensional piece, a textural composition, a nature object, or any other method desired. The effectiveness of the visual study, like the sound study, relied in part on the reactions from classmates, teachers, or directors. Baker often reminded us, "What are you communicating? What is the quality of the work in progress? How is the actor connected to the character in action or word? What personal associations do you (the class) have to the work in progress?" The class or cast examined the visual studies, and their objective reactions were noted. The actor working alone on the visual study explored the character through color, texture, design, motif, shape until it served as iconography for the character.

Movement study afforded the actor an important medium through which to explore and express the character. Facial expressions, mannerisms, body movements (sitting, walking,

People have to see you as a method, one that works for the spirit and growth of a human being outside of the circle of artists in the theater.

You need to become not a guru, but an artist that can change the world through Integration of Abilities. A new way to think and enlarge one's being with what is around him in his search for balance and productivity.

Sara Hess Roney

gesturing, handling objects) and overall movement patterns were investigated to connect outer movements to the inner motivation. The movement study was often composed of a series of pantomimic moments or scenes from the play. Other actors chose to express their characters through abstract movements. Students were advised to refrain from a choreographed or "danced" presentation. Often students discovered those issues of body strength, flexibility, energy, or stage movement (i.e., stage combat, period dance, etc.) that needed to be addressed. Through the use of this exercise actors learned that movement was the most expressive element of the character and that an in-depth study of the inner and outer movement patterns led to greater credibility in the actor's portrayal.

One way of conducting movement study was to approach it through the Laban effort theory. Rudolf Laban classified all human movement into categories called *efforts*. He explained in his numerous books on the subject that when movement was executed, energy was expended. This expended energy emphasized four motion factors: flow, weight, time, and space. The inner or psychological motivation that preceded movement was significant to the actor, and the effort classification of movement provided him with a viable description of psychological and physical movement. The efforts were outlined as punch, slash, dab, flick, press, wring, glide, and float. Punch was straight in direction or flow and heavy in weight. Slash was curved and heavy, fast in flow. Dab was straight, light and fast; flick was curved, light and fast. Press, wring, glide, and float were all slow in time, yet they differed in space and weight. Press was straight and heavy; wring was curved and heavy; glide was straight and light; and float was curved and light. The efforts provided the actors with a working vocabulary through which they could define clearly the essence of an intended attitude or movement.

Choice study was used to explore any aspect of the character that the actor felt needed additional investigation. Any of the preceding studies could be repeated for more in-depth work with the exception of the word study because word study was ongoing. The choice exercise was especially valuable for historical characters, Shakespearean characters, or characters who had specific physical or vocal adaptations. Period dance, stage combat, physical challenges, and handicaps were explored whenever appropriate. Sometimes it was necessary for an actor to research the historical time frame of a play, the style of theatrical production (Theater of the

Absurd, Expressionism, or Theater of Cruelty), or the life of the playwright. This study allowed adequate time for the actor to explore any aspect of the character, play, historical context, or ideology affecting the play.

Each study was built upon the preceding one until the final ten-line study. This exercise was a synthesis of all character exploration done until that time. The actors selected approximately ten lines from the play that they believed displayed a variety of emotional levels and facets of the character and demonstrated the progression of the character during the course of the play. The lines, in most cases, were in chronological order as they appeared in the play. The ten-line study was, in effect, the performance of the character through the entire play as expressed through ten lines from the play. The transitions from one line to the next usually involved abstract movements, sounds, rhythmic phrases performed vocally or physically, pantomime, or Laban effort explorations. The ten-line exercise pulled the other studies into a coherent composition that had dramatic meaning to the actor.

In her acting classes Netzel stressed that the actor must learn that the creation of a character is an ongoing process. Knowing one's lines and stage blocking are not enough. Yet many actors have no way of knowing how or where to go on from there. Baker gave us that knowledge. In a classroom lecture, Netzel stated, "movement does not stop when vocal delivery is begun and vice versa. The delivery of the line is part of the character you have spent so much time developing, not an isolated or special technical thing to be tacked on. This is the central point of all the earlier exercises—the unification of voice, body, intelligence and imagination."

Stage Movement Class, Dallas Theater Center

Michael Chekhov stated in his book, *To the Actor*, "If in the beginning or from the very first entrance you already have a vision of yourself playing (or rehearsing) your last scene—and, conversely remembering the first scene as you play (or rehearse) the very last scene—you will better be able to see your whole part in every detail, as though you were viewing it in perspective from some elevation. The ability to evaluate the details within the part as a well-integrated whole will further enable you to play each of these details as little entities which blend harmoniously onto the all embracing entirety" (17).

Each human being possesses unique creative gifts. Wherever artists are given the freedom to explore their hidden talents wondrous things can happen. I am not sure that I was aware of these things while I was a student in Dallas more than a quarter century ago. It was as I began to teach that I realized the boundless gifts bestowed upon me.

Paul Baker usually went against the traditional modes of making theater happen. He gave us the courage to do the same. Not only have our theaters been transformed but our lives also. His work has changed us, our ways of working, our ways of seeing one another, our ways of perceiving the world. Mostly, he taught us that *we* were important, that *our* ideas were valuable, and that we could change the world. For that we are grateful. ∎

End Notes

[1] Paul Baker's theater is the world; he continues to direct it well. I'm thankful to be a continuing part of his cast. *Marvin Smith*

[2] Throughout his career [Baker] sought to influence parents, schools, and churches to cultivate and encourage the love of beauty and the pursuit of truth. Baker has been a prophet in the wilderness challenging our society not to fear openness in thought and expression . . . children . . . were taught to think and to give form to their thoughts through music, dance, painting, sculpture, and drama. They were taught that play was part of their work and that their expressions, whatever form they took, did not have to conform to some preconceived adult end.
The Reverend Raymond Bailey

3 Although I stayed only two semesters in the theater it was a life-changing experience for me. I have gone on, as a musician–record producer, to contribute original music and score to *Paris, Texas*; *The Border*; *Streets of Fire*; *Long Riders*; and *Alamo Bay*, among other Hollywood films. I have produced or recorded with musical artists from Arlo Guthrie and the Rolling Stones to Aretha Franklin and Carmen McRae. I have passed on what I learned from Prof to two generations of artists. *Jim Dickinson*

4 I was working on a Restoration comedy role one day when Baker jumped onto the stage, took me by the front of the shirt, and pulled me up so that my toes touched the floor first. That is how I learned to walk like a Restoration "dandy." *Henry Carter*

Othello, Baylor University

From the Baylor *Othello* to the Dallas Theater Center

Mary Bozeman

"Paul Baker is a nut. He's a good nut, but he's a nut." Thus spake not Zarathustra but Joseph Gifford, my first director in the theater. This remark was made to me after he viewed Baker's tradition-breaking presentation of *Othello*, in which I played one of the facets of Desdemona. The year before, Gifford had seen Baker's production of *Cocklebur* by Ramsey Yelvington and had come away from it so impressed by Baker's staging that when it came time for me to leave the Gifford theatrical nest, he saw to it that I enrolled at Baylor University to study with Paul Baker for a master's degree in theater.

I received my early training at Centenary College in Louisiana from Mr. Gifford, a wonderful gentleman of the old school and a marvelous, dynamic director, whose philosophy embraced the advice attributed to the late Noel Coward: "Know your lines, speak up, and don't bump into the furniture." (Advice at which I by no means scoff.)

No wonder, then, that Baker's *Othello* left him less than enthusiastic. He had encountered the creative genius of Paul Baker, and it left him more than a bit shaken. *Othello* broke new ground in the theater on a worldwide scale. Baker's concept and the production that evolved were both startling and revelatory, the latter because the complexities of Othello, Iago, and Desdemona were revealed in razor-sharp relief. Baker broke the roles of Othello, Iago, and Desdemona into the three major facets of each, with a separate actor/actress playing each facet, all onstage simultaneously.

The other two Desdemonas and I first worked together to determine the major facets of her character. Next we worked through the entire text of the play, weighing carefully which actress should speak which lines and which lines should be spoken together for emphasis. Because we were all three components of the total Desdemona, we knew that we needed to find a way to feel that completeness. We accomplished this through moving together, arms linked, thoughts attuned. We worked in this method, moving from one stage to another, thinking as our particular facet of Desdemona. We came to move as component parts of one unit. Instead of individuals with divergent directions, we moved as one. If one of the trio directed her thoughts and body in a direction, the other two members anticipated the movement and moved with her. This entire process involved concentration, rhythm, control of body tensions, and a feeling for space.

At Baylor, I was plunged into classes in theater history, scene design, playwriting, directing, and repertory acting. In the latter course, we explored the styles of various periods in theater history: medieval, Greek, Roman comedy, Restoration, and Shakespearean. The only area in which I had thought I had some expertise was acting. Suddenly I was expected to have something to contribute in all of these other areas. At the ripe old age of twenty, I found myself stirred up, questioning, and confused . . . but more alive mentally and creatively than ever before. That year at Baylor studying and working in Baker's master's program was the most influential year in my life as a theater artist. It turned all of my ideas inside out and left me in a state of complete dismay, barraged with self-questioning: Do I have a feeling for time and space? How do I give texture and depth to a performance? Where are my body tension points? And on and on ad infinitum. Truly terra incognita.

For the first (and only) time in my life, my knees knocked together as I stood before my fellow classmates to perform a scene from *Medea*. How could this be happening to me? I had played a half dozen or more major roles at Centenary—Juliet, Elizabeth I, Anastasia, etc.—and had always felt secure, scarcely nervous at all. Now it seemed I was undone, my comfortable old stage ideas shattered, my security blanket torn to shreds by the ideas of Paul Baker. Through work with him, I was asked to step outside the comfortable niche of "actress taking direction" and into the role of "thinking person respecting one's own ideas and translating them into creative work." Quite a leap that was . . . but what a rewarding one.

Whereas my previous work in theater had involved taking down blocking and then acting a role without much introspec-

180

tion, Baker's guidance led me to a richer, fuller way of working. As an example, while exploring the role of Mrs. Alving in Ibsen's *Ghosts* under the direction of Mary Sue Jones, Baker's assistant, I wrote the following stream-of-consciousness piece for an exercise she assigned.

Broken pots with rich brown dirt strewn in piles and rivulets. Juice of the broken stems and leaves lying in a shaft of weak, white, pale, milky sunlight. Why does Alving's foot rest at such a grotesque angle? Saliva hanging in suspension along the side of his face. Hanging attenuated between his jaw and the cool tile floor where it ends in a smooth flat pool. His face is that of a child . . . a little boy . . . all the wrinkles there, but smoothed over by the release, the release . . . the flat nothingness of his stupor. Where is he this moment? I see his body stretched out in the clothes. I hear his steady breathing. But where is he? Who is he? My mind clicking . . . organizing . . . setting aside. Am I?

There's the patter. Sharp rain drops. I want the fire again, tea sizzling over the fire, clean sparkling hard white cold china. Everything beautiful and easy and safe. And the room. My sitting room. Velvets. Soft and enclosing. But I can't ever go to that room and stay there. As soon as I lean back in the chair and sigh and close my eyes . . . it is cold and damp and I shiver. Slate gray sunlight through cold glass. Brown dirt. Grainy. Dirt smell. Carrots and onions and radishes and green fresh plants. Broken, smashed, bone . . . lying flat.

Under the table I see two bright inquiring eyes . . . soft and wet . . . startled, darting, not afraid. Not yet. Hold his little body close to mine. Feel his head on my breast. Comforted. Safe. Warmth and ease. Melting all of the jerks and wires when my baby my baby my baby, my Osvald, part of myself, is next to me. I feel almost whole. Not singing. But whole. Not wavering anymore. Not darting.

Push and set aside. Stand him firm and tall. Put a railing in his hands. Fill his eyes with ideas. Brush up the fears into a bundle and put them in a drawer in your room. Slip the bar across the door. Find a hard core and a rock slab and stand on it. For him.

During our rehearsals and performances of *Othello*, Charles Laughton coached the members of the cast individually. Etched in my memory is the power of his presence as I stood on the stage beside him and looked into his eyes. So strong was his spirit, his creative force, that had he asked me to leave with him and become his servant, I would have done so. (I was twenty years old, remember.)

I can still recall how nervous I was about meeting him, about even attending the rehearsal at which he was to work with us. Dressed comfortably in a brown gathered skirt, blue work shirt, and ballet slippers, I joined the rest of the cast at the theater. One by one he worked with us. Once onstage with him, all of my fear departed. He urged me to take more time with my speeches, time to "be a woman" whenever I spoke to or of Othello. To "turn on my femininity." After our *Othello* performance, we were all milling about backstage in the scenery shop when I heard Laughton calling, "Mary, Mary." I assumed he was seeking Mary Sue Jones. But no, it was Mary Bozeman. He came up to me, looked me in the eye, and said, "Very nice. . . ." My all-time favorite review.

Paul Baker and Charles Laughton

In thinking back on Mr. Gifford's evaluation of Paul Baker as "a nut," I decided to go to *Webster's Dictionary*, whose first definition of nut is "a hard-shelled dry . . . seed." I laughed aloud at the truth unwittingly spoken by Mr. Gifford. If ever there was a human being who has been an artistic seed, it is Paul Baker. Through those whose lives he has touched, his ideas and his influence continue, year after year.

Practical lessons learned from Baker became part of my theatrical armamentarium. My husband, William Osborn, optioned an interview that Jeannine Hager had done with her Aunt Sim (Mrs. Elma Beale Beck of Yoakum, Texas) about her experiences as an undertaker. He created a one-person show, *Sim: One Night with a Lady Undertaker ffrom Texas*, based, in part, on her wonderful stories that ran the gamut from humorous to tragic but were all true. It has garnered excellent reviews everywhere it has been played, from New York to New Orleans. Near the end of a performance of *Sim* in the French Quarter Theater in New Orleans, the lights suddenly went out. I did not skip a beat but continued in the darkness, guided by a long-ago lesson to keep on going no matter what happens. Soon, the beam of a flashlight hit the stage, and I completed the performance in its soft glow.

Only later, as the audience filed out of the darkened theater, did I become aware of what had instinctively carried me through. I remembered that decades before during a performance of *Othello* the same lighting problem occurred. There we were, clad in black tights and leotards, net skirts, and ballet slippers atop a ten-foot-high platform, no railings, no safety net . . . except . . . in only moments, there was the sight of Baker, looking up at us, a flashlight in each hand that cast beams at just the correct angle to allow us to proceed unafraid with the scene until the stage lighting was restored.

Hodges Gardens is a four-thousand-acre forest preserve in the Piney Woods of North Louisiana. I now stage a Shakespeare play there annually in a 125-by-250-foot rose garden, with audience members seated on folding chairs among the roses that surround three thirty-foot square grass plots upon which the plays unfold. Open to the sky above with the waters of a nearby lake glistening in the background, and with some ten entranceways onto wide concrete walks that intersperse the roses and the grass plots, it is, for me, the ideal space for Shakespeare. Had I not been exposed to the thinking of Baker, I never would have envisioned it as such.

One day, five years after my studies at Baylor, I sat at the Alley Theater in Houston waiting to audition for Eugenia Leontovich, who was casting a production of *The Cave Dwellers* that she was to direct for Nina Vance. The role I was to read for was only two or three lines long, yet I waited eight hours, so hungry was I to act again. Later that same night, I received a call from Baker inviting me to join the Repertory Company of the Dallas Theater Center. He needed an actress and somehow remembered me. There followed four richly rewarding years of working as a resident artist in true revolving repertory.

Designed by Frank Lloyd Wright in collaboration with Baker, the Dallas Theater Center nestles into the rocky terrain of Turtle Creek Boulevard in Dallas. Its color and curves combine to create a sense of belonging where it is. The structure seems to emanate from the earth rather than being imposed upon it. Beige and gold, warm and open, these are the images that spring to mind when I recall first entering its space.

The circular stage itself reached out to the audience rather than separating what occurred on it from the spectators. The connection was immediate and alive. Its huge round revolving floor provided a fluidity not achievable with the usual static platform stage. It seemed to fit all of Baker's requirements for a clean

Kalita Humphreys Theater, Dallas Theater Center

184

uncluttered space in which to create. But the building was not what made the Dallas Theater Center pulsate with the creative life force. That can only be attributed to Baker. A ruggedly handsome man, usually clad in comfortable clothes, including two shirts, one of them a blue work shirt worn unbuttoned and open as a sort of make-do jacket, he was everywhere, orchestrating his company of directors, designers, actors, writers, students. What a juggling act that must have been! I used to wonder why he addressed most females (including me) as "Girl." In retrospect I realize he meant no disrespect; he had so many people to deal with he could not always remember all of our names. He seemed always to be traveling at high speed, his consultations and evaluations rapid but to the point. His rhythm of existence was accelerated, no longer the contemplative Baylor rhythm of academe. It was as if the Dallas Theater Center was a giant bubbling cauldron of creativity and Baker was the wizard who put in all of the ingredients and then continued to stir the pot. Cultural chef extraordinaire.

Work in a true revolving repertory company is like nothing else in the world: pure paradise for the actor. Rehearse and open a show; play it for several weeks. Move on to another play. Rehearse and perform the second play for several weeks. Then return to the first play. Then move on to a third and continue the revolving schedule through the entire season, with spans of time occurring between performing a particular role. Time in which to reflect, contemplate, refine, and deepen one's performance and then return to it: Clara the maid in *Hayfever* this week; Claire Zachanassin in *The Visit* the next; Mother Fletcher in *Sister* a month later; then back to *Hayfever*. Never the worry of becoming bored or growing stale. Truly the actor's "heaven on earth." This is what Baker provided to his company.

There were dissatisfactions, complaints, thwarted dreams. But as I look back on those years, I realize how minor all problems were. When I arrived at the DTC to play Mother Gibbs in *Our Town*, there was trouble in the ranks with a few of the actors in the company who had come only to act, not to paint scenery or hem costumes. Eventually, they left.

Occasionally, we actors were invited to elegant, sumptuous parties given by wealthy patrons of the DTC. The food was always superb, and the champagne flowed. The setting might be poolside at the home of the president of a world-class airline or beneath huge tents on the lawn of a local oil baron's mansion. These events were truly lagniappe, as we say in Louisiana.

185

As a resident artist, in addition to acting and pulling duty on various crews (costumes, sets) from time to time, I also worked in the box office on certain days, taught acting classes, and eventually directed one major production, Federico Garcia Lorca's *Blood Wedding*. Part of my casting task was to use various actors from other countries, if possible. While this seemed to be a negative at first, this policy turned out to be a major plus. Actresses from South Korea, Turkey, and Peru brought an exotic quality to the finished product, adding to the poetic essence of the piece.

Roles actors love remain a part of them through the years. Two stand out in my memory: Juliet at Centenary, when I was eighteen, and Katherine of Aragon at the DTC. In preparing for the role of Katherine, I discovered a biography of her from which I learned of her love for Henry. He was a magnificent physical specimen in his early years (not the corpulent degenerate of the Charles Laughton film). The biography revealed that the words of the speech in which she pleads with Henry "Sir, I desire you do me right and justice. . . ." were actually spoken by the real Katherine herself before the court of the real Henry VIII. The Katherine I played was not from Shakespeare's *Henry VIII* but in a contemporary play about Cardinal Wolsey, *Naked to Mine Enemies*, by Charles Ferguson. Mr. Ferguson also used that same wonderful speech as the lynchpin of Katherine's character in his play.

As an actress, it was exciting to originate a leading role in a fledgling playwright's first play. During my tenure at the Dallas Theater Center, it was stimulating to work with guest artists Baker brought to the center: Angna Enters, Burl Ives, Eva Le Gallienne, Fernando Colina, and others.

Baker brought artists from around the globe—Australia, Chile, England, Korea, Mexico, Peru—into our midst, enriching all of us. One could say he created a factory of theater. But instead of Andy Warhol's factory, peopled with druggies and weirdos, Baker's was a workplace of dreams, ideas, creativity, and personal growth . . . an esprit de corps flourished, without the tense atmosphere of commercial theater. Imagine the day the company performed for the visiting Eva Le Gallienne: in the afternoon, *The Taming of the Shrew* (designed by Chile's brilliant Fernando Colina and directed by Ivan Rider); and that night, Baker's innovative *Hamlet*. What a twenty-four hours!

Memorable advice from Paul Baker: "You must realize that the world is a lonely place. Somehow each of you, in your own way, must find within yourself the strength and determination

186

to stand alone, even when no one believes in your talent or cares about your development as an artist." Those words from him, spoken at a company meeting at the Dallas Theater Center, carry more and more weight with me as the years roll by. "Never work with an end result in mind." This seemingly innocuous statement is perhaps the most powerful of Baker's tenets to remain with me. It opened and keeps open the door to searching, experimenting, and growing in my work.

Begging the pardon of the Bard for a happy change in verb tense: "He is a man, take him for all in all, I shall not look upon his like again." ■

Of Time and the River, Baylor University

The Tempest, Dallas Theater Center

"Those Old Boats Don't Float"

Frances Swinny

Prior to 1944, speech courses at Trinity University, depending on their content, were offered in an array of departments. In 1883, speech was taught in the department of elocution and oratory. In 1899, elocution and oratory moved to the department of fine arts. Later, oratory was taught in the department of Greek. Since 1944, speech and drama shared physical facilities and mutual academic respect.

Because oral expression and delivery were prized and considered mandatory for ministerial students at the Presbyterian school, the faculty and administration strongly supported membership in two highly competitive literary societies. Members met weekly, in a room with excellent library resources, to debate questions and deliver orations. The best oration was often included in commencement programs.

In 1908, after Trinity moved from Tehuacana to Waxahachie, two men's debating clubs were established. Then the Texas Inter-Collegiate Debating League was organized, with three member schools—Trinity, Southwestern, and Texas Christian University. Trinity students competed for positions on the debate squad. In 1930 Waxahachie resident O. J. Chapman offered twenty-five dollars to the top two Trinity contenders. The winners were I.T. Jones, first place, and Paul Baker, second place. No one predicted at that time that Paul Baker would eventually become chair of the Trinity University speech and drama department.

When Trinity University left Waxahachie and moved to San Antonio in 1942, completing a speech major required eight courses in speech and four in theater. Two years later the department was named department of speech and drama, at last correctly reflecting course offerings. World War II veterans, taking advantage of the GI Bill, became the "new Trinity students," along with many others whose education had been put on hold.

The physical facilities were grossly inadequate, faculty were asked to teach heavy overloads, and the department budget was slim. Speech and drama students built and painted flats outdoors, praying it would not rain. They fashioned stage lights from giant juice cans and designed and made their own costumes. They rehearsed in a large hot classroom—no air-conditioning in the building. The university rented San Pedro Playhouse, home of the San Antonio Little Theater, for dress rehearsal and opening night—the only night of performance. Cast and crew had to journey across town.

In 1952, Trinity made her final move to Trinity Hill, a northeast location high above San Antonio. Only three buildings were complete. Space for speech classes was adequate, but there were no facilities for play rehearsals and performances. Students built and painted sets on a small cement slab on lower campus, beside the makeshift university physical plant.

On the new campus the speech faculty numbered two, plus a very competent technical director who taught a few sections of public speaking. With Dr. James Laurie, a dynamic president, at the helm, Trinity dedicated itself to a well-planned, aggressive building program, and soon the department of speech and drama moved from the administration building to the new music building. Now audiences attended productions on a small music concert stage or in a large adjoining art gallery where shows were played in the round.

The next building completed in the Ruth Taylor Fine Arts Complex was the art building. The speech and drama department moved to offices in that space, but there seemed to be little hope for a theater. Plays presented during summer months used the cement slab on lower campus for productions.

While undergraduate speech courses had little need for more classroom space, there was not enough faculty when the department added graduate speech courses in order to meet student demand. With skillful scheduling and teaching overloads, along with reading and conference courses, the department remained on course. The faculty numbered two in drama and one full-time and one part-time instructor in speech. Despite the struggle, students received personal attention and training that grounded them in speech and theater basics and strengthened their resolve to work through obstacles.

At this juncture Paul Baker joined the Trinity University faculty as chair of the speech and drama department, bringing with him five drama faculty. (Other faculty members commuted from Dallas each week.) In 1963, Paul Baker's *Long Day's Journey into Night* was a short day's journey into Trinity and also into my life. President Laurie, a man of vision and action, not only opened our halls to Baker but also to his fearless faculty who would not only bring experimental theater to Trinity but perhaps even some of those daring ideas. That was exciting; it was stimulating and it was awesome.[1]

What greeted Paul Baker and his Baker's half dozen when they came to Trinity? Not much.

A relatively new campus only half as large as it is today, with no theater building or facilities. (I often said that at Trinity we thought a box office was an office shaped like a box.) There was no department secretary, five drama majors, and two tenured professors, one of whom was close to retirement and soon left. I remained as the only link between what had been and what was to come. And it wasn't long in coming.

Twenty-four new courses were added to the curriculum. Those courses to be taken by drama majors and those to be taken by the speech interest major were listed under separate headings in the university bulletin.

As if taken for granted, a theater emerged. Baker laid claim to the third floor of the science building. He made it our theater. I emphasize "our" because he demanded that the space must be ours exclusively. And it was. The Attic Theater became an intimate temporary space for many memorable productions. Notable among many were *The Crucible* and *The Visit*.

It was not long before Baker's reputation and tenacity brought about groundbreaking for a new theater, the final building in the Ruth Taylor Fine Arts Complex and the final and most welcomed move for the Trinity University speech and drama department. The Ruth Taylor Theater—fifty-five thousand square feet of space for offices, classrooms, scenery and costume shops, a real box office, and three stages—represented the result of Paul Baker's courage, perseverance, and vision.

One might expect that the speech program would be curtailed by the launching of such a strong theater program. The opposite prevailed. Baker visualized the synergism between speech and drama. He encouraged continuation of current speech offerings and strongly supported activities that were in place, such as the Trinity University High School Speech Festival. Initiated some fifteen years earlier as a recruiting tool, it gave the department statewide visibility. The festival grew to be the largest in the state and attracted financial support from the Sears Roebuck Foundation. The festival was discontinued after twenty-five years when it became unmanageable because of limited physical facilities and overburdened faculty.

Baker invited me to sit in on the Integration of Abilities class. I was singularly struck with his concern that I, a non-Baker product, understand that the IA class was the common bond and philosophy beneath the entire curriculum. I registered for the class along with some of my own students. I clapped out my rhythm study of a person I knew and even today share with others the amazing accuracy of Baker's interpretation of it. Although my discipline was speech communication, not drama, the course was the foundation for my understanding the process of discovery and the discovery of a process.

My exposure to the process as well as the arts vocabulary facilitated communication with students. This was especially true when invited by directors to critique productions prior to opening night and to coach actors needing additional speech practice. Jesse Ramos attributed his continuation in college and in the arts to the individual encouragement and speech instruction he received.[2] James Hill regularly asks me about his speech performance after a local sports broadcast. Willie De Los Santo, currently artistic director of the Castle High School Performing Arts Center in Hawaii, persistently and tenaciously worked for speech improvement.

With national recognition of the unique theater space in the Ruth Taylor Theater came significant growth in the department and a pressing need for additional faculty. The budget did not allow for an additional full-time speech instructor, but the need was temporarily addressed by several drama instructors who taught a basic course in speech.

Baker disciples of all ages, from all strata of society, lined up to hitch a ride on the Baker bus that was headed for self-discovery or rediscovery of their creative potential. The Women's Fine Arts Committee, composed of influential women in the arts, volunteered many hours of work and provided funding for arts programs. Other townspeople enrolled in a noncredit evening drama workshop directed by a well-qualified instructor who taught a basic speech course and several courses in creative writing and theater production. Many nontraditional students repeatedly enrolled in this workshop and appeared in a variety of theatrical productions that emerged from the class.

In 1971, Baker invited Arthur Lessac, distinguished author and widely acclaimed teacher of voice and diction, to Trinity to conduct an intensive seven-week graduate voice and diction workshop. Graduate students from across the country applied to study with Lessac and his staff of five. Baker requested that I attend the workshop and achieve certification in the Lessac method of voice and diction, after which I resumed teaching undergraduate courses the following fall.

Because the Lessac method employed a heuristic philosophy, it was compatible with the IA course—a process of discovery. It demanded a total awareness of self and body. Arthur Lessac insisted that voice was the study of one's self, a continuous process to be applied in each acting role and in every speaking situation. Students embracing the Lessac system discovered this meaningful gestalt: "Nothing stands alone, isolated or encapsulated. Everything is a part of something and nothing functions well until it functions in balanced relationship with every other part."[3]

I worked with many drama students for whom voice and diction were required and with scores of students across the campus who elected to take the voice and diction course . Even today frequently a former student, whose face is no longer familiar, greets me at a chance meeting with "Those old boats don't float"—a familiar call focus phrase (Lessac's term for a familiar mantra) practiced by all students.

In 1974, the Trinity administration authorized an additional full-time instructor. This was a significant step, enabling the expansion of speech offerings and the resumption of a forensics program. The speech curriculum added courses in rhetoric, history and criticism of public address, and group process and leadership, satisfying a long neglected area of speech discipline. The department also hosted speech and drama workshops for high school students and their teachers. These workshops were practical educational events, and attendance grew from two hundred to more than eight hundred in a few years.

Speech and drama majors increased from five to more than one hundred. Course offerings mushroomed from twenty-four to sixty. Rather than three play productions a year in rented or borrowed space, there were six major productions and a variety of others, including an active children's theater, numerous student-written, -acted and -directed one-act plays, several touring shows from the Dallas Theater Center, and a Happening event that utilized every acting space in the theater, including Theater One, Attic Two, the Cafe Theater, the outdoor patio, the foyer, and the carpentry shop. Every space but the roof atop the building.

With the Dallas Theater Center shows came professional actors and actresses who lectured to undergraduate students and brought new perspectives and insights to all of our students. All the while, Baker commuted from San Antonio to Dallas each week. For a lesser man, one theater was enough, perhaps too much. For Baker, two was company, and he made sure they were good company.

Although some parts of the nation came to know Trinity University because of its championship tennis team, and we did have one—one year the Davis Cup resided at Trinity—the speech and drama department had truly become the flagship of the university.

The speech program achieved excellence in large part because of the support and collegiality of Baker and the drama faculty. The unique relationship between the two disciplines is rare in higher education, but, at Trinity, faculty recognized the interrelationship of the disciplines and capitalized on it. Speech and drama majors benefited. When Baker retired from Trinity he left a large legacy that continues to enrich the lives of hundreds of former students. ∎

Trojan Women, Trinity University

194

End Notes

[1] I remember very well when it was announced that this whole respected team of Paul Baker and associates was leaving Baylor because their artistic freedom had been curtailed . . . and Dr. Laurie . . . welcoming them saying that we encourage artistic freedom and different voices . . . and then the fact that he got somebody and his whole huge team that were so big league . . . and that they walked out of Baylor over principle . . . and we thought, my god, that Trinity is welcoming these artists that this other big school wouldn't give them the right air to breathe, or whatever. All of that was so exciting. *Joe Armstrong*

[2] I had auditioned for every play .,. . but I was not getting cast. Dr. Swinny pulled me aside and brought my speech impediment to my attention. Through (her) patience, dedication, guidance, and endless Y-buzzing I turned my deficiency around. In less than one year I was cast as the lead . . . I have led countless seminars and am currently director of volunteers for Miracle House, an AIDS/cancer organization. I am the special event producer, which is everything like directing a show. I continue to periodically stage shows Off Off Broadway simply for the joy of it. *Jesse Ramos*

[3] The other day someone with a heavy New Jersey accent asked me about improving [his] diction, and I found myself teaching the Lessac method from what I could remember from Frances Swinny's great voice classes. . . . My last production, a new play called *The Size of the World*, starred Rita Moreno, Frank Whaley, and Louis Zorich and was directed by Austin Pendleton. . . . I still do the occasional voice-over as time permits and serve as an artistic advisor to a group of theater angels in New York. *Charles Rucker*

Teen Theater, Dallas Theater Center

Booker T. Washington Arts High School

Louise Mosley Smith

Early one February morning I was setting up the stage in the Dallas Theater Center for a Teen Theater performance by my Shakespeare class. Paul Baker walked in from upstage left and called, "Girl, I just got a call from the superintendent asking me to be the director of the arts high school. Since you're going to be doing most of the work, you might as well be hired, too."

Thus began a long journey for me—developing a school for the arts that has become one of the most successful in the country. The invitation followed years of involvement with the schools and the community, beginning with working with Kitty Baker at Baylor as she taught theater to the children of Waco and continuing at the DTC.

The Children's Theater was a strong component of the original plan for the DTC. Ruth Byers recruited children for the theater classes in coffees and teas in the homes of the board of directors in the Park Cities while the building was being constructed. Children's classes were held in the midst of the construction site. I became the assistant director of the Teen and Children's Theater in 1960 and developed the curriculum for the teenagers. Through the years as the size and number of classes for children and teenagers increased, the size of the building and the number of theater productions possible limited expansion of the program.

We looked for convenient spaces nearby. Six blocks away was Sam Houston, an elementary school that was not being used because of the population shift in that area of town. Baker and I wrote a proposal to use that school for children's classes in the afternoons and for workshops for teachers. The superintendent of schools did not accept our proposal, but it remained a dream of which the school district was aware.

As the DTC expanded and the graduate program developed, more graduates wanted to remain in Dallas as members of the resident company. Baker's philosophy that every company member should also have a "day" job in the running of the theater meant that more programs and community projects involving productions must be developed, and they were. Among them were the Down Center Stage, the Magic Turtle shows for children on Saturday mornings, New Playmarket to showcase new scripts, mime troupe performances in the public parks, and touring shows first to Trinity University, then throughout Texas, then throughout the United States.

Touring shows into the public schools were a natural outgrowth of this expansion. Every production had preparation classes in the English or social studies classes and was followed by evaluation sessions after the students saw the production. At these sessions we answered questions and correlated the lesson of the play with the course of study. These productions went into every Dallas high school and some middle schools. There were so many that Baker developed another department with Joanie Meister and Cookie MacInroth as the codirectors of the DTC In The Schools project. Additional personnel wrote teacher curriculum guides, workbooks, and handouts to give the students.

When Nolan Estes, an innovator in education, was hired as superintendent in the late sixties, Baker told him of the success of the productions in the schools and asked to expand the program to staff development for the teachers. In the 1968–1969 school year several of the Teen Children's Theater staff developed and taught an ongoing course in creativity for the teachers of the Dallas ISD.

During the sixties the concern in education circles was that schools, with their traditional courses and ways of teaching, were not interesting to teenagers and that they were not providing people who could think in new ways and solve problems creatively. Traditional education did not engage the whole person or relate to life. Students were not given enough responsibility for learning on their own and at their own pace. Teenagers were not interested in learning for learning's sake; they wanted to be able to apply what they learned immediately to their world. Career education was suggested as a way to solve these problems. Funds from the business community and federal vocational programs were available to help Dallas change the focus of the education of its children.

A large tract of land was purchased on the outskirts of Dallas in the northeast section, and Nolan Estes worked with the business community to create a career development center at a state-of-the-art, campus-style school called Skyline. Skyline opened in 1971. Required high school classes were taught for half the day; then students worked on practical projects in their chosen career field. Some students in their junior and senior years worked half a day off-campus in businesses and banks applying their learned skills. The training required one to three years in a group of progressively detailed classes called clusters. The innovative program brought in

198

vocational and career professionals to give hands-on learning in plumbing, air-conditioning, plastics manufacturing, construction, engineering, fashion design, advertising, printing, visual arts, music, theater, dance—a total of forty-four fields.

New ways of teaching and experimental curricula were developed. Learning was measured by successful completion of behavioral objectives as well as traditional tests. Educators from all over the world came to see this successful experiment.

In 1975 Dallas was ordered to desegregate its public schools. Estes and the school board identified this as a problem for the city of Dallas, not just for the schools. He called again on the business community as well as other citizens. They formed a group known as the Alliance. Career-focused high schools or magnet schools were being developed in large cities, and the federal government made money available to establish these schools. The Alliance decided that Dallas should pull eight of the career clusters out of Skyline and develop magnet schools for law, health, business, social services and education, science, talented and gifted (college track), auto mechanics, and arts. Thus began the long-held dream of establishing a school where talented and creative students could work toward their goals of becoming artists while they completed their high-school education.

The Alliance worked closely with the Chamber of Commerce, the pastors of churches who were vitally concerned about the best school opportunities for all children of Dallas, and leaders in each career field targeted for magnet status. Career directors were selected for their excellence in their field, their commitment to educating young people, and their ability to draw populations stipulated by the court order.

The directors were hired by DISD for three years to set the goals and tone of the professional training in each magnet, including the design of the studios, seeking and approving qualified professionals to write and teach the specific curriculum, and making connections with the professionals in their field for eventual internships for the advanced students. Baker was chosen as director of the arts magnet, as one Chamber of Commerce member explained to visiting tourists, because he had the confidence of the northern part of the city, and he could bring in the middle- and upper-middle-class white students from Park Cities and further north.

After Baker and I rejoiced about his selection, we sobered to the thought of "What do we do first?" What was a magnet school? Where would it be located? What arts would be included?

Who would attend? Who would teach? These questions had to be answered during the five or six months before classes were to start in the fall of 1976.

We discovered that there was to be a National Conference of Magnet Schools in Houston and signed up to attend. While we were there we also wanted to visit with Ruth Denney who had been a drama teacher and then started the Arts High School in a former synagogue that she and her staff had renovated into a wonderful performing arts space.

We went to the conference for only one morning session and read the program and could find nothing about the arts. Every magnet school represented was for a different career field, which made us believe that we were wasting our time. We called Ruth Denney and asked her to meet us.

We asked how she got started, what problems she had encountered, and how she had solved those problems. She said one of the things we must insist on was a budget to bring in professional artists to teach workshops or specialty courses. She had not foreseen the need for student connection to professionals in the community and had to find monies to provide it. Professional artists would raise the level of the teaching and also the acceptance of the school in the professional community.

Baker demanded an extra $100,000 budget from the district for part-time professionals. Denney gave suggestions for faculty and pledged to bring her staff to Dallas to meet with our staff to share ideas and encourage each other as the only two arts high schools in the state. We became sister schools and have visited each other several times over the years.

DISD would provide principals to run the everyday business of the schools and make sure that the schools complied with local, state, and national mandates. The heads of each selected department at Skyline and the staff who wanted to start the new schools would go to the magnets.

One of the first meetings Baker and I had was with the teachers of dance, drama, music, and visual arts at Skyline. He wanted to hear their goals and philosophies and learn something of their personalities and methods of teaching. He looked for a commitment to creativity rather than the result-type emphasis on technique for its own sake. I took notes, and we talked after each meeting to share perceptions.

Music and visual arts were the largest departments with the largest faculties. Drama had one full-time teacher, and dance had a teacher for half a day. Several faculty members were concerned that Baker would be partial to theater and would not be able to oversee all the arts. He had to convince the staff that even though his field was theater he would be fair to all the arts and would give each of them space, supplies, recognition, and freedom to grow. Most of all he would listen to their needs and provide for them.

All the magnets were to be clustered around the downtown area for ease of busing the students. We were given two possible sites. An old Dr Pepper warehouse was strongly recommended because of its proximity to Fair Park with the music hall, the art museum, and the Margo Jones Theater. The other possibility was the no-longer-used Booker T. Washington High School that had been the first African American high school in Dallas County. It had been used for an elementary school and then as a meeting place and a storage area for the citywide PTA. Because it was closer to the DTC we visited Booker T. Washington first.

It was love at first sight and smell. As we walked through the halls with the high ceilings, the lovely wooden cabinets and floors, and the courtyard next to the cafeteria, we envisioned a small theater in the former choir room and a drawing classroom in the old homemaking room; we began planning how to turn the auditorium with its balcony into a usable theater with a light booth and dressing rooms. We even planned a commons area in the courtyard. We never visited the warehouse. We felt at home in the much-loved historic building.

Baker and the two principals began interviewing faculty and staff. Baker wanted every teacher to have some artistic background. The arts faculty should have professional experience as well as training in their field. Each should be a practicing artist. Another factor was willingness to spend extra and even unpaid time in teacher training and in working with students before and after school and possibly on weekends. The court and DISD mandated that the faculty and staff be ethnically diverse.

Baker brought the arts department heads to the school, and we decided which cluster would have which rooms and areas. The first cluster heads were Rosanne McLaughlin Cox, dance; Douglas T. Cornell, music; Louise Mosley Smith, theater; Margaret Hull, visual arts; and Alphonso Jordan, academics.

The size of the rooms determined what would be taught there. The arts classes would be clustered toward the back of the building so that their noise and action would not bother the academics. Baker asked the district to hire architect Art Rogers to renovate the spaces in the old building and to design a new extension at the back of the building for a dance studio, music studio and library, and several visual art studios that would have huge windows open to the south and west. Unfortunately we had no control over the hiring of the contractor. Most of the building renovations were completed using inferior products.

Spring was passing, and students had to be recruited. The Skyline teachers were expected to encourage their students to come, and I was sent into the high schools and middle schools the last weeks of April and the first weeks of May with personnel from the other magnets to talk about our schools and encourage students to apply. I also talked up the school in the Teen Theater classes, and many of those students applied.

I spent the summer writing the integration of abilities curriculum for ninth-grade students; it was to be the core arts course. All students would take this class the first year, as it set the philosophy of the school. Summer had hardly begun when Baker asked the faculty to meet at the DTC for a three-day workshop. We got into our grubby clothes, and members of "Learning About Learning" from San Antonio led us in creative exercises based on the vocabulary of the arts. In order to know each other better, we were invited to drop into each other's classes during our planning periods, to take a dance class or throw a pot in ceramics.

Baker talked with us about his philosophy, how it applied in each academic area, and how he saw the faculties of each area working together to help each student develop to his or her fullest. He announced that there would be ongoing faculty meetings in which each area would be called upon to relate that teaching field to the elements of the arts.

As the first day of school approached, the faculty worked frantically to get their classrooms ready, with books and supplies in place. We had lists of names of students on paper but we had no idea if they would show up. We had been given a projected number for each ethnicity and been told that we must meet that quota. Just before we started, Baker met me in the hall and said, "Do what you have to do, girl, but make it work." We waited nervously for the first yellow bus to arrive. As we saw it pull in front of the school, the principals went out to greet the first students. The day was a bit chaotic, but every student was made to feel comfortable and looked forward to learning about his or her art form. At the end of the first week we discovered that we had met the ethnic goals set for us without effort, and we settled into a comfortable schedule.

Throughout the fall we held faculty meetings on Wednesdays to talk about the elements of the arts, and each department presented the relation of the course of study to the elements. Baker recorded the presentations and made them into a chart that he published in *Making Sense of the Five Senses*. On Monday mornings each cluster faculty met with one of the academic department faculties—music with English, drama with math, etc.—to discuss individual students, their talents, strengths, weaknesses or problems, and their work habits. We went into depth discussing the students having the most difficulty; sometimes we spent a session on one or two students. We invited the academic faculty to observe the students performing in their cluster, and together we tried to find ways to make the students more successful.

The cluster faculties worked on ways to correlate what we taught to the academic areas. In theater, we related basic measuring for costuming and stagecraft to ratio and proportion in math; lighting and physics were related; color and character motivation were related to psychology, and plays were easily related to literature and history. Kitty Baker, a former math professor, spent hours in the fibers studio setting up the looms, weaving, and relating weaving to math.

The academic department heads and the cluster coordinators met on yet another morning of the week to discuss the activities of the week. Someone from the DTC attended these meetings and typed up a calendar so that we knew what all of us were doing and where we were. We, in turn, shared these with the faculty in our departments. Everyone worked to make the students successful which, in turn, made the school a success. When a staff or faculty member was not working well, someone offered help. During one year we lost a registrar, and there was not a replacement, so Dolores Arnold, a co-coordinator with me, volunteered to take the job. She organized the school and was able to communicate helpful information about the students to each of us. At the same time she functioned as a nurse some days, as a counselor at other times of the day, and even a disciplinarian. She is presently head of the English department.

The first year everyone took IA for fifty-five minutes a day for nine months. We met in the upstairs dance studio that had been the old gym because it was the largest open space in the building. Because the surface was flat, Baker had Carl Fairleigh, the carpenter at the DTC, build a twelve-foot-high platform with a railing around the top and steps at the back. The platform was on rollers with brakes on them. A microphone was placed on the platform, and that was where I led physical and vocal exercises and gave general group instructions for the projects. When other teachers explained projects, they, too, came up on the platform. We all laughed that it looked like General Patton's platform when he talked to the troops.

To familiarize the students with the elements of the arts we made signs and attached them on the walls around what had been the gymnasium. The signs were at least three feet high and four to six feet long, depending on the length of the words: texture, line, rhythm, space, color.

Every arts teacher had a group of ten students—at least two students from each arts cluster. There were weekly planning meetings for the teachers of IA. Baker worried that the course would not be successful, so he arranged for the district to hire graduate students from the DTC as part-time teachers. One of them was assigned to work with each magnet teacher. They, too, came to the early morning planning meetings for the course. The presence of the graduate students strengthened the course because they could answer questions that the teachers had and could encourage those teachers who might have been hesitant.

Movement studies started each class with stretches and general warm-ups and developed through the course into yoga positions, dance patterns, and the Laban efforts that grew from recognition of movements in time, weight, and shape into character studies. One effort was introduced each week and exercises developed around that effort.

Vocal exercises started with basic warm-ups and clarity of diction, then continued through the course with Arthur Lessac (*The Use and Training of the Human Voice*, New York: DBS Publications, 1967); exercises in the "call," Grace Nash (*Creative Approaches to Child Development with Music, Language and Movement*, New York: Alfred Publishing Company, 1974), exercises using words, choral reading, and finally into listening and matching pitches to hearing and singing harmony. Many of the nonsense words and phrases used for diction warm-ups were in Spanish or "Spanglish" as well as English.

The first major project was making a "me" collage. The students worked in small groups of ten, learning to say their name clearly and tell their interests and cluster study area. After answering a series of values-oriented questions for the purpose of making them think more deeply about themselves and their beliefs, each student selected a partner and helped that partner draw

204

around his or her body on butcher paper.

A group lesson on collage suggested interesting ways to use the paper and add more bits of paper and other items to express individuality. Materials were introduced or brought from home and adhered to the paper. Once the collage was finished partners interviewed each other and made outlines, which were then shown to the group. The partner told about the significance of each item included on the collage. These collages were hung around the room and through the halls for the first six weeks.

Introducing the vocabulary of the arts took some time. Each art form assigned a project that demonstrated the unique way that discipline used vocabulary. The visual art faculty felt most secure and in possession of "their" vocabulary developed and codified at the Bauhaus School. They were helpful in suggesting and leading exercises to exemplify further the elements that they worked with daily. For instance, they added value and its properties of quality and intensity to clarify the element of color. Students had a workbook that included a color survey, with the added attraction of personality profiling. There was a demonstration of mixing color in pigment; the theater faculty demonstrated mixing color in light. The English faculty introduced color poems, and then each group chose one poem. They performed it in choral reading with added movement, costume pieces, music, and light.

Each discipline made worksheets and developed exercises to clarify the use of the element in that art form. For example, line was explored by making a drawing using many different kinds of lines. The theater group introduced improvisational scenes developed from the line drawings of Sol Steinberg (*The Labyrinth, The Passport, The Art of Living, All in Line*, New York: Duell, Sloan and Pearce, 1945).

Music faculty and students helped students trace musical lines and melody lines, and dance faculty and students used their bodies to make a variety of lines cutting space.

Some exercises did not work. In focusing on space the theater faculty took the students through a variation of Mary Sue Jones' play space exercise. Her thesis was that individuals have a space that is comfortable for them; most often this space is similar to one that the individual played in as a child. In the play space exercise a student was to rediscover his or her "child" through recreating the games, sounds, textures, thoughts, and space experienced. The presentation took the form of a movement and sound exercise with some words. Honesty in the rediscovery was stressed.

The more mature high school students enjoyed exploring and recreating the imaginary and real games, the friends, the sounds made in their play spaces. The immature were either uncomfortable having to recall details that may have been painful or embarrassing or were trying so hard to be accepted as adults that any suggestion of childhood was abhorrent to them. Those who were from lower economic situations were often reluctant to share their experiences. The exercise was abandoned and instead the students were asked to design a personal space in which they could work, relax, and create.

The nature object became the culminating exercise of the course. The object was first experienced through all the art forms—drawing, movement, sound, etc., and these experiences and thoughts were written in a journal. The dance faculty gave a worksheet and took the class through the steps of creating a dance from the natural object by using words that described the object and then creating movements that fit those words, finding a design in the object and repeating that design in various levels and tempos and floor patterns, or by creating a story from the object and letting the story inspire the movements. The strong structure of the exercise helped students become successful in areas that they had never experienced.

After long work and many ideas had been gathered, each student created an original work inspired by the natural object in the cluster art form. Then another original work was assigned in a different art form of the student's choosing. Those were shared with the small group along with an explanation of the creative process used to develop the work. Each student wrote a final paper on his or her individual creative process.

In addition to sharing the original works, each student practiced explaining their reaction to what they saw, heard, felt, and experienced. We taught them to start with an example of something good that was experienced or observed and to connect suggestions for making the performance better with an "and" not with a "but." Suggestions for strengthening the performance were to be positive with phrases such as "would be even stronger if you . . ." or "try clarifying what you said by . . ."[1]

The nature object exercise developed into yet other performances called *Creations*. Each creation performance piece had to have at least three artistic components. A musical number must also include a dance and perhaps lighting. A painting must include perhaps a scene and some music. Through the years the inspiration of the natural object has been dropped in *Creations* but the combination of expression in three art forms remains. This performance has also been opened to any student in any grade rather than just the new students.

The Texas Education Agency and DISD demanded more academic courses and, consequently, demanded that some of the arts courses be sacrificed. IA was dropped as an all-school course although I continued to teach it as a semester course in theater. Each art cluster drifted into becoming more competitive for space and performance time, and there was no longer a feeling of unity. Discussions and workshops followed in which it was suggested that IA not be offered until the senior year or that advanced IA be offered. Some thought that by the time the students were seniors they would understand and value what they had experienced perhaps reluctantly as freshmen.[2] Cluster teachers, however, were loath to give up advanced courses. The culmination of the discussions later reestablished IA as the core course for one semester for all incoming students. (Several theater courses bring in the nature object study as a three-week revisiting exercise at the end of the year for graduating seniors.) The name, however, was changed to EA for the elements of the arts. IA was in the curriculum books as introduction to algebra and confused computers and those who made the schedules.

Audience decorum has become more important as the school has grown and accepted a widely divergent group of students, many of whom had never been to performances or art galleries. A great deal of time is spent now in teaching terminology and etiquette for observing and enjoying a variety of arts performances from visiting an art gallery or museum to attending a dance performance, jazz concert, or opera. Respect for artists of all ages and disciplines is stressed. This is taught and practiced in performances by peers in the first weeks of school and in at least one field trip a semester to a professional performance.

The arts curriculum for the first few years of the school was lumped into three-hour blocks with no particular course titles. Each art cluster could designate what subjects or techniques students would learn during that time period. Goals were called behavioral objectives, and teachers filled out long forms called progress reports each six weeks to communicate to the parents how their child was progressing toward those goals.

Dolores Arnold and I decided the first year that all theater students would take beginning acting except her students from Skyline and mine from the classes at the DTC. They would be in advanced acting and the first year would work on Shakespeare. All students worked in voice and diction although specific vocal techniques were related to classes in acting styles. In addition, all students would be introduced to costume construction, basic stagecraft, beginning costume and set design, beginning stage lighting, and sound for the stage. We trained interested students one-on-one as stage managers for the performances, but there wasn't yet a formal course in stage management. Stage movement was required for all students, and mime techniques were taught so that students would have a readily available performance medium to take to community events.

The block of time for the arts allowed for workshops with individual artists who were in town performing. From the start the school asked professional artists in all art forms to talk to the students about their area of expertise or to give workshops if time permitted. Baker selected a diverse theater faculty from recent graduates of DTC and had the DISD hire them.

The philosophy of our department followed that of Baker: Every student is creative, and that creativity applies to all areas of the student's life; therefore, every student should try every aspect of theater. I challenged every teacher of the ninth- and tenth-grade students to find individual talents and interests as they taught the introductory courses and to encourage each student to build on those discovered interests, asking for challenging opportunities. We say to the students and parents that if people love theater this school will train them in several aspects of theater so that they can find a job and wait for the leading actor to break a leg or the lighting designer to leave for another job. Our student will be ready to take the leading role or design the next show.

The students guided me in adding and developing advanced courses. Developing the courses also depended on the abilities of the full-time teachers and the availability of experts to teach part time. We included a beginning course in plays that introduced ninth-grade students to the structure of plays and to various styles of scripts. We also added a beginning playwriting course for those who wanted to write a play, but we believed that high school students would only be able to write one play usually involving, we thought, teenage problems and angst or comedy over those problems. We found wonderful playwriting teachers who inspired the students to write, to see new plays, and talk intelligently about them. We had to create two advanced playwriting courses so

208

that students can now take four full years of playwriting. The same process happened in costume design and costume construction.

We have become known among colleges as the high school that teaches more technical theater than any other high school in the United States. Our students have reaped wonderful scholarships and career opportunities from this reputation and their own talents and eagerness to learn. Several former students working in theater in New York have told us that although they have graduated from college and even done graduate work, the name of this school on their resume has gotten them jobs.

Baker set the example of full faculty workshops in creativity and in problem solving. Through the years as new administrators and new faculty came into the school the staff suggested and then demanded more of these workshops. Some years the faculties of the arts clusters led the workshops. Individuals who attended other workshops and brought back those ideas led others. We shared our reactions and compared the way we worked with other methods. The advisory board was in charge of several of the workshops. They were particularly strong and supportive in preserving our history and philosophy. The strength of the school is that few faculty members have left. It is said in DISD that someone has to die before a new teacher can get into the arts magnet school.

As the school district has changed and the principals of the school have changed, staff development has become institutionalized. We have less freedom and less support and have lost focus. We have become mainstreamed and no longer meet as a special group. DISD instituted "Job Alike" sessions in which each teacher attends meetings with colleagues who teach similar subjects in other schools. Hours are spent discussing the UIL (University Interscholastic League) one-act play contests although we chose in 1976 not to participate in UIL. We recognize this as a problem and have taken steps and written waivers to enable us to rekindle that spirit of a whole faculty. One principal asked for and received corporate donations to take the arts magnet faculty to a Network of Performing Arts conference that gave us a common experience and made us grow. We continue to be pulled by the district and the courts, but the faculty is ornery enough to fight, and we have been lucky to have principals who helped us.

After twenty-five years the school has been recognized many times for intense training in the arts and academics, from the Rockefeller Foundation grant during the first four years to its current role as a mentor school in Texas, hosting faculties of other arts schools in the state and throughout the United States. One of our first principals helped to start the Network of Performing Arts Schools that has international memberships and serves as a support group to beginning programs.

The arts magnet is unique among arts schools because we insist on students' achieving in academics as well as their chosen art form and because each art cluster is strong. In many schools one form, usually music, dominates, but in this school all are strong. Dance has trained and produced eight presidential scholars in the arts. Music has won more *Downbeat* magazine awards for outstanding musicians than any other high school in the United States, and music students have been invited to perform at the International Jazz Festival. The theater department has been nominated by eight professionals to represent Texas at the American High School Theater Festival at the Fringe in Edinburgh, Scotland. Visual art can point with pride to student murals, sculptures, and paintings that decorate the city of Dallas and offices in Austin and in Washington, D.C.

The 2001 graduating class had 150 students. They were offered over $5 million in scholarships. The impetus for these scholarships is the Senior Showcase and Portfolio Day. Five years after the school began I believed that the theater students needed a way to show their abilities to colleges and professional schools. I contacted the schools and asked them to send theater faculty representatives and recruiters one weekend for a presentation of monologues and technical portfolios. The following year when Charlie Helfert from Southern Methodist University returned from a similar weekend in Kentucky he brought me a program that helped immensely in organizing two days of workshops and presentations. As various programs became stronger, we added presentations of short plays and then presentations of mime scenes.

The visual art department decided to join the showcase. Then the dance department joined. Expenses mounted for printing the programs as well as headshot books and materials for the portfolios. We asked the Junior League to help with volunteers, and they offered to help finance the weekend. When the music department joined the other three departments, the amount of scholarship grants soared past $5 million.

The graduates have become Grammy winners, young jazz classicists, and lighting designers for rock concerts all over the world as well as operas and theater productions of all genres. Set designers work regularly in New York and on Broadway. Dancers are members of companies all over the world. Artists are getting top dollars for their works. Actors are seen on television, in films, and on stages across the United States.

Even better for Dallas, students return to share their talents with the city. Several former theater students have started a theater company that produces a season of plays, including a new plays festival each year. This five-year-old company mentors our current students by using them to help teach children's classes, giving them jobs in their productions, and performing their plays. Many of our current and former students work with Robyn Flatt at the Dallas Children's Theater. They perform and work in theaters all over the Metroplex. Many former students are teaching arts in the Dallas public schools. Eight former students are now full-time teachers. One former theater student is now a full-time physics teacher.

We had no idea that the Arts District would spring up around us—the Dallas Museum of Art, the Morton H. Meyerson Symphony Center, the Arts District Theater of the Dallas Theater Center, the Dallas Black Dance Organization, Artists' Square with the Nasher sculpture garden—and make us its educational heart and center. Once we were joined by the other professional arts organizations, DISD tried to sell the building. Again we called on Baker as well as our advisory board and the Washington-Lincoln Alumnae Organization for help. The other magnets were moving across the river, but we needed to stay in the Arts District. After countless phone calls, meetings, visits to officials, and protests, the building was designated an historical site and the name of the school altered to "Booker T. Washington High School for the Performing and Visual Arts," the educational wing of the Arts District.

What Baker began has followed his philosophy and taken his strong all-stops-out approach to life, creating a living monument to his beliefs and ideas and teachings. ∎

End Notes

[1] When you criticize, talk about what you saw in the work, not how you would have done it." As a media critic, I use this as a guideline for writing about film, theater, television, music, and art. It was one of the first lessons Mr. Baker taught us, and it remains one of the most important things I learned from him. *Elaine Liner*

[2] When I first took integration of abilities at Baylor, I thought it a waste of time. . . . I took the course again at Trinity and still didn't get it. It was only after taking it a third time at the Dallas Theater Center, in graduate school, that the lightbulb went on. . . . Integration of abilities has been the most important course I have ever taken and continues to serve as a potent tool for my own creativity and understanding that of others.

When I took a teaching position at Dallas' Arts Magnet School, I taught integration of abilities but always felt the class was not that successful. However . . . when the performing arts organization I co-founded was seeking funding from a major corporation, a member of the corporate funding team reminded me of that course. . . . She told me she had been a student of mine from the magnet school and went on to tell me how meaningful, important, and beneficial that class had been for her. Even though she now worked in the corporate world, she still drew on the lessons learned and tools acquired from that class. *Tom Adams*

Children and Teen Theater

Kitty Baker, Irene Corey, Ruth Byers, Linda Daugherty, Robyn Flatt

Paul Baker did not view theater as diversion or escapism but as a way to confront problems in a creative and educational manner that brought delight and enlightenment. That was as true for children as for adults.

The children's art and drama class begun by Kathryn (Kitty) Baker and Lenora Schultz grew into the Children and Teen Theater at both Baylor and the Dallas Theater Center, Learning About Learning in San Antonio, the Dallas Children's Theater, and less directly, the Dallas Arts Magnet High School.

Many of those involved in children's theater did not pursue a career in theater. Josie Whitley became a psychologist.

That influence has been visible in my relationship with my daughter (and now my granddaughter), the children's theater productions I directed or wrote stage adaptations at Our Lady of the Lake College, the creative dramatics program I ran with my college students at an Hispanic elementary school and in a black public housing community, the kindergarten classes I taught, my relationships with emotionally disturbed children and adolescents with whom I worked over the years, and even in my work with individuals as a psychologist. Her [Jearnine Wagner's] . . . concepts . . . helped me to see the miracle present in each individual. In my current work . . . I ask, "Who cared for you, who believed in you, who gave you permission to dream?"

Retta Baker Van Auken pursued a career in journalism and is presently director of capital community development for the Austin-American Statesman.

From age four to eighteen, it [children's theater] was a place [I] could count on: space, excitement and discovery. We gathered weekly, first with Mary Sue Jones, then Ruth Byers, and finally with Jearnine Wagner.[1] One day we might spend the entire hour talking about a color. The next time we might fan out and pick up interesting shapes. . . . Often there was no particular "product" desired at the end of the exploration, just the joy of the experience itself.

One of the most memorable experiences was writing and producing The Tin Man *and* The Painted Town *. . . about being different and in my mind, much of the content grew out of trying to accomplish that in Waco, Texas . . . also this was the fifties, so some of the play dealt with our*

213

frustration with our town's racial biases. Listen in on one of the major characters, Mr. Painter, as he talks to Tin Man who is chartreuse: "I think your main trouble is your color. People around here are very conscious of color. They haven't had a change of color for the past fifty years. They never want a change. And your color, it kind of clashes with the colors they do have. You've got to blend in with the town, or else they won't like you."

Baylor Children's Theater was our lifesaver: it gave us permission as well as the tools to not blend in.

Two children who did become theater professionals are Linda Daugherty, playwright-in-residence at the Dallas Children's Theater, and Robert Wilson, director, author, and designer of the internationally acclaimed multidiscipline works Einstein on the Beach, *with Philip Glass, commissioned by the French government, the* CIVIL warS *[sic], and* The Life and Times of Joseph Stalin. *His current projects include* Sustainable life in the 21st Century, *commissioned by Aventis Foundation; an adaptation of* The Cabinet of Dr. Caligari, *for the Deutsches Theater in Berlin; a musical,* WillmS, *about the life and death of Shakespeare, written by Edward Padula and Robert Mansell; and the opera* Osud/Fate *for the national theater in Prague.*

"He [Baker] opened a door for me," said Robert Wilson. "My interest was in visual arts and painting. I hadn't thought to work in theater. He encouraged me to use those talents in theater. Most important, he taught me to trust in myself, in my body as an instrument."²

The Editors

Baylor Children's Theater: The Beginning

Kitty Baker

In the spring of 1941, Baylor Children's Theater was born. Something had to be done to avoid being dubbed by our children as the meanest parents they knew. Although our refrigerator was always supplied with ice cream, we did not allow soft drinks, junk food, and mind-wasters like

Saturday morning movies, afternoon radio, or even comic books—never mind if the local shoe store put one into the Buster Brown shoebox. Our philosophy was that a child's mind—which is so impressionable—should not be wasted.

To fill the gap, I organized a Saturday morning play group with the help of another faculty wife, Lenora Schultz. We gathered a small group of children, aged three to ten years, and met for two hours each Saturday morning in the Baylor Theater green room. The program consisted of crafts—painting at an easel and clay modeling, which I directed, and impromptu movement and play-acting on the stage, with Lenora at the piano. The idea was to let the children create their own scenarios. Each Saturday, we mothers returned home exhausted; the children were exhilarated, and their parents, most grateful.

Later that year when two theater students, Irene Lockridge and Jeanne McRae, chose to direct Maeterlinck's *The Blue Bird*, we were delighted to let them choose their cast from our play group. ■

Children's Theater

Irene Corey

In 1947, Jeanne McRae and I were asked to lead classes for children. Our work ultimately grew into a main stage production of Maurice Maeterlinck's *The Blue Bird*. This emphasis broke the common practice of using "leftover" theater for children, and instead used the same standards as those for adults but with materials appropriate for their age group.

The Color Conscious Conscience, my play for children, was included in *New One-Act Plays* produced by the Baylor drama department in 1948. It was first staged as a student production, and came to be the first live telecast in the state of Texas, on WBAP-TV out of Fort Worth.

Baylor Children's Theater

Although television was still in its infancy at that time, Baker brought Layton Mabrey onto his staff to teach the basics of television and film production. Never mind that there was no equipment. With viewing holes cut into cardboard boxes mounted on wooden legs, we learned "close up," "long shot," and "point of view"! By using the dummy cameras, the student actors developed a sense of camera movements and positions before they transferred their stage productions to the Fort Worth station for performance in front of actual cameras. ∎

Teen Children's Theater: Baylor and the Dallas Theater Center

Ruth Byers

Upon completing my master's degree in drama, I wanted to teach on the college level, and I had been in correspondence with Orlin Corey about teaching with him in Kentucky. Baker offered me the opportunity to teach introduction to drama, but children's theater was central to the job description. When I became director of children's theater at Baylor, I was unaware of my interest in working with children. I soon discovered new talents in myself: an ability in management, writing curriculum, teaching, and directing. It was exciting to discover a child's creative ability and natural talent. It was obvious that this was the place for me.

The former director, Mary Sue Jones, had done interesting work with children on the historical periods of theater. That captured my interest, because classes in repertory and theater history had excited me about history. In repertory class I had been introduced to a period piece in drama and shown its relationship to music, art, literature, math, and the cultural and political climate of the times. Baylor professors were invited to lecture or demonstrate that period in history through their art form. I saw the interrelationships, and my mind and imagination were ignited. I saw for the first time the importance of the arts in a society, indeed, the arts as a reflection and forerunner of the direction of a culture. A culture was more easily approached and understood when reduced to elements of form and sound that Baker taught and his staff applied in their areas of expertise.

Comparing the history of art to the growth of a child was intriguing. Starting with the primitive period of art, the children and I studied the beginning of drawing (a child's first drawing of man was a circle—this later led to the creation of a TV series, *JOT*). Simplicity of the life and art of early man was natural to the young child, who was learning about size, shape, line, form, color, pattern, design, and the realities of sound and space. Children were encouraged to hear and see and learn and do. Working with their hands in many media and learning to use their bodies and voices as means of expression and communication, the children were brought into a new dimension of thinking and feeling, of expressing and understanding.

As the children grew older, we progressed through the Egyptian, Greek, Roman, medieval, and Renaissance periods, and into contemporary times. Field trips provided vicarious experience of the times. To understand what it was like to be a Greek actor projecting in an amphitheater, students were taken to the center of a football stadium and told to speak so that all in the stands could hear. To understand the weight, size, and richness of Egyptian architecture built to last "for eternity," students visited an exceptionally beautiful Masonic Temple in Waco. The children worked with mosaics and stained glass when studying the medieval period; when students made and used large head masks as characters of a Greek drama, they realized that the identity of an actor had to be magnified for the amphitheater.

When the Dallas Theater Center opened in 1959, I became an assistant professor in the graduate school and director of teen-children's theater. I taught beginning and advanced classes to the instructors who worked with children, ages eight through eighteen. Should a child have the rare opportunity of participating in teen-children's theater for eight to ten years, he or she would have been introduced to the major periods of theater history through art, writing, movement, drama, music, and other creative activities. This knowledge could find expression in writing a play, designing and executing costumes, makeup, set, and props, as well as performing in the play.

My book, *Creating Theater: From Idea through Performance with Children and Teens*, published by Trinity University Press in 1968, recorded these ideas that evolved from teaching theater history through art, writing, movement, drama, music, and other creative activities. The book discusses the source of these ideas and how they were developed into theatrical production. It included creative interpretations of period drama by young

Teen Cildren's Theater

people. But how can one put together all the years of creative thought and action that led to the establishment of such a theater for children and teenagers and convey its essence over a period of one or two hours a week for nine months?

Several students completed their graduate degrees majoring in teen-children's theater and writing their theses on some aspect of the program at the DTC. Among them were Synthia Rogers, Louise Mosley Smith, Emily Jefferson, Jayne Randolph, and Miskit Airth. The integrity of this approach to learning and the synthesis of ideas into a concrete form of expression were far reaching. Years later, contact with former students whose eyes, ears, and mind had been opened to new ways of doing things proved the depth of their experience and gave the program validity. ■

A Playground of Ideas

Linda Daugherty

At five years of age everything in the world seems enormous. I was five years old when I took my first class at Baylor Theater. Through the doors, I entered the long, cool lobby, always hung with paintings that made me linger. The lobby led to a gigantic theater with not one but three stages where I was enveloped in an oversized, soft leather swivel chair.

Off the lobby in another direction was Weston Studio—a surprising, cavernous theater space often filled with tiered platforms of directors chairs. The giant platforms for the audience and the fantastic sets were always changing and were wonderful to play on and under. Then there were those magical stairs leading up, up, up to the mirrored dressing rooms that smelled of years of pancake and clown white. Baylor Theater had a catwalk to spy from, hundreds of secret hiding places, and a tunnel connecting stage right and stage left, reportedly inhabited by a ghost. The "guts" of a piano for making mysterious sounds lived stage left, and a tall metal sheet stretched up into the grid for creating terrifying thunder.

Baylor Theater was my playground, but it was so much more. It was a playground of ideas.

219

In that building I lived the extraordinary on both sides of the heavy, velvet curtain. *Three Zeros and One One* was a creation hilarious to both my parents and me, with moments reenacted for each other at home. In other productions I heard achingly beautiful words spoken as actors moved through colored lights and disappeared behind smoky scrims. In *Caucasian Chalk Circle* an actress in a faraway world that seemed as real as my own actually ate a whole onion onstage! The velvet curtain also rose on me as I performed hundreds of "plays" that somehow seemed very important— "plays" made from a collection of ideas discovered and nurtured on that playground. At Baylor Theater I played hard and joyfully and never wanted to leave.

But I did leave. The doors of Baylor Theater closed with the production of *Long Day's Journey into Night* and the controversy that followed. Those of us in the children's theater who had felt so grounded in that wonderful building were devastated. Thankfully, we had our ideas, each other, and two wonderful women who made a place for us in their homes—Luanne Klaras and Virginia DuPuy. We carried on with "our theater," acting and painting, beating out rhythms, exploring, dreaming.

The next year with Baker's help I headed for Trinity University's drama department. On that beautiful San Antonio campus there was no exciting, ever-changing Weston Theater, and there was no old, friendly theater with ghosts and mystery and three stages. For that first college class I climbed up to the third floor of the science building to discover a chemistry lab converted into a theater with risers of folding chairs facing a stage with a black floor, black walls, black dusty curtains. "This is it?!" This was it, but it soon became filled with "it!"—wonderful, exciting rehearsals, remarkable classes and ideas. Later a new gorgeous theater was built, and I grew to love it too, but a part of me always missed climbing those three flights to that surprising, dark, little theater at the top of the science building.

The move from Waco to San Antonio was refreshing. The new children's theater began in a city filled with music and color and different cultures. The amazing Jearnine Wagner developed the program. The children's theater started with afternoon and Saturday classes but soon developed into the nationally known Learning About Learning. This innovative dream of Jearnine's took on the schools, the neighborhood, and each and every child it met—exploring and nurturing the growth of the creative spirit.

220

The Dallas Theater Center was the next stop for those of us who knew that theater was our path. Following the principles of the famed IA class, we "integrated" all our theater abilities. I learned to do everything—make costumes, design sound, build sets, manage the house, as well as act and write plays. And I learned so much more—I found I was able to work and create when I thought I was out of energy and ideas; I learned my resistances to work and how to make a stab at conquering them; and what I learned as a child was reinforced again—that creative work in itself is its own fulfillment.

After the DTC's resident company was disbanded, my move to the Dallas Children's Theater was a natural progression. Robyn Flatt wanted to recreate for a new generation the world that had also nurtured her as a child, and I am honored to be part of that journey. At DCT my title is playwright-in-residence, but I continue to "integrate my abilities" as an actress, teacher, propmistress, and more.

The Dallas Children's Theater is a place for ideas, a place to tackle difficult feelings, celebrate fantasy, honor storytelling, and uncover new voices, a place to see ourselves as we are and as we could be, a joyous playground to nurture and honor what is special in every child.[3] ■

Dallas Children's Theater

Robyn Baker Flatt

My father Paul Baker's practice of bringing a diversity of great minds to the Baylor Theater brought me face to face with America's first solo mime artist, Angna Enters, in 1962. When asked the meaning of the word "mime," Angna answered, "Mime is everything the actor does on stage beyond words." Certainly I'd known that, but somehow her statement was so very clear. It stamped bold letters on my brain. Perhaps I was ready to absorb its meaning. Perhaps her words summarized and brought into focus my primary love in the world of theater—the poetry of movement in space, the dynamics of an actor cutting across a stage in a particular rhythm and silhouette, the

Journey to Jefferson,
formerly *As I Lay Dying,*
Dallas Theater Center

wheels of a wagon defining time and travel as they rolled over Baylor Theater's multiple stages.

Later that same wagon traversed the Trinity University Ruth Taylor Theater's three stages and the revolving stage of the Dallas Theater Center. William Faulkner's *As I Lay Dying*, adapted for the stage by Robert Flynn, was printed deeply into my muscle memory. We also took the production to Paris, France, where it won the coveted Special Jury Award at the Theater of Nations in 1964. The rustic motion of its Faulknerian wheels captivated the imaginations of the aesthetic French.

Ever since I can remember I have wanted to dance. That could be my mother Kitty Baker's fault for teaching me Martha Graham moves before I could walk. She can also be accused of starting my theater career, because she was instrumental in launching a children's theater at Baylor. Thanks to her efforts, at age eight I became one of the founding participants in the new Baylor Theater Children's Theater. I stepped into the world of creating plays. We explored ideas through art, movement, music, and dialogue. We finger painted, we danced to live piano music, and we made up stories. We presented our creations on Baylor's multiple stages of Studio One. Remarkable artists such as Irene Lockridge Corey, Jeanne McRae, and Mary Sue Jones inspired our explorations, directed our plays, taught us to build flats, and created a world in which the hard work of developing a concept or making a play were the thrills of our lives.

As I approached college years, my father identified a great mind of the dance world, Juana de Laban. He persuaded her to join the Baylor Theater staff. A celebrity in her own right, she was also the daughter of Rudolph von Laban, recognized internationally as the father of dance notation. I was thrilled with this development. At last I had a formal opportunity to explore the world of dance, movement for the stage, mime, and *commedia del arte*. The history of dance in Europe, the fascination for tribal ritual, the analysis of motion—all this and more exploded before me in a kaleidoscopic display of possibilities. I had the good fortune to work with Laban for more than twenty years. She fanned the flames of my yearnings and pointed me to the doors of my future.

Laban's energy and experience complemented and reinforced one of the predominant approaches to the play by the Baylor Theater staff. My father's most acclaimed works were rich in the language of movement. Eugene McKinney's *A Different Drummer* utilized a jungle gym set over all three theater stages at Baylor with the actors in vertical motion, silhouetted against a cyc-sky. *Othello* and *Hamlet* both made use of designer Virgil Beavers' brilliant ramps that swept boldly across the stage spaces, thrusting the actor's every move into the laps of the audience. Against those raked floors, action crystallized in breathtaking eloquence. These images and experiences all made indelible impressions on my kinetically inclined soul.

Years later at the Dallas Theater Center, where I became a member of the original resident professional company, I was asked to create productions that could be performed in parks throughout the city of Dallas. Realizing that words would be lost in the great outdoors, our creations relied on the language of movement, music, and mime. The success of this approach continued for seven years. We performed in every neighborhood throughout the city, providing a multigenerational event where thousands of families, friends, and neighbors enjoyed theater in spite of the impossible heat of our Texas summers.

Each year the park presentations grew out of collaborative group explorations and improvisations, much the same way as *Of Time and the River*, *Journey to Jefferson*, and *Three Zeros and One One* had evolved. As before, the raw data was refined and shaped into final form by directors, choreographers, and designers. One of the highlights of these years was the production of *Alice in Wonderland* designed by Irene Corey, with design and script evolving out of dynamic exploration of the text through movement.

Irene's magnificent sculpted foam rubber costume pieces and character heads for such figures as White Rabbit, Cheshire Cat, the Red and White Horses, Mad Hatter, and certainly the

Magic Turtle Series
Dallas Theater Center

Jabberwock were magical, each a work of art. Movement and masks merged, supporting and amplifying each other until Alice's encounters delighted audiences, simultaneously crossing all language, ethnicity, and age barriers.

Reaching entire families, capturing the imaginations of children, crossing cultural barriers, employing the universal languages of movement, music, and design as foundations for theatrical production became increasingly compelling to me as a person in theater. Thus, the next step: founding Dallas Children's Theater.

Never to be narrowly defined, this theater was envisioned as a direct outgrowth of the rich fabric of experience of prior years, with a conscious focus on the kinetic experience. Multigenerational theater, in my mind, has to be imaginative, kinetic, poetic, visually dramatic, and exciting to the ear. The mission of Dallas Children's Theater is "to inspire young people to useful and productive lives through the art of theater. This mission is accomplished through innovative educational programs built on the basis of sensory experience and a season of professional theater productions that feature the concerns and perspectives of youth while speaking to all generations and ethnicities."

Founded in 1984 with $500 by a group of artists determined to make this project a reality, the theater has grown to a $2.4 million budget and serves approximately 245,000 people each year. It has a nationally recognized ten-play professional season, a national tour, a theater arts school for children ages three to eighteen, and extensive arts-in-education programs based on the innovative Curtains Up on Reading curriculum that was developed in collaboration with the faculty of an inner-city Dallas public school. The methodology is a direct application of Baker's

224

Making Sense with Five Senses, and his integration of abilities philosophy. The Curtains Up curriculum is now in multiple Dallas schools and is used as a basis for arts-integrated curricula in a number of locations in Texas and beyond.

When using the Baker philosophy, school students, actors, and directors alike base their explorations of ideas, whether they be school-determined curricula or playwright-inspired scripts, by exploring elements such as space, rhythm, line, sound, and color. This approach gives all individuals a way to find themselves in relation to the subject at hand, to make that personal connection, to ground their journey in what they know (their sensory experience) while providing a tangible link to that which they are trying to discover.

Dallas Children's Theater is planning a permanent home. We want a space where ideas can be nurtured, where families can come together to rejoice, to explore, to question. Classroom space is important. The new building will allow the theater school to serve three times more students and expand programming for teens. There is so much we want to do. There is so much that needs to be done.

However, the theater's performance space must be the heart-beat, the pacesetter for the organization. The performance space must be intimate so that the young and the new theater-goers of whatever age can feel contact. It must offer maximum flexibility, allowing spatial change according to the needs of the play. It must provide room for motion, because a play is often a journey. There must be a space that can highlight the drama of time and travel. This space must challenge the "one-view-TV-box" by providing the possibility of multiple images, changes of perspective, and maximum contact with the audience.

Interweave, Dallas theater Center

225

Thanks to architect Richard Flatt and Hidell Associates Architects, plans have solidified for a new Dallas Children's Family Theater. The performance space allows for the audience to be surrounded by stage one, stage two, and stage three—with at least one-third of the audience captured in between. Baylor's Studio One was my childhood play space. Its shape and its rhythm are in my bones. It is my dream to bring it alive again to inspire actors, directors, and designers to think in new dimensions and to captivate the young and the young at heart who will know they can reach out, touch, and be part of a theater throbbing with ideas for them. ∎

End Notes

[1] The children Jearnine taught and mentored were encouraged to follow their truest paths. And many of them, no matter what their professions, their careers, still honor a part of themselves that they otherwise might not know existed because of her great imagination. Jearnine died but lives on in the hearts and souls of many of us formerly known as children. *Susan McAtee Monday*

[2] Quoted by Everett Evans, "Admirers Salute Baker's Career in Theater," *Houston Chronicle*, August 13, 1990, D1, 4. Unable to attend a celebration of Baker's career at Baylor in 2001, Robert Wilson wrote a poem honoring Baker. (see pp 248–9)

[3] Linda Daugherty began her career in the theater as an actress, performing at the Dallas Theater Center, on Broadway, and in regional theaters around the United States. She began writing when her children were young and has written more than twenty plays premiered at the Dallas Children's Theater, where she is playwright-in-residence. Favorite titles include: *Bless Cricket, Crest Toothpaste and Tommy Tune; African Tales of Earth and Sky*; a new musical version of Hans Brinker (written with Danny Ray); two adaptations of Steven Kellogg's books: *The Island of the Skog* and *The Three Sillies* (also with Ray). Her plays have been performed at the Kennedy Center; Stage One; The Louisville Children's Theater; Baltimore's Children's Theater Associatio; Atlanta's Alliance Theater; Richmond's Theater IV; Portland's Northwest Children's Theater; the Children's Museum of Indianapolis; as well as community theaters and colleges. She is especially proud that her play, *Bless Cricket*, the story of a girl dealing with her brother with Down syndrome, is the featured play of the Jellybean Conspiracy, a program that promotes understanding for people with disabilities.

Learning About Learning

In addition to theater productions some ideas developed through Children's Theater evolved into books such as:

Kitty Baker and Jearnine Wagner. *A Place for Ideas: Our Theater*. San Antonio: Principia Press, 1965.

Ruth Byers. *Creating Theater: From Idea through Performance with Children and Teens*. San Antonio: Trinity University Press, 1968. (Rumanian translation, *Editura Didactica Si Pedagogica*).

Cynthia Herbert. *I See a Child*. New York: Doubleday, 1974.

Susan Russell and Cynthia Herbert. *Everychild's Everyday*. New York: Doubleday, 1980.

Robert Flynn and Susan Russell. *When I Was Just Your Age*. Denton: University of North Texas Press, 1992.

Robyn Flatt, Amy Shoults, and Melissa Deakins. *Curtains Up on Reading*. Dallas: Dallas Children's Theater, 1999.

Mime Park Tour, Dallas Theater Center.

Day of Absence, The Janus Players, Dallas Theater Center

228

Learning About Learning

Susan Russell, Julia Jarrell, Susan McAtee Monday

Fact number one: If you are born, sooner or later you die. Fact number two: In order to capitalize on the space between birth and death, each individual should grow in a vital, creative way; each must live his inner personal, sensitive life. Fact number three: This creative, imaginative life comes most easily and naturally to children. It is their soul. It is the God in them. . . . Paul Baker in the foreword to A Place for Ideas: Our Theater *(Kitty Baker and Jearnine Wagner, Principia Press, 1965)*

One of the most creative outgrowths of Children's Theater was the highly imaginative nonprofit educational foundation, Learning About Learning. The body of work of LAL had deep roots in the philosophy and practices of Paul Baker. The foundation itself, incorporated in San Antonio in 1968, grew out of Jearnine Wagner and Kitty Baker's children's theater programs at Baylor and at Trinity, documented in the voices of children in *A Place for Ideas*. In San Antonio, Wagner began expanding the children's theater program beyond the campus of Trinity with Ideas in Motion and Unlimited Potential, both programs that utilized the talents of volunteers among the theater students and the philosophy of creative growth and integrated abilities.

In 1968, Jearnine and a small staff, who later became the founders of LAL, created the Children's Garden at Hemisfair in San Antonio. Children from all over the city, the country, and the hemisphere participated in drama and integrated arts programs, ranging from the workshops for the creation of the environmental artwork used in the innovative exhibit buildings to short-term programs designed for children who visited the fair with their families. Today it would be called multimedia—then, it defied definition.

The San Antonio Independent School District, an institutional partner of the Children's Garden, also engaged LAL to create arts curricula for teachers and sponsored a summer-long institute that involved local teachers and teachers from Mexico City.

At LAL's imaginative fund-raisers guests might be greeted by children on a flower-decked donkey or find themselves implored to dress as a family ancestor. Wagner recruited the president of the board of the IBM Foundation by waltzing, without an appointment, into his office with six teenage students in tow. Many of the board members and supporters found themselves sewing hundreds of dolls for a Fiesta parade float, dyeing bolts of army-surplus silk for gala tablecloths,

229

decorating that donkey with flowers, ushering hundreds of children though an imaginary spaceship while trying to keep donated PCs online in what must have been San Antonio's first electronic interactive exhibit.

The staff began looking at children through the lens of "education." Wagner wondered how to save children's emotional and creative lives that otherwise might wither or stagnate for want of attention. Her genius was her ability to know in a flash, with incredible intuition, what a young soul needed not just to live but to thrive.

Wagner asked, "What keeps children from bringing the creative behavior developed in the protective world of A Place for Ideas to other aspects of their lives—school, home, peers, relationships, and problems? Why do children do brilliant intellectual work in the arts but do poorly in school? Why doesn't this innate creativity transfer? Why don't children use the skills they learn here when they go back to their classrooms? Where is the breakdown?"

From this puzzle, more specific questions were asked within the framework of Learning About Learning over the next twenty-two years: How can more successful learning climates be created in schools and other institutions that help all children succeed? What kinds of tools— ways of looking—can be taught to children to help them successfully enter academic, social, and cultural worlds? How can children be in the "driver's seat" of their own learning? How can children reach their individual creative potentials? These questions drove our applied research with children, families, and teachers.

Every program began with the assumption that each child is unique and uniquely gifted. The "elements of form" vocabulary, now called the "sensory vocabulary," was a basic part of a child's experience at LAL. Children learned these elements by using them in open-ended exercises designed to produce original and thoughtful results. They became aware of how to use the creative process, work in many media, ask big questions. These generative thinking processes were an outgrowth of Baker's inanimate object exercise. Children reflected on their own work, contrasting it with others, noticing their own patterns and favorite ways of thinking and working. They learned how to work out of their own strengths. These thinking processes are now referred to as "metacognition."

Children built giant robots and giraffes, wrote operas, dug their own clay for pottery, made a movie about a trash monster at the city dump, spent the night at Mission San Jose, designed murals for Hemisfair, published their poetry, traveled to Washington, D.C., to star in the Smithsonian Institution's "Celebrating the Year of the Child," and saw their ideas come to life, often in ways that transformed their perceptions of themselves. To Jearnine, teaching was theater, too.

The curricula for children's programs developed at Learning About Learning had in common an approach to learning that (1) affirms learning as an experience-based, discovery process of investigation and creation, (2) gives children many different entry points and routes to learning, (3) requires that the learner creates his or her own outcomes based on individual discoveries and curiosities, and (4) directly teaches thinking processes and entry skills into various disciplines, situations, and settings.

These characteristics were applied to experiences as diverse as producing an original play, exploring historical sites such as the San Antonio missions, mastering the skills and perspective of an academic discipline, studying a period of art history, or visiting a college class. Children were exposed to this philosophy and practice in short week-long intensive programs, through after-school and weekend classes, in family-centered summer neighborhood activities, through semester-long projects developed in classrooms in the San Antonio and Edgewood school districts, and in long-term community arts programs such as the Kenwood Players.

Kenwood, one of many inner-city communities where LAL provided summer arts programs, was a neighborhood poverty pocket between more prosperous San Antonio communities. The community was blessed with cultural diversity and with Joyce Sowells, principal of the local elementary school, Sojourner Truth. Through her support and collaboration many programs were created for the youth in the area. The Kenwood Players, teenagers working together as an improvisational theater company, created original plays and facilitated workshops for other students on issues vital to young people: family and peer pressures, problem solving, friends, roles and relationships, stereotyping, ethnic and racial tensions, wishes and dreams, etc. Directed by Johnny Gutierrez and Charles Jarrell, the project became a program of the San Antonio school district, working to defuse racial tensions in schools.

In 1975, LAL began a serious endeavor in applied research in education, launching a full-day lab school funded by a five-year cooperative funding partnership including the National

Endowment for the Arts and the Moody and Sid Richardson foundations. Ordinary children from a variety of ethnic and socioeconomic backgrounds attended the lab school full time. The challenge was to develop, document, and assess the applications of the LAL methodology to academic fields of study. The results were gratifying. The LAL lab school was cited by the National Endowment for the Arts as a pacesetter for learning through the arts in the 1970s.

The Hogg Foundation for Mental Health funded the monograph on the lab school and LAL, written by Dr. Sylvia Farnham-Diggory, H. Rodney Sharp Professor of Education at the University of Delaware. In her 1979 evaluation, A Creative Arts Model for a School, Dr. Farnham-Diggory wrote,

Just as a physical education program trains athletes, so LAL trains minds. It does so visibly and concretely. The children's resulting work is striking. Children—normal children— emerge from this program looking like geniuses. All children, they say, are geniuses. They simply need direction in understanding how their own genius works. That is what LAL provides. That is why the LAL program is, in my judgment, the most significant educational program on the scene today (39).

The lab school was just one of LAL's arenas. The staff worked in museums, training arts educators and designing interactive exhibitions for children, most notably at the Kennedy Center for the Performing Arts and during the Smithsonian Institution's "Celebrating the Year of the Child" symposia. Books and materials were packaged for the retail market under the name of "Imagination Works." For the children of San Antonio, the after-school programs and Saturday specials of the Idea Workshop were a continuing local resource.

Concurrent with the children's programs (often using them as ongoing internships for adults and college students), LAL created many professional development programs for teachers, museum professionals, community service providers, and university faculty, training educators in techniques of integrating these ideas into their domains and venues. Although LAL was a local organization, its programs had a far-reaching effect, not only in its region but also nationally. Among the dozens of programs for children, parents, and educators were

232

• "Thinking Historically," in collaboration with the Smithsonian Institute, funded by the National Endowment for the Humanities.

• "Imaginations at Work," a middle school program, with workbook and video, developed with the San Antonio Independent School District and the Texas Commission for the Arts. This project culminated with a special collaborative project with the Smithsonian Institute, "Celebrating the Year of the Child" (1979) and the opening of the new I. M. Pei Wing of the National Gallery of Art in Washington, D.C.

• "Kids Invent Theater," developed in collaboration with the Smithsonian Institute.

• "Kids Introduction to the World of Opera," a special project developed for Opera America.

• "KidTechnics," a sensory exploration of technology designed to inaugurate the Houston Children's Museum at the Blaffer Gallery of the University of Houston.

• "Profitable Thinking, a Kid's Guide to Entrepreneurial Thinking," funded by the San Antonio Chamber of Commerce.

• "City Senses," a child's leadership development series for exploring cities, funded by the Texas Commission for the Arts.

• "Learning to Look," a middle school program and book developed with architect O'Neil Ford, funded by the Texas Commission for the Arts and private donors.

• "Future/ Past," an early prototype of a "Parks as Classroom" Program developed for the San Antonio Missions when they were part of the state park system with a program narrative and activity guide. Developed in cooperation with San Jose Mission State Park and the San Antonio Independent School District.

Neiman-Marcus and other retailers sold Imagination Works, a retail line of interactive kits that included books and toys. Books included English and Spanish editions of *Me, Yo*; *Ideas*; *Celebrations*; and *The Neighborhood Explorer*.

These exhibits, professional development programs, books and materials, programs, and activities were grounded in the Baker philosophy that each of us is an unrepeatable opportunity. By bringing habits and ethics of creative work into our professions we can make great contributions and find personal rewards in ourselves. First, we must remember who we are and where we come from, find and exercise our creative abilities, and put them to work. These programs allowed the staff and those involved as volunteers, parents, teachers, and children to explore their own creative potentials, work in new media, stretch, and try out new ways of working in a supportive and nurturing environment. This process created an ever-growing family of lifelong learners, adventurers and risk takers—adding more branches to the Baker family tree.

Learning About Learning closed its doors in 1985. Jearnine Wagner, the "spiritual mother" of LAL passed away in 1998. The rest of the founding staff—Susan McAtee Monday, Julia Jarrell, Dr. Cynthia Herbert, Steve Bailey, Dennis Poplin, Charles Jarrell, Nancy Busch, and Susan Russell—have gone different directions, although they continue to build on the rich legacy of ideas and experiences for children and for the future. ∎

Theater of the Spirit

The Reverend Raymond Bailey

The theater has often been viewed as a place of escape for those on the stage and those in the audience. For some, it is a hiding place, but, for others, it is a finding place. Theater at its best is an experience of discovery. The theater of Paul Baker was always designed to arouse in persons a capacity for encounters with truth, truth about themselves and the world around them.

Baker's legacy is a view of life that understands all humans as potentially creative beings with the ability to see the world as it is and to see it as it might be. Anne Tyler, in her novel *Breathing Lessons*, longs for lessons for living that would come with each new child, but every birth is the beginning of a new adventure, and each person needs to be an artist who can create a life.

Irwin Edman's book *Arts and the Man* was on the required reading list for Baker's courses in creativity. Edman crossed the boundaries of the commonly accepted concept of "art." He wrote that life is an experience and that the province of art is an "intensification and clarification of experience." "Far from having to do merely with statues, pictures, and symphonies, art is the name for that whole process of intelligence by which life, understanding its own conditions, turns them to the most interesting or exquisite account."[1]

Other required reading included *The Creative Process*, by Brewster Ghiselin, and *Works of the Mind*, edited by Robert Heywood. These books applied creative principles to the work of politicians, architects, administrators, historians, and a whole range of occupations that seek to give form to ideas. It is easy to understand why Baker's courses were profitable not only for those pursuing careers in the dramatic arts but also for educators, business entrepreneurs, engineers, and ministers. Baker inspired students to approach every facet of life as an opportunity for invention.

Paul Baker throughout his professional life has been in Tennyson's words "a bringer of new things." His innovative staging of plays new and old sent ripples of delight through theater professionals. His productions captured the creative energies of diverse artists who collaborated to imagine and invent art that was truly alive and combined space and time to a degree rarely achieved. Always the teacher, Baker challenged his students to be bringers of new things, whatever their media.

Baker's influence had an impact on more than professional goals. His students were probably better parents because of his influence. Baker urged parents, schools, and churches to cultivate and encourage the love of beauty and the pursuit of truth. Most of his career was spent in the context of religious communities. This was as it should be because Baker's aesthetics are rooted in a belief that every human being is created in the image of God. Baker's life work suggests that the essence of God instilled in human flesh is the ability to create. The image of God is not in gender, skin pigmentation, the slant of one's eyes, but in one's capacity to be a world maker. In the mind and heart of each child born is a drive to give form and to participate in God's ongoing work of creation.

Artistic communities, especially theater companies, are among the most open and inclusive. Individuality is affirmed and experimentation encouraged. Barriers of ethnicity, sexual preference, or gender rarely are to be found backstage. Provincialism is overcome not only through the scripts performed on stage but also through the collaboration necessary to produce drama.

Many students who found their way into his classes had been trained to stifle their creative impulses. They had been conditioned to control sensory experience and creative impulses in order to conform to cultural expectations. At home, they were rewarded with parental approval by being mommy's or daddy's little man or princess. In school, they were taught to look for preconceived ends and answers and the one acceptable method of arriving at the "right" answer. By the time they got to college, they just wanted to know the requirements to make an "A." Even in the fifties, the goals of education were shifting toward utilitarianism.

From their birth, my wife and I sought to affirm our daughters as unique creations of God with innate worth. We encouraged them to experiment with their senses. The girls were encouraged to play with mind, voice, and body. We soon learned that our values were not universally shared. When our oldest daughter was six years old, I arrived home one day to find her on the porch crying. When I asked her the cause of her sadness, I was told that she had received a "bad" first report card from school. She could read before she entered school and had read her teacher's comment that she needed to improve because she did not color within the lines. Her trouble with the schools went back through her father to Paul Baker, who taught us that it was not necessary to color between the lines. We pressure our children to conform to convention even if it means stifling creative instincts. Children need freedom within reasonable boundaries to become who they are rather than who we or a community or school system want them to be. After the Baker experience, those of us who became parents should have been parents who joined their children on journeys of discovery rather than training them to perform acceptably on cue.

I came to Baylor as a ministerial student in the fall of 1955. Except as a school with athletic teams in the Southwest Conference, I had never before heard of the university, and I had never heard of Paul Baker. A sense of religious vocation during my senior year in high school led me to seek counsel from a local minister who urged me to attend Baylor to prepare for seminary. My first months at Baylor were not happy ones. I had not come from a church family and was not comfortable in the religious culture of the campus, nor did I have the social background or finances to fit into college life. I wandered into the Baylor Theater in the hopes of losing myself or hiding behind characters I might play onstage. In the theater I found self-esteem, respect, and acceptance. Not only would the experiences of the theater contribute to personal actualization, they would also indelibly imprint my theology and shape my life's work.

One of the reading assignments in Baker's class was an article by Frank Lloyd Wright on the creative process. Wright, recognized as one of the outstanding architects of all time, wrote that the work of the architect is a combination of head, heart, and hand. This concept has guided my ministry of ethics, worship, and proclamation. One might say that the shaping of a successful life is a matter of intellect, feeling, and physical labor. The work of the church should be to create an environment to love God with mind, spirit, and strength.

Every worship service is a drama with all the classical elements: plot, character, thought, rhythm (dance), and spectacle. The structures of the performing spaces in Baylor Theater were designed to catch the audience up in the drama. Audiences were often engulfed by sound, sight, and action. The excitement of experiencing a drama in Studio One or Weston Studio was the "willing suspension of disbelief" that allows purgation (catharsis) and heroic redemption of human dignity. Sadly, too many churches are designed like lecture halls that suggest that information is to be passed down. Good theater shows rather than tells and seeks to generate an experience of revelation. Good worship should lead to transformation and empowerment through revelatory experience.

Many of the problems that have plagued religion through the years have their roots in prepositional faith, i.e., faith as content controlled by dogma. Religious education and worship suffer from the notion that being Christian in the world results from the infusion of certain information. The generative power of the experience of scriptures is suppressed by biblical rationalism.

Not only were Baker's productions experiences, every class was a dramatic encounter. One of the theatrical masterpieces produced during the Baker years was a stage adaptation of Thomas Wolfe's *Of Time and the River*. A scene in the play re-created a drama class filled with pseudo-aesthetes who played academic games. The mood of the scene is oppressive; the dialogue is a battle of clichés. The scene ends with the narrator explaining that in those students' bleak class-room, "no birds sang." Paul Baker created an open classroom in which every bird sang. This is the spirit that needs to be duplicated in Sunday school classes and worship services.

Long after my days at Baylor, I discovered Søren Kierkegaard's drama paradigm for worship. He observed that a popular view of worship in his day was the minister as actor, God as prompter, and the congregation as audience. Kierkegaard argued that a better paradigm would be to view the congregation as actor, minister as prompter, and God as audience. Out of my experience with the theater of revelation, I might see God as playwright, with the congregation acting out the drama of creation and redemption for a world in despair.

For much of my career I taught preaching and worship to graduate students. I adapted the techniques for entering a text learned at Baylor Theater to the entering of biblical text. Baker was willing to trust texts to students to a degree few other teachers would. One of his most daring ventures at Baylor was to break Thomas Wolfe's massive novel into blocks and give different sections to student teams to develop the material into dramatic scenes.

Biblical texts are often viewed through the lens of dogma and creed. Preachers accept an interpretation of the text but never really encounter the story. They in turn tell the congregation what the text "means" instead of leading the congregation to discover themselves and the world in the text. Preachers often talk about the text rather than preaching the text. Someone described the special character of the dance of Isadora Duncan by observing that while other dancers danced to the music, Duncan danced the music.

I have encouraged young preachers to attempt to enter the biblical text free from doctrine and predigested interpretations in order to find scenes for their particular congregations. If they can have an experience with the text, meet the characters, share the smells, tastes, sounds, and movements of the scenes, then they can lead the congregation into similar experiences. Study of the text begins with the senses, moves to character, and then to plot. Because of who I am, I may

238

experience a text quite differently from someone else. The purpose of preaching and worship, like good theater, should be to evoke the illusion of the first time. The congregation should have the feeling that what is happening has never happened in exactly the same way before.

Baker set the tone for this kind of experience with his directing style. I never saw him begin with a preconceived interpretation of each character or a blocking blueprint requiring every actor to move from x to x. He encouraged actors to feel their way into characterization, interaction, and blocking. Good actors then created an environment of discovery. A good preacher does not ask, "Did they understand?" but rather, "Did they encounter incarnational truth?" We do not interpret the biblical drama; it interprets us.

A particular theater company brings to a production their combined experiences drawn from intellectual and emotive memory. Each audience brings to a performance a collection of life experiences, and their response makes each night's performance unique. Each biblical text is an encounter in a particular moment of the minister's life cycle and in the life of the congregation, as well as the cultural context and the collection of individual stages on life's journey.

A text like the story of the prodigal son in Luke 15 is an invitation to personal catharsis. The story can be approached from the point of view of the father, the absent mother, the younger son, the elder brother, companions in the far country, those who gave nothing to the down-and-out son who was in need, the citizen who exploited and humiliated him, or the servants. I have at different times in my pilgrimage identified with nearly every character.

In the Exodus story, different congregations might understand the fears of the Egyptians more than the oppression of the Hebrews. The plots of the biblical stories are universal, and the creative preacher seeks to express unique empathy in a moment in time. Each text should be explored for its value for a particular time and group. A minister should enter into a text as a director does a play and through collaboration with other worship leaders create an experience for a participating audience.

The church should be a theater in which the glory of God is revealed through the service (or work) of people reflecting the image of a creator God. There is a need for the church to recover a theology of play and openness to new thought and forms. When one looks at the history of the church, it is astounding to see the architecture, painting, music, and drama inspired by a sense of sharing in the work of a God whose creative work never ends. Too many worship services today take the form of pep rallies or offer cheap imitations of pop culture.

A service that incorporates dramatic elements might follow a plot used in our church. The service begins with a simple invitation to contemplation, the opening of mind and heart to the presence of God in the company of seekers. A musical prelude can be chosen to stimulate the emotions or quiet them. The use of familiar hymns for the prelude will fill the mind with old memories, and familiar lyrics may block new images. A choral summons from a choir behind the congregation, scattered throughout the sanctuary or surrounding the main body, can create a sense of true community. A processional hymn with choir and clergy coming through and out of the congregation symbolizes pilgrimage and encounter. A call to worship, which may be a psalm of praise and adoration, confession of sin and absolution, or a contemporary original piece, unites the congregation through the spoken word.

On the Sundays when baptism and communion are included in the service, the result is a play within the play (a device often employed by Shakespeare). Baptism and communion are dramatic reenactments. Baptism by immersion (the form of my tradition) symbolizes the death, burial, and resurrection of Jesus. The subjects in our service are asked to give a spoken declaration of their faith. As they arise from the water, the presiding minister lays hands on the head of the baptized and blesses them as new members of the priesthood of believers called to salvation and service. Through the ritual of baptism, believers act out the drama of redemption. This centuries-old practice allows the performer to identify with the church of the ages while inviting contemporary observers to cathartic memory of their own baptism. We often use printed meditations in our order of service, recognizing that some respond better to hearing, others to seeing. In a recent baptismal service, we used the following:

> Baptism affirms that if I grow into the likeness of him who created me, if I continue within the fellowship to which I am wedded in baptism, and if I become a functioning member of the Body, it will be in great part due to God's loving actions toward me, for me, in spite of me, through the agency of the believing and baptizing community. I never cease being dependent upon the baptizers. Thus, to the perplexing question, Who am I? Baptism

240

responds: "You are the sum of your relationships. You are not a self-made man as if you existed in isolation from the web of life, the events of the past, and the claims of others. You are not parentless. The discovery of your identity is group product. You have a history that will take you the rest of time to unravel. You are who you are in great part because of the way you were conceived, nurtured, birthed, and loved by the household of faith. This is who you are."[2]

Those present were asked to recall their baptism and remember those who had influenced their decision to be baptized. They were encouraged to ask what baptism had meant for them as they emerged from the water and what it meant for them today. An illustration in the sermon described the baptismal scene in the movie, *Tender Mercies*, and the dialogue between stepfather and stepson, both of whom had been baptized. The boy asks the older man, "Do you feel any different?" to which the adult responds, "Not yet." The congregation was asked what difference being a baptized Christian made in their lives. At one point in the service, water was sprinkled on the congregation as a reminder of their baptism, whatever form they may have experienced.

The experience of communion is a repeated drama in which every person is an actor. Communion may be approached as a reenactment of the last supper, a representation of the encounter with Christ, or an anticipation of a heavenly banquet. The congregation is encouraged to think about the relationship of communion and community. This ritual involves all the senses. There is taste, smell, touch, hearing, and kinesis. Participants may come forward to receive the elements, or pass the trays, either requiring physical action. When the cup and bread are passed among the worshipers, they are reminded that as they serve one another, they act as priests, represent brother and sister to God and God to brother and sister. Often they use words such as "the body of Christ" or "the blood of Christ." In the particular service referenced here, the final meditation was:

We go out now and resume our journey. Down the mountain we live out what we have seen, glimpsed, perceived of new possibilities, challenges, hopes. Go forth with a thirst for more life that will lead you up other mountains where you will meet another in your life who is waiting to show you more of themselves, of you and of God. Be prepared to be disoriented and fearful. Remember, however, as you choose to see or not to see that, either way, you will be touched and sustained by the Holy God who is in every valley and upon every mountain—opening eyes—giving courage to look and granting courage to live with whatever you see.[3]

The service included a period designated the "discipline of silence" that allowed worshipers to think about that which they had seen and heard. We do not have a recessional in our service, but I believe that one can be a terrific symbol of the church leaving the gathered community and sanctuary to enter the world for reconciliation and redemption.

We encourage members of our congregation to participate in service according to their gifts. In the Baker tradition, we affirm the giftedness of each person. A gift may be as simple as welcoming members and guests in a way that affirms them. In a typical year 150 people read scripture, lead calls to worship, or pray. Children, youth, elders, male, and female participate according to their interest and ability. Members are invited to submit original artwork for bulletin covers and original meditations. Different groups receive the offering each week; sometimes families, sometimes college students, youth, elder adults, or whoever will symbolically represent the body. There is an effort to move beyond a performance mentality that limits telling the story to a special class, such as deacons or ordained clergy. All members are encouraged to learn and to teach through play.

We have too often yielded to the temptation of imitating pop culture in our education as well as our worship. Sunday school teachers do not lead a class into an experience of learning but try to inculcate the answer provided by a book that is safe. Worship is too often designed to make one feel good or guilty depending on the tradition of the particular religious body rather than freeing the divine image.

The church has too often treated theology, worship, and ethics as finished business. When this happens, the church stifles the most active minds—the dreamers and visionaries. To freeze thought in the work of any council, creed, discipline, or age is to act as if God's work is finished and the Spirit is silent and still.

242

Church should not be a factory that pours doctrine into passive minds. Church should be a community devoted to freeing women and men to work out their salvation in fear and trembling as those created in the image of God and entrusted by God with stewardship of creation. Our worship should be designed to arouse in persons their innate capacity for encountering God. The finest in music, symbol, work, and action should stir hearts and minds to call a world into being. Organized religion has too often yielded to culture rather than transforming it.

A dose of Baker's theology might stir the dry bones of orthodoxy to life and let the church become the facilitator of true integration of life. The vocation of the church is to liberate the human spirit that all might share the final vision of the priest of George Bernanos' *Diary of a Country Priest*—"all is grace."

I am not sure that Paul Baker made me a better actor, although the performing techniques that I learned from him and the Baylor staff have served me well in more than forty years of pulpit ministry. I do believe that he helped me become a better person, parent, teacher, and minister. Aristotle said that drama is an imitation of life. Paul Baker's style of drama is a paradigm for life. ∎

End Notes

[1] Irwin Edman, *Arts and the Man: An Introduction to Aesthetics* (New York: W. W. Norton & Company, 1939), 10.

[2] William Willimon, *Worship as Pastoral Care* (Nashville: Abingdon Press, 1979), 154–155.

[3] William L. Dols, *Just Because It Didn't Happen . . . Sermons and Prayers as Story* (Charlotte, NC: Myers Park Baptist Church, 2001), 8.

. . . one of the richest experiences I have ever had. There are no high Broadway production costs, no limit on student energy and enthusiasm, no fear of commercial failure; the only goal a high standard of learning.

Eliot Eilsofon
Life Magazine *photographer*

Funeral scene in the Baylor theater's stage presentation of Thomas Wolf's novel, *Of Time and the River*

244

Paul Baker Biography

Born 1911 in Hereford, Texas, to Retta Chapman Baker and
William Morgan Baker.

Bachelor's degree in drama, Trinity University, 1932.

Studied at Yale University department of drama until forced to
leave for financial reasons.

Began teaching career, Baylor University, 1934.

Married math professor and artist Sallie Kathryn (Kitty)
Cardwell, 1936. Father of Robyn Cardwell Baker, Retta
Chapman Baker, and Sallie Kathryn Baker.

Chair of drama department, Baylor University, 1939–1963.

Studied theater in England, Germany, Russia, and Japan, 1935.

Designed Baylor Theater, 1941.

Completed master's degree in fine arts, Yale University, with
Rockefeller Foundation scholarship, 1939.

Received Rockefeller Foundation grant to engage
professional staff for Baylor drama department, 1942.

Special Services entertainment officer in Iceland and Paris,
France, during World War II. Request for actresses led to
the formation of the Civilian Actress Technician Corps
(CATS).

Named chief of entertainment branch for European
theater of operations; awarded the Legion of Merit for
reorganizing the entertainment branch of the European
theater of operations, 1944.

Rockefeller grants to study the use of drama in relation to the
community and leisure time, 1946, 1959.

Presented *Green Grow the Lilacs*, by Lynn Riggs, at the Theater
Babylone in Paris, 1952.

President, Southwest Theater Association, 1956.

Honorary doctorate of fine arts, Trinity University, 1958.

President, National Theater Conference, 1958–1961.

Brussels World Film Festival Award for *Hamlet*,
    filmed by Eugene McKinney, designed by Virgil Beavers,
    directed by Baker, 1958.

As managing director, helped found the Dallas Theater Center
    and graduate drama school, 1959.

Recipient, first Rogers and Hammerstein Award for
    outstanding contribution to theater in the Southwest,
    1961.

Chair, department of speech and drama, Trinity University,
    1963–1978.

Special Jury Award, Theater of Nations, Paris, 1964,
    for Dallas Theater Center presentation of *Journey to
    Jefferson*, an adaptation of William Faulkner's *As I Lay
    Dying* by Robert Flynn.

Taught four-week seminar on theater in New Zealand, 1964.

In association with Arthur Rogers, designed the Ruth Taylor
    Theater at Trinity University, 1967.

Elected to the board of governors, American Playwright's
    Theater, 1967.

Elected to the board of governors, American National Theater
    and Academy, 1967.

Faculty, American Studies Seminar, Salzburg, Austria,
    1968, 1972.

Toured Yugoslavia at invitation of U.S. State Department, 1968.

One of four American directors selected by the German government to tour West German theaters, 1974.

Integration of Abilities. San Antonio: Trinity University Press, 1972.

Founder and first director of Booker T. Washington School for the Performing Arts, Dallas, 1976.

Distinguished Alumnus Award, Trinity University, 1978.

Honorary Doctorate of Humanities, Texas Christian University, 1978.

Awarded Thomas De Gaetani Award for service to American theater by the United States Institute of Theater Technology, 1983.

Texas Commission on the Arts Special Merit Award, 1994.

Making Sense with Five Senses. Waelder, TX: The Baker Group, 1994.

. . .the center's main claim to fame is that of a theatrical powerhouse from which Britain, as well as the rest of the United States, has something to learn.

FOR PAUL bAKer FOR HiM HiS HYMN
is todAY to SAY HiS WAY HiS WAY
beCAME ouR wAY oF being oF Seeing
oF HeARing oF LeARNiNg About LeARNiNg
oF thiNKiNg iN WAYS always All wAYs
opeNiNG to SAY ANd HeRe WiTH A
                        HeAR
QuEstioN About QuEstioNs ANd NOT
ANSWERS butSAYiNG wHAt iS it ANd
NOt wHAt SomeTHiNg iS iS oNE oF
the tHiNgS tHAt I LeARNed FROM HiM
tHiNKing todAY oF SAYiNG tHeRe iS
tHAt iS iN HiM tHAt HYMNs tHeRe iS
tHAt iS tHeRE ARE tHeSe wAYS wAVes
oF wAYS tHere ARE tHOSe tHAt ARe
HeRE ARe tHOSe WHO ARE WiTHiN US
tHAt SiNG tHiS HYMN oF being ANd
SAYiNG tHeSe tHiNgS tHAt HYMN SiNG
SiNgs SiNgiNg ANd SAYiNG tHeSe WAYS
HiS WAYS tHAt iS HiS iS ouRS ARe
ouRS HiS WAY wAYS iN SAYiNG MY WAY
oF SAYiNG tHiS WAY wAYS SAYiNG tHeRe
iS tHAt iS iN HiM tHAt HYMNS tHAT iS HiM

248

THAT IS ME SAYING THIS TODAY FOR HIM

WE FIRST MET IN 1955 THROUGH VIRGINIA
DENNARD/LYNCH IN A HOUSE ON A HILL
BY A LAKE IN A ROOM WITH SIX PRIMITIVE
PAINTINGS BY CLEMENTINE HUNTER WHO
DEPICTED LIFE ON A PLANTATION IN
NATCHITOCHES LOUISIANA SOON AFTER THAT
I BEGAN WORKING WITH RUTH BYERS AT
THE BAYLOR CHILDREN'S THEATRE. IT WAS
THERE I MET RHETTA AND ROBIN AND AND
AND AND AND AND LATER ONE DAY A DAY
IN ONE THERE WAS A VERY SPECIAL ONE DAY
I MET FRANK LLOYD WRIGHT THAT DAY
TODAY IS VERY SO VERY CLEAR I CAN
SEE THE WAY HE TIED HIS TIE THAT HAS
MADE THE TIE IN SAYING

THAT THIS IS HIS IS MINE IS OURS TODAY
SHARING THIS HYMN FOR HIM FOR THEM
FOR US TODAY WE CELEBRATE THIS SEED
REMEMBERING THE WAY WE SAY THANK YOU THANK
YOU MR. BAKER FOR ALL FOR ALWAYS BEING
YOU WHICH IS US ME SAYING THAT I
WE ARE CONSTANTLY CHANGING IN WAYS
WAVES THAT IS US HYMNING THIS HYMN

ROBERT WILSON JUNE 5TH 2001 WATERMILL CENTER

250

Paul Baker's Theaters

Baylor Theater—an inclusive term for two theatrical spaces, two lobbies also used as art galleries, offices, shop, dressing rooms, green room, costume storage, and stage spaces used for classrooms. Theater spaces included:

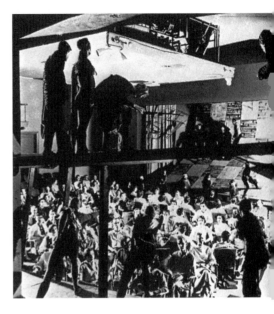

Studio One—stages surrounded audience seated in swivel chairs. Chairs could be placed on the stages to convert the total space into an arena theater. In the rear, sliding doors could transform the front lobby into a proscenium stage or a sixth stage with a balcony.

Weston Studio (designed by Bill Tamminga in association with Paul Baker)—a large open space with movable risers for staging or seating. Could be used as a film or television studio.

Sidewalk Theater—a former cafe turned into a rectangular camera theater with a stage at one end of the room and a light booth at the other; used for student productions.

Dallas Theater Center (designed by Frank Lloyd Wright) —an inclusive term for two theatrical spaces with offices, shop, etc.; adjunct spaces for off-location storage, instruction, and performances.

Kalita Humphreys Theater—a caliper-arm stage, based on the classical Greco-Roman amphitheater, containing a thirty-two-foot center revolve with two side stage arms; an audience of 480 to 520, depending on the use of the balcony and lodge sections, sat in three pie-sections of an octagon.

Down Center Stage—created by the DCT staff in the basement directly under the revolve chamber of the main stage, between two support pillars. Seating fifty-five, Down Center Stage became a home for playwrights, showcasing approximately fifty world premieres, and the Magic Turtle series for children.

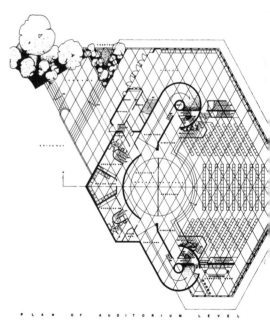

PLAN OF AUDITORIUM LEVEL

251

Trinity University

Attic Theater—former classroom space in a science building turned into temporary theater space.

Ruth Taylor Theater (designed by Arthur Rogers in association with Paul Baker)—included classrooms, offices, shop, dressing rooms, drafting and costume design room; the lobby was also used as art gallery and theater spaces. Classrooms designed for stagings and rehearsals.

Theater One—a large theater with side stages, movable proscenium posts that could define the width of the proscenium opening, and swivel chairs that could be placed on stages to convert to arena-style productions.

Attic Two—smaller rectangular theater with the stage against one long wall, seating seventy-five.

Cafe Theater—a small theater with concrete stage against the theater wall; also used for classroom and refreshments during intermission

Patio—an open space between the Ruth Taylor Theater, Laurie Auditorium, and Ruth Taylor Art Building; used for intermissions, classroom, sculpture shows, and Happenings.

Contributors

Darrel Baergen: M.A., Baylor University, Ph.D., University of
Denver; taught directing, acting, and radio-television-film
at Hardin-Simmons University, Southwest Texas State
University, and Southwestern Baptist Seminary; currently
department chair at Hardin-Simmons University.

Raymond Bailey: Ph.D., Southern Baptist Seminary;
postdoctoral, University of Chicago Divinity; taught
theology at Hardin-Simmons University and Southern
Baptist Seminary; senior minister, Seventh and James
Baptist Church;adjunct professor of theater at
McLennan Community College.

Kathryn (Kitty) Cardwell Baker: B.A., Randolph-Macon
College; M.S., University of Chicago; math professor for
thirty-nine years; volunteer in art and math at Arts
Magnet High School in Dallas; continues work as artist
in watercolor, print making, fiber arts; married to
Paul Baker since 1936.

Mary Bozeman: M.A., Trinity University; actor and/or director
for fifty years; cofounder and artistic directorof the Sabine
Parish Players, Shakespeare in Sabine, and the Statewide
Louisiana Shakespeare Network Festival.

Ruth McKissack Byers: B.A. and M.A., Baylor University;
assistant professor of drama and director of Teen
Children's Theater at Baylor University and Dallas
Theater Center; presently writer, educator, drama consultant.

Raymond Carver: Ph.D., attended Baylor University, the
University of Denver, and Yale University School of
Drama; director of theater at Angelo State University
until retirement; directs the Living Room Theater in
Salado, Texas.

Irene Corey: theatrical designer; studied at London Central
School of Arts and Crafts; taught at Georgetown College
(Kentucky); designer and cofounder of the Everyman

Players; awarded Thomas De Gaetani Award by
the United States Institute of Theater Technology, 1994;
author of *The Mask of Reality: The Face Is a Canvas*.

Linda Daugherty: M.F.A., Trinity University; actress, teacher,
propmistress; playwright-in-residence, Dallas Children's
Theater; more than twenty plays produced including
performances at the Kennedy Center, Atlanta's Alliance
Theater, and Richmond's Theater IV.

Bill Doll: Ph.D., Texas Tech University; director of university
theater and associate professor of drama at Angelo
State University.

Robyn Flatt: M.A., Baylor University; member of
Dallas Theater Center; resident professional company
for twenty-four years; cofounder and executive artistic
director of the Dallas Children's Theater.

Julia Jarrell: B.A., Trinity University; educational program
designer; founding director of the LBJ Heartland Network;
currently overseeing professional development programs
for rural teachers from Central America through the office
of International Programs of the Alamo Community
College District.

Susan McAtee Monday: B.A., Trinity University; Baylor
Children's Theater student; founding member
of Learning About Learning Educational Foundation;
founding director of exhibits and programs for the
San Antonio Children's Museum; fiber artist, writer
and professor at University of the Incarnate Word and
the Southwest School of Art and Craft.

Arthur Rogers: member of the American Institute of Architects;
graduate in architecture from Miami University in Ohio,
Rice Institute, and L'Ecole des Beaux Arts in France;
designer of more than twenty theaters and auditoriums;
architect for the African-American Museum, the Arts
District Theatre, and St. Alcuin Montessori School;

254

a collection of his poetry is being prepared for publication; serves on the board of directors of the Dallas Black Dance Theatre.

Susan Russell: designer and author; consultant with museums and educational organizations; recently established The Foundry to create programs and products for children in new media.

Glenn Allen Smith: M.F.A., Trinity University; playwright of seventeen plays, most of them receiving multiple productions, including Off Broadway; taught playwriting at several institutions and has served as playwright-in-residence in various theaters.

Louise Mosley Smith: adapted the integration of abilities curriculum for high school students; served as theater coordinator for the Arts Magnet program and has directed many of its productions.

Claudia Sullivan: B.A., Butler University; M.F.A. Trinity University; Ph.D. University of Colorado at Boulder; professor of theater and communications at Schreiner University; author of six books, including two texts on acting.

Frances Swinny: Ph.D., University of Texas; longest tenured faculty member in Trinity University's speech and drama program beginning in 1948; directed the department's speech program, and greatly expanded its curriculum and activities during Paul Baker's chairmanship.

Harry Thompson: M.A., Baylor University; director of theater at Hardin-Simmons University and Austin College; consultant and designer of theaters; independent movie and television producer; currently a successful painter.

You may not like it,
but you won't have any doubt
about who did it.

Paul Baker

255

Index

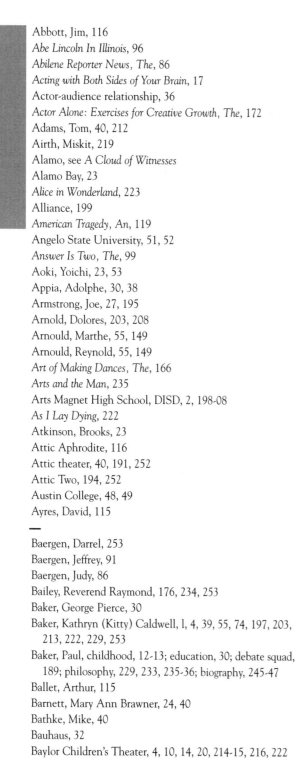